RENEWALS: 691-4574
DATE DUE

WITHDRAWN
UTSA Libraries

Beyond Security

PRIVATE PERCEPTIONS AMONG ARABS AND ISRAELIS

John Edwin Mroz

Published for the International Peace Academy

Pergamon Press
New York   Oxford   Toronto   Sydney   Paris   Frankfurt

The International Peace Academy is pleased to sponsor publication of this book. The Academy, however, is not responsible for the views expressed by persons interviewed by the author nor for the analysis and presentation made by the author.

Copyright© 1980 by International Peace Academy, Inc. All rights reserved under International and Pan American Copyright Conventions. No part of this book may be reproduced or transmitted in any form or by any means, electronic or mechanical, including photocopy, recording or any information storage and retrieval system, without the prior permission in writing from the publisher. All inquiries should be addressed to International Peace Academy, Inc., 777 United Nations Plaza, New York, New York 10017.

Library of Congress Cataloging in Publication Data

Mroz, John Edwin.
  Beyond security.
  "An International Peace Academy publication."
  Bibliography: p.
  Includes index.
  1. Jewish-Arab relations--1973-   --Public opinion. 2. Public opinion--Arab countries. 3. Public opinion--Israel. I. Title.
DS119.7.M73 1981   327.5694017'4927   80-82857
ISBN 0-08-027517-6   AACR2
ISBN 0-08-027516-8 (pbk.)

Library of Congress Catalog Number: 80-82857

Printed in the United States of America
Book design by Dean William Rudoy

Dedicated to my best friend, Karen Marie,
and to my parents with deepest gratitude
for making it possible

Contents

Maps	6
Preface	7
Preface to the Second Printing	10
Acknowledgements	11
Summary	13
Introduction by Major General Indar Jit Rikhye	16
1 New Dynamics in a Protracted Conflict	21
Perceptions	27
Threats	32
Special Concerns	38
2 Perceptions of Threats	44
Israel	45
Jordan	61
Syria	70
Lebanon	80
Palestinians	88
Egypt	97

	Observations	101
3	**The Search for Security**	**105**
	Primary Military Security Threats	109
	Secondary Military Security Threats	124
	Non-Military Security Threats	129
	Observations	133
4	**Some Options for Resolving Security Threats**	**136**
	A Neutral Palestinian State	138
	A Confederation of a Palestinian (West Bank/Gaza) State with Jordan	163
	Other Ideas for Consideration	173
	Conclusion	**184**
	Footnotes	**190**
	Bibliography	**196**
	Glossary	**206**
	Index	**211**
	About the Author	**215**

Maps

Overview of the Middle East Region	20
Iraq	30
Arab-Israeli Conflict Area	33
Israel	46
Golan Heights and Vicinity (including the Hula Valley)	48
Israeli Maps Showing Geo-Strategic Dangers	52-3
Persian Gulf Area (including Strait of Hormuz)	58
Jordan	62
Jerusalem	67
Syria	71
Golan Heights (including UNDOF area)	73
Jewish Settlements in Israeli-occupied Golan Heights	77
Lebanon	81
Southern Lebanon after Israeli Invasion, March 1978	82
West Bank	89
Egypt	98
Jewish Settlements in Israeli-occupied West Bank	116
PLO Views Partition of Palestine	120-1
Israel Views Partition of Palestine	122-3
Road Map of Israel/West Bank/Jordan Area	128
Syrian Map of the Region	176

Preface

The materials presented in this publication were gathered in the Middle East during 1978 and 1979 by the author as a member of the Middle East Task Force of the International Peace Academy.[1] In 1977, the Academy's governing Board of Directors[2] decided to establish this Task Force and charged it with the responsibility of gathering information and updating the Academy's understanding of the current trends in thought on the Arab-Israeli conflict. This timely information would be used to design problem-solving exercises, background readings, simulation games, and other teaching materials for the international training seminars which the Academy conducts for diplomats and military officials from 114 nations. Also, the Task Force would produce additional Academy publications on various aspects of the Arab-Israeli conflict.

Since 1970, training seminar participants frequently have explored questions relating to both the security requirements and the failure of the peacemaking process in the Middle East. The 1979 Task Force visit focused primarily on the security dimensions of the conflict and especially on the attitudes and roles of third parties in facilitating or hindering agreement.

The Task Force conducted private discussions in 1978 and 1979 with more than 175 government leaders and non-government officials including journalists, businessmen, defense analysts, and scholars in Egypt, Lebanon, Jordan, Israel, Syria, Kuwait, and Sudan; with Palestinians on the West Bank and Gaza; and with officials of the Palestine Liberation Organization (PLO). The success of the Task Force visits in 1978 and 1979 is directly related to the willingness of most of these Arabs and Israelis to discuss privately their personal attitudes and reservations about critical issues. Task Force members agreed that any resulting publications would adhere to a policy of non-attribution. Most of the meetings were conducted as private discussions, rather than as opinion polls or surveys.

The periodic reference in this publication to the *1979 Middle East sample*[3] refers to the 108 Arabs and Israelis who participated in the 1979 discussions with Task Force members in Egypt, Jordan, Israel, Lebanon, the West Bank, and Syria. In addition to the Task Force discussions, a concerted research effort was undertaken to verify the collected data and information. This research included an attempt to locate supporting evidence for each of the major arguments raised by the *sample* participants, resulting in a collection of English-language quotations which are referenced in the footnote section of this publication for those who wish to pursue a particular contention. Several arguments presented by each of the parties in public discussions with Task Force members were made for obviously propagandistic reasons. These arguments bore little correlation to proven events, data, or searches for confirmation and, for the most part, they have been avoided in the text that follows. The arguments most frequently raised by Arabs and Israelis in the *sample* are given special consideration, as are the private views of the protagonists during 1978 and 1979 toward both the threats they perceive and the security requirements which might meet those threats. The Task Force made efforts to conduct conversations even with persons whose views differed from the mainstream, e.g., those Arabs and Israelis who are considered extremists by their countrymen. These minority opinions are presented periodically in this text when deemed to be important to discussion of a particular issue.

This presentation of the protagonists' private views may appear to some readers as surprising if not almost naive in light of today's negative headlines and official pronouncements. The reader is assured that the views in this publication, expressed by prominent persons in each country and the PLO, were carefully analyzed and reviewed with leaders and experts in the region. An Israeli defense correspondent argued, "I remember well our previous discussions [of security issues in the Arab-Israeli conflict].... I noticed in my [later] review of the galleys that most distorted arguments — by Arabs and Israelis — were removed or deemphasized.... I cannot accuse you for [sic] falling victim to flimsy, or false arguments.... I'm pleased you've exercised some discretion in your presentation."

Author's Appreciation

I would like to express personal appreciation to all the officials in the Middle East who have been so helpful and to my colleagues at the International Peace Academy. General Rikhye has been a personal and professional adviser from whom I have learned a great deal during my four years at the Academy. Ambassador Arnold C. Smith, Chairman of the Board of the Academy and former Secretary General of the Commonwealth, has provided encouragement and advice during the project. In addition, I would like to thank General Wilhelm Kuntner for his professional and personal guidance and friendship. Finally, appreciation is paid to Austrian and Swiss officials and scholars for their advice and assistance.

I owe special thanks, for their advice and guidance, to the members of the Manuscript Review Committee that was established for this publication by the Board of Directors. The members are: General Rikhye; Mr. Elmore Jackson, Special Adviser to the Aspen Institute for Humanistic Studies and author of *Meeting of Minds;* and Dr. Oscar Schachter, Co-Editor-in-Chief, *American Journal of International Law*, and author of numerous works in the field of conflict settlement and international law.

I am also very grateful to the entire staff of the International Peace Academy. In particular, I must thank Henry Wiseman, Jennifer Borchers, Jeff Helsing, Dick McDonnell, Lauranne Pazhoor, Anne Meenan, and Joyce Hellew for their special efforts which helped make this publication possible. Our late colleague, Brigadier E.M.D. Leslie (Canada), provided all of us with a special sense of renewed spirit. Ted will be sorely missed and long remembered personally and professionally.

Personal gratitude is expressed to the trustees of the Miriam and Ira D. Wallach Foundation of New York and to the Columbia Foundation of San Francisco for their continued confidence and support. Ira Wallach has been a particular source of encouragement and assistance. The readability and attractiveness of this publication is due to the generosity of Dean William Rudoy, a clinical psychologist and personal friend, who has devoted many hours toward making its physical presentation appealing. Appreciation is also offered to Janet Francendese for her assistance, patience, and advice.

Finally, and most importantly, I owe the deepest possible gratitude to my partner and best friend, my wife Karen Linehan Mroz. Together with my good parents and associates at the Fletcher School of Law and Diplomacy, she has encouraged me to devote more time to writing.

Most books on the Arab-Israeli conflict are prefaced by a statement claiming that efforts were made to present an impartial and factual picture of the conflict, although certain readers with vested interests might read an intended bias into the content or presentation. The testimony this author would like to present is that some twenty Israeli and Palestinian experts reviewed copies of the first galleys of this book. Without exception, they stated that although they cannot agree or accept everything in this publication, they do believe that the intention, approach, and final product is as objective as possible.

Responsibility for errors or misinterpretation of data or events are solely my own. Comments, questions, or suggestions are welcomed from the reader.

John Edwin Mroz
New York City
January 31, 1980

Preface to the Second Printing

Several important events have occurred since the release of the first printing of this study. The Iranian-Iraqi war has seriously weakened the *Eastern Front* military capabilities, undermined the argument that simply resolving the Palestinian problem would bring peace to the region, and bolstered Israeli confidence that America would see Israel as the only reliable ally in the region. The growing tensions between Syria and Jordan/Iraq, combined with the recently concluded Treaty of Friendship and Cooperation between Moscow and the Syrian regime of Hafez Assad, are additional developments that escalate the perceived sense of threats in the region. The election of Ronald Reagan together with a highly conservative Senate has similarly disrupted traditional thinking throughout the region vis-a-vis future American intentions and capabilities in the area. The future of the Camp David peace process and the nature of East-West relations have become further complicated. Despite these events, defense analysts and officials in the region have argued that the approach and contentions of *Beyond Security* remain important for serious students of the Middle East crisis to understand, as they underlie the perceptions of threat held by each of the disputants: Israel, the Palestinians, Syria, Jordan, Lebanon, and Egypt.

This edition includes an index and a bibliography. The latter includes a great variety of materials used by Task Force members since 1977. Its listings represent a wide variety of ideological and methodological approaches to the Arab-Israeli conflict. As such, these sources have served as useful aides in both the preparatory and analytic phases of this study.

I would like to convey my appreciation to Basil Larthe, David Kellogg and their colleagues at Pergamon Press, Inc., for their encouragement and capable handling of this endeavor.

John Edwin Mroz
New York City
December 1, 1980

Acknowledgements

The continuation of the International Peace Academy's Middle East Project is due in largest measure to the strong cooperation and encouragement that has been given by governmental officials in the Middle East. In particular, appreciation is given to the Ministries of Defense and Foreign Affairs of Jordan, Egypt, Syria, and Israel, and to the political and academic leadership of the Palestinians in the West Bank and Gaza and within the Palestine Liberation Organization. Scores of non-governmental professionals — including journalists, strategic analysts, businessmen, and scholars from throughout the region — have facilitated the project since 1977. Particular appreciation is expressed to the Al Ahram Centre of Political and Strategic Studies in Cairo, the Centre for Strategic Studies at Tel Aviv University, the Faculty of Law and Sharia at Kuwait University, and the Faculty of Bir Zeit University on the West Bank.

The Middle East Project has received considerable assistance from United Nations and Arab League officials. Special appreciation is given to Brian Urquhart, James Jonah, and George Sherry of the United Nations Secretariat, and to Generals Ensio Siilasvuo (Finland), Emmanuel Erskine (Ghana), Rais Abin (Indonesia), and Hannes Phillip (Austria). Government officials and scholars in Lebanon, Sudan, Kuwait, and the United States have also assisted the project.

Many diplomats assigned to Permanent Missions to the United Nations lent valuable assistance in facilitating and clarifying matters. In addition to the 175 persons in the region with whom Task Force members visited during 1978 and 1979, these officials provided useful ideas and analyses of difficult events and data.

The Academy is grateful to the Miriam and Ira Wallach Foundation of New York and the Columbia Foundation of San Francisco for their strong support of this project during 1978 and 1979. The trustees and staff of both foundations have been most cooperative and understanding of the Academy's need to retain its impartiality in this work.

Research aid was provided by Ken Wyker of Trinity College (Hartford). Library assistance was provided by the staff of the Dag Hammarskjöld Library at the United Nations, and the Middle East Institute. Particular appreciation is paid to Mrs. Khairallah at the latter library who provided valuable assistance. Map and documentation assistance was provided through the courtesy of the PLO, the Government of Israel, the State Department, *The New York Times,* and the *Christian Science Monitor.*

The entire staff of the International Peace Academy has been most supportive of this project, oftentimes offering to lend assistance in their personal time. Appreciation is paid to the members of the Board of Directors and the International Advisory Board of the Academy for their advice, assistance, and direction. Particular appreciation is paid to the Government of Austria for making available the services of Lt. General Wilhelm Kuntner, Commandant of the Austrian National Defense Academy during the 1978 and 1979 Academy Task Force visits. General Kuntner serves as a member of the Advisory Board.

A number of private individuals lent important assistance during various phases of this project, including P.G. Bjorlin (Sweden), Awn Al-Khasawneh, Joseph Rubel, and Rashid Khider. The Academy expresses its appreciation to these and the many other persons who professionally or personally have contributed to this Middle East Project during 1978 and 1979.

Summary

An analysis of the research conducted in the Middle East during 1978 and 1979 has led to the formulation of a series of observations and conclusions regarding the peacemaking process in the Arab-Israeli conflict. Much of the information was collected during 1979 in the aftermath of the Egyptian-Israeli Peace Treaty. Subsequent developments in the region will have affected public policies and personal attitudes of the six protagonists: the Syrians, Palestinians, Lebanese, Jordanians, Israelis, and Egyptians. Nonetheless, it is our belief that the basic views and sentiments expressed to us in 1979 still prevail. The following is a summary of the private Israeli and Arab views which are more fully presented in the body of this study.

- The overwhelming majority of Arabs and Israelis have personally accepted the fact that Israel and the Palestinians have the right to exist as permanent actors in the region.

- The public statements and attitudes of both Arabs and Israelis appear to be as uncompromising as ever. However, their personal attitudes, as expressed to Task Force members, show that Arabs and Israelis are privately undertaking a reassessment of their future relations with each other and of the nature of a future comprehensive settlement. In contrast to publicly expressed positions, these personal attitudes are much more flexible and tolerant of the problems perceived by the other protagonists.

- Nine out of ten Israelis and Palestinians who met with the Task Force members believe that the Palestinian issue is the most crucial one to be resolved. Eight out of ten believe that there could be no peace in the Middle East unless there was a fair solution to the Palestinian issue in all its aspects.

- An overwhelming majority of all Arabs as well as a majority of all Israelis who exchanged private views with Task Force members believe that a comprehensive settlement requires the establishment of some form of Palestinian entity in areas of the West Bank and Gaza through the exercise of some form of self-determination. There was not agreement among Israelis or Arabs as to the nature and authority of a Palestinian entity.

- Most Arabs and Israelis believe that the status quo is unsatisfactory and that all of the protagonists would have to make concessions if a comprehensive and full settlement is to be reached. Most believe that this time is the most propitious for a settlement and comprehensive peace.

• Neither the majority of Arabs nor the majority of Israelis believes that the other's current leadership truly desires a peaceful resolution of the conflict, although each agrees that the populace of the other probably did desire full peace.

• Each of the protagonists believes that all of his perceived threats are real, and feels that the other protagonists are insensitive to these threats. More than 150 threats were listed by the Arabs and Israelis during the Task Force private discussions. One-fifth of these threats could be considered widely shared by the populace of the region.

• These threats have been categorized by this author into three primary sets of security considerations. These categories include: 1) primary military security threats, such as a full-scale armed attack; 2) secondary military security threats, such as terrorism and the efforts to transform the character of the occupied territories; and 3) non-military security threats, such as a severe change in relations with a guarantor state, or penetration of institutional and cultural mores. Contrary to expectations, the strongest perceptions of imminent danger were found in the secondary military security threats, rather than in the primary military security threats.

• Most of the Arabs and Israelis who talked with Task Force members agreed that basic security requirements could probably be met without overwhelming difficulty, if all of the protagonists were first convinced of the others' genuinely peaceful intentions.

• The Arabs and the Israelis consider the two-fold question of third-party involvement crucial. First, great power involvement is seen to be necessary, but is not enthusiastically welcomed. It is understood that without the direct intervention of the great powers neither war nor comprehensive peace is likely, since they alone possess the capability of providing the arms and exerting the pressures for changes in policies. *Impartial* third parties compose the second category of third-party involvement. Arabs and Israelis doubt that there are many truly impartial parties; however, they recognize that some states, international organizations, and private groups which seek to provide positive services may be very helpful. The distrust and hostility among the protagonists are so intense that the impartial third parties are considered to be necessary for implementing phases of agreements and for promoting confidence-building components. The general belief is that the great power third parties would eventually help to make a peace, while the impartial third parties would help to carry it out.

- Two of the most frequently mentioned *compromise options* for resolving the Palestinian issue were a neutral Palestinian state on the model of Austria or Switzerland, and a confederation of a Palestinian entity or state with Jordan. Although neither of these alternatives meets the full list of requirements demanded by the Palestinians and the Israelis, many Arabs and Israelis consider them as potentially acceptable forms of compromise, provided that they are part of a larger agreement for complete peace. It should be noted that neither of these options is espoused here. Rather, an examination of each is provided as an example of an agreeable solution that could provide for the security and political concerns of all six protagonists.

- Current peacemaking efforts are severely hindered by problems that relate to the process as well as the substance of such undertakings. These hindrances include: publicly enunciated demands to an adversary to accept some rigid preconditions prior to formal negotiations; tactical uses of sabre-rattling and antagonistic language to convey policy statements or views on conflict issues; tendencies to reject options for resolving problems without adequate study or discussion; and demands for immediate answers to specific questions when there is no agreement on the principles for settlement, or even limited confidence of good intentions on the part of the other protagonists in the conflict.

Introduction

The October 1973 war between the Arabs and Israelis ushered in a new era in the Middle East. It is a sad parody on history that wars have resulted in greater change, sometimes for the better, rather than long periods of peace. The October war led to altered perceptions and the first serious moves to reconcile Arab-Israeli differences. After twenty-five years, Israel had become a reality that could no longer be ignored by the Arabs. Israel's illusion of invincibility against Arab attack and hesitancy to barter Arab-occupied lands for peace led to perhaps the most serious threat to the young Jewish state.

The last days of this war witnessed the mobilization of the airborne forces of the Soviet Union to relieve the beleagured Egyptian Third Army east of Suez, causing President Richard Nixon to order the first American global nuclear alert. Any intervention by the Soviets in the Sinai would have led to a clash with the Israeli air force and the making of a global conflict with all its terrible consequences. Such a war was averted through the determination of the Americans and the Soviets not to allow a proxy war to escalate into a nuclear holocaust and the will of the international community to control this conflict.

The withdrawal of the first UNEF (United Nations Emergency Force) from Gaza and the Sinai in May 1967 and the ineffectiveness of the U.N. Security Council to deal with that crisis led to a worldwide disappointment in the United Nations system. But when the call by the two superpowers to end hostilities in October 1973 went unheeded, it was the medium and small powers, represented in the Security Council, who called for a cease-fire and established an international peacekeeping force along the Suez Canal. These measures became a prelude to Secretary of State Henry Kissinger's step-by-step diplomacy, President Anwar el-Sadat's historic visit to Jerusalem, and a peace treaty between Egypt and Israel negotiated by President Jimmy Carter at Camp David.

Since its founding, the International Peace Academy has maintained a deep interest and concern in the Arab-Israeli conflict. Many of the participants of the Academy's training seminars, starting in 1970, were from states directly or indirectly involved in the Arab-Israeli conflict; others included those serving or likely to be assigned as U.N. peacekeepers, representatives of interested regional and non-governmental organizations, and scholars.

Because of this interest, each seminar has paid special attention to this conflict with the invaluable participation of Arabs and Israelis, scholars, political and military experts, and U.N. leaders in studying third-party roles and analysing available options to resolve this prolonged struggle.

Although in the early 1970s Arab diplomats and military officers, and by mutual consent Israeli scholars (almost all military reservists or members of recognized institutions), had participated in the Academy's seminars, which afforded many informal contacts between them, attempts to organize an off-the-record meeting between the parties involved in 1973-74 were aborted by one or the other side. The publication of *The Middle East and the New Realism*, a special report by the Academy written by John Volkmar and me, and *The Elusive Peace in the Middle East*, edited by Malcolm H. Kerr in 1975, concluded this phase of the Academy's work in this area.

The faltering momentum of Kissinger's step-by-step diplomacy after concluding an Israeli withdrawal east of the Mitla and Gidi passes in the Sinai and a partial withdrawal on the Golan Heights, the heightening crisis in southern Lebanon, and the realization that a durable peace would not be possible as long as the future of the Palestinians remained unresolved led the Academy to have a fresh look at and review of its Middle East project. A Middle East Task Force was established to determine (1) what possible reduced, altered, or increased roles third parties might be called upon to perform in the Middle East in the implementation of a possible agreement by the disputants, and (2) what options are available for establishing new forms of security arrangements in the Middle East if there is an agreement by the disputants.

The Academy was fortunate in obtaining the acceptance of Lt. General Wilhelm Kuntner, Commandant, Austrian National Defence Academy, an expert in European security matters and confidence-building measures, to join the Task Force. John Edwin Mroz, Executive Vice President of the Academy, became its third member with me and agreed to write a report. The Task Force visited Egypt, Israel, Jordan, and Syria in 1978, meeting with high-level political and military leaders, and diplomatic and U.N. representatives in the area. In 1979, John Mroz carried the main burden by not only spending several months of his time, including his evenings and holidays, in preparing the report, but also often traveling and researching alone throughout the Middle East. General Kuntner accompanied him part of the time, and they both joined me, together with James H. Binger, former Chairman, Honeywell, Inc., and a member of the Academy's Board of Directors, in visiting the U.S. Sinai Field Mission. I am sure General Kuntner will agree with me that this publication is the result of John Mroz's ingenuity and months of relentless work.

In his summary, John Mroz has indicated — a view shared by other members of the Task Force—that though the Arabs and Israelis, more so the latter, have little enthusiasm for third-party roles in helping to resolve their conflict, they do accept that such help is needed for further progress in the negotiations. Both sides recognize that the United States must remain the key mediator; they agree that the Soviets play some role (although Egypt and Israel would prefer their exclusion) and that other third-party assistance should be limited to helping implement agreements already reached. The Israelis publicly maintain little faith in the United Nations, yet privately concede its importance and have found at least its peacekeeping capability useful. When the Security Council refused to redeploy a U.N. force in the Sinai to supervise withdrawal of Israeli forces from Egypt as part of the Camp David accords, a price paid for isolating the Soviets from these negotiations and dividing the Arab world, both Egypt and Israel were disappointed. However, the United Nations did agree to redeploy some additional military observers, part of the U.N. Truce Supervision Organization, to patrol the zone between Egyptian and Israeli forces from east of El Arish to Ras Mohammed. In the meanwhile, the U.N. supervises the cease-fire on the Golan Heights and maintains a shaky truce in southern Lebanon. Thus, the international presence and its peacekeeping role remain essential to prevent renewal of hostilities and allow the peacemaking process to continue.

The slow progress of the Palestinian autonomy talks and questions relating to Jewish settlements on the West Bank on the one hand, and the sustained challenge to Israel from the Arab rejectionist block and the PLO left wing on the other, hinder a better understanding between the Arabs and Israelis.

The revolution in Iran, developments in North Yemen and the Horn of Africa, and the Russian military intervention in Afghanistan have resulted in a chain of events that will cast their shadow over the future of peace negotiations between the Arabs and the Israelis. Indeed, the security of the oil supply lines remains vital to the economic life of many nations dependent on Persian Gulf oil. Although such outside events should not interfere with the Arab-Israeli peace negotiations, attitudes of the protaganists have hardened somewhat between the spring of 1979, when the Task Force visited the Middle East, and this fall, when John Mroz completed the manuscript. Only a solution of the Palestinian question will prevent the disintegration of Lebanon and decide the future of the West Bank, as well as Jerusalem and Gaza. Only then will the security of Israelis and Arabs be assured, peace between Israel and its neighboring Arab states become possible, and comprehensive settlement be achieved in the Middle East.

There are, John Mroz argues, two levels of perception: the public and the private. He has taken on the challenges to bring some of those private thoughts to light and suggests means of dialogue to break the absoluteness of polarized public policies. There are, of course, no magic techniques that can override the problems in the area. But men interact in war and in peace. It is how they interact that determines whether it be one or the other.

The International Peace Academy is hopeful that the ideas presented in this book are worthy of examination and may prove effective in generating open discussion and new concepts which could become key strands in the sensitive task of building bridges between the Arabs and the Israelis.

Indar Jit Rikhye
Major General (Ret.)
President
International Peace Academy

Overview of the Middle East Region

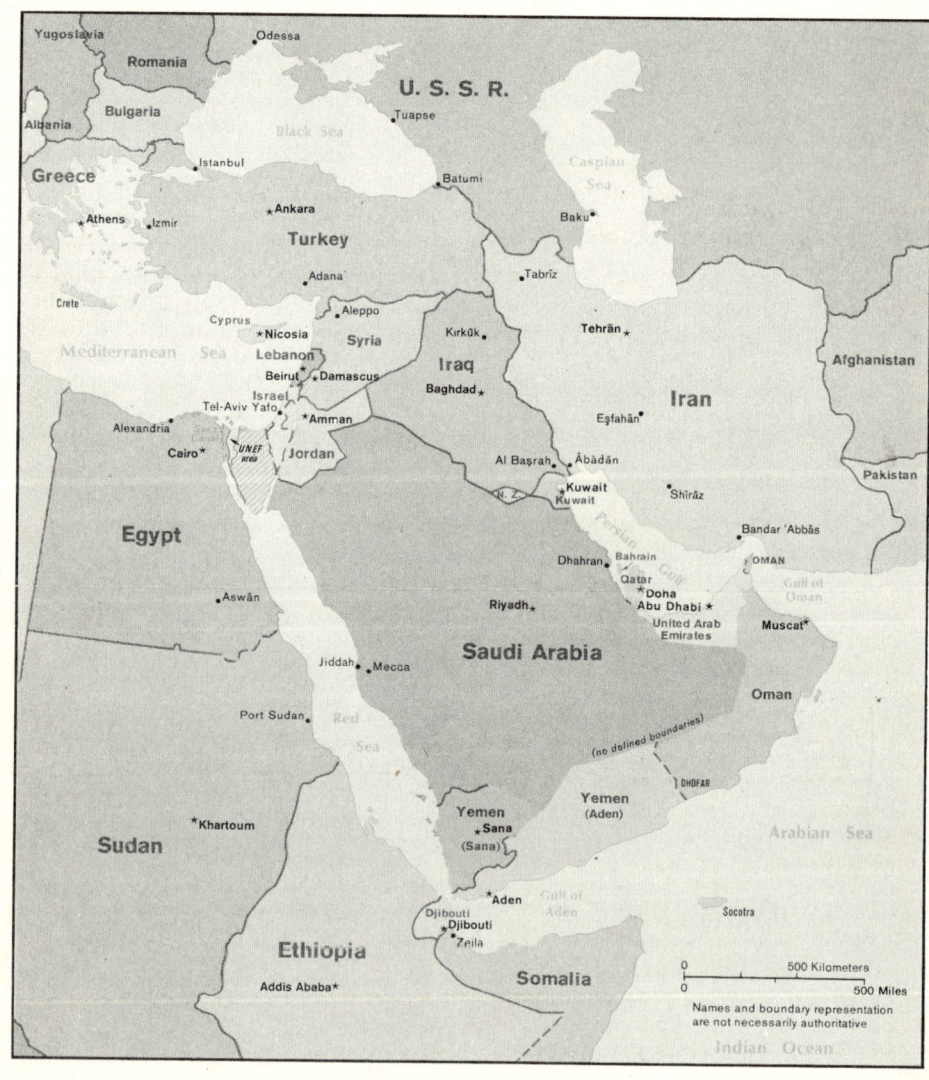

1
New Dynamics in a Protracted Conflict

Many Arabs and Israelis privately believe that the decade of the 1980s could become a turning point in the persistent Arab-Israeli conflict. A widely shared, private realization among Arabs and Israelis is the awareness that neither the Israelis nor Palestinians will disappear or be done away with through resort to violence. Traditional alliances and immutable policy positions have given way to events and policies that were unthinkable just several years before. This willingness to accept the right of the Palestinians and Israelis to exist permanently within secure and recognized borders is a new development in the history of the conflict.

At the same time, the region has experienced a new era of unprecedented internal turmoil. Few governments in the region enter the 1980s with as much stability as they possessed during the previous three decades. Growing economic disparities within and between states in the region have exacerbated tensions and strained the ability of governments to cope with demands for rapid changes. Ideological, religious, socio-economic, and political movements have gained adherents who willingly transfer their belief in certain causes to actions which undermine existing authority and policies.

Both of these broadly defined trends emerged out of the late 1970s. They have caused numerous policy-makers and analysts in the region to express privately the belief that a new attitude is developing in the Middle East about the future of the Arab-Israeli conflict. Some Arabs and Israelis feel that if certain confidence-building measures were taken, the attitude could be strong enough to lead to decisions which would break through the perceptual barrier that has hindered the peacemaking process. For example, mutual recognition by Israel and the Palestine Liberation Organization of the other's right to exist would mark a radical departure from the past and reinforce those truly seeking a comprehensive peace among both peoples. The Israeli perception that most Arabs privately would like to drive Israel into the sea is counterbalanced by the Arab perception that Israel seeks to destroy the Palestinian people and exert a domineering influence over the region. The delicate relationship between perceptions and reality strongly affects the potential impact which these attitudes have upon the policy-making process, as will be seen later in this study.

The attitudes that prompted the writing of this publication were based upon the information gathered during the Task Force discussions in 1978 and 1979 with more than 175 governmental officials and non-governmental leaders in Egypt, Jordan, Israel, Lebanon, and Syria, as well as with the Palestinians, including the PLO. The formal, surface discussions reinforced the prevailing belief that positions and attitudes in the Arab-Israeli conflict remain as uncompromising as ever. However, during private discussions, there were numerous indications that both Arabs and Israelis were seriously reassessing the future course of their relations and the nature of a possible comprehensive settlement. Inherent in the reassessment was a personal acceptance, oftentimes reluctant, of the fact that Israel, the other Arab states, and the Palestinians had all become permanent actors in the region. It might be more accurate to call the acceptance a *spirit of resignation* rather than an act of willing acceptance. But it could represent a turning point in the conflict. A vast majority of Arabs and Israelis privately noted that they had arrived at a personal acceptance of the existence of an Israeli state and a Palestinian homeland. Most doubted, however, that their traditional antagonists were also undergoing such a process of reassessment and resignation. Most argued that if no progress was made in this decade, then a fundamental shift away from this concessionary attitude could take place.

A Jordanian civic leader noted that "the argument can be viewed not as whether Israelis or Palestinians *will exist* but rather *how their existence* can be accepted into a workable framework for the region." Most Israelis were privately unenthusiastic about the establishment of any form of Palestinian state. Similarly, many Arabs were unenthusiastic about admitting that Israel has become a permanent actor in the region. But both were willing to agree that the question was indeed changing from one of the *right of existence* to that of establishing principles that could govern an accommodation for permanent co-existence. The status quo is not accepted as an adequate mode of living by Arabs or most Israelis. Regarding change, there is a notable concurrence of unofficial suggestions on possible accommodations. Some of these will be explored in greater detail later in this volume.

Emerging private opinions often contradicted public policies and official pronouncements. Their emphasis was frequently placed on the need to resolve the Arab-Israeli conflict before time runs out leading to another full-scale war, or what one senior Arab political official called "the near total military and economic domination of our region by outside powers." An Israeli journalist noted that the great powers, in the name of their respective allies in the Arab-Israeli conflict, have "gradually been able to raise their level of influence over the Arabs and us [Israelis] that it surpasses, one could say, any of their own so-called required needs." The need to alter the status quo was also reflected in private Arab and Israeli statements that noted the long-term damage which is being done by delaying settlement. A Lebanese lawyer argued, "The psychological damage increases by geometric proportions."

These trends of private thinking in the region appear to be related to the dramatic upheavals that have shaken the Middle East since 1977. Included in these are the Iranian Islamic revolution, the responses and adjustments made after President Sadat's initiatives, the Camp David process, and the separate peace treaty between Egypt and Israel.

These private opinions also reflect the changing dynamics of regional and global politics, including the nearly universal acceptance of the right to self-determination for the Palestinian people, the recognition by most of the world community of the Palestine Liberation Organization (PLO) as the sole representative of the Palestinian people, and the profound economic and social impact of the pricing policies of the Organization of Petroleum Exporting Countries (OPEC). The uncertain situation is further aggravated by the rampant inflation, economic dependency, and political instability in most countries of the region, including Israel and the so-called Arab confrontation states.

Looming over the horizon for most government leaders is the military and economic influence of outside powers over local affairs. The bold Soviet military moves into Afghanistan in late December 1979 and earlier Soviet activities and commitments in the People's Democratic Republic of Yemen (South Yemen) have given rise to serious concerns. Similarly, the *shopping* by American officials for possible new military bases in the region, including frequently mentioned sites in Israel and Egypt, has caused concern as well. A Jordanian business leader summarized these concerns with the following statement: "For several years we breathed a sigh of relief that the great outside states were fighting their battles in the schoolyard of the Africans. . . . Now we see that they prefer to spar right here in the Middle East. . . . There is too much at stake in their fights and we are not interested in providing them the opportunity or surroundings. . . ." In addition, a score of lesser powers have become crucial actors in the economic, political, and military dimensions of the conflict.

The continuing escalation of conventional arms sales to states in this region has raised fears, as has the increased capability of several important states including Israel, Iraq, and Libya to develop a nuclear capacity which could one day be translated into a nuclear weapon capability.

Analysis of the materials gathered by the Task Force members during private discussions, particularly those in 1979, shows a clear concern by

Middle East officials that another decade of the Arab-Israeli conflict could only worsen the situation. An Israeli military officer expressed his concern: "I am afraid in the 1980s we are all going to face the question, not of what would we like to do if we had our entire way, but what must we do to maintain control ourselves of our region and prevent this whole prolonged struggle from escalating to the point where none of us will benefit and all will lose what is most dear to us."

Each of the six protagonists in this conflict relies heavily upon outside parties for its economic stability. Critical needs such as weapons, food, and energy supplies are among the areas where dependency is most extensive. The role of *impartial* third parties has been largely restricted to firefighting measures when violence has erupted. Throughout the region there is constant discussion of the impact and intentions of third parties.

A brief review of Middle East history demonstrates that third parties have long played a critical role in this region. The resilience of the local peoples to withstand waves of foreign intervention of all types, including such forces as the British, French, Ottomans, Persians, and Romans, is worth noting. Special skills and procedures for coping with regional rivalries and outside influence were perfected in this region and include alliance formation, underground violence, and intrigue. Today the peoples of the Middle East continue to demonstrate these skills. A Westerner seeking to apply logic or standards of ideological commitment to explain Middle East actions will be disappointed. A political leader on the West Bank told the author that "political ideology is not critical for us . . . we will extend our hands to the devil to get Israel out of our land. But we will always be the master of the relationship, sometimes unbeknown to our new ally."

Despite the distrust of outside parties, all but a dozen persons of the *1979 Middle East sample* believe that substantial, impartial third-party involvement would be required to help implement the transitional phase of a comprehensive settlement, regardless of the particular objections and preferences of any of the protagonists. Nearly the same number foresee the need for an extended third-party role over time in helping achieve implementation of an agreement. It is worth noting that the role of *impartial* third parties is highly regarded as a confidence-building measure, but held in low esteem as a vehicle for achieving a break-through in negotiations. An Arab political official summarized the problem: "Third parties with clout make a settlement; third parties with neutral and noble aims help implement it."

The frequent inconsistencies in attitude about third parties must be understood in the context of the conflict itself. The protagonists view certain third parties as being both part of the central cause of the problem and essential as allies to one or more of the protagonists. Hostility and distrust are so pervasive that impartial third parties are often seen as necessary for implementation of specific components of the settlement process. It is generally agreed that these third parties will be most useful as auxiliary actors in a comprehensive settlement.

It is often argued that the greatest danger in the Arab-Israeli conflict is the risk of great power confrontation. An overwhelming majority of the *1979 Middle East sample* believe that another Arab-Israeli war is possible during the 1980s. More than two-thirds believe that such a war is probable in the next ten years if progress is not forthcoming on the Palestinian problem. Perhaps most important, all but a few argue that such a war is likely to exact high civilian and military casualties on both sides.

The Arab-Israeli conflict has demonstrated that it is one of the most complex conflicts to resolve. Not only have specific events and problems been extended and generalized over time in terms of principles, values, and emotions, but also outside powers and influences have become totally intertwined in the process of exacerbating and resolving the conflict. A Palestinian official inquired from the Task Force members:

> Who [what interest group] is not a party anymore? . . . and who are those who are most immutable in their positions? Is it not the American and European Jews? The Russians and the Libyans or the Pentagon and the Kremlin experts? The arms merchants in Paris and São Paulo and Prague? I heard that the Beirut banks are making money better than ever before and making the Frenchmen and Swiss who own interests in them rich despite the civil war that has ripped Beirut apart since 1975.

The Arabs and Israelis understand the changing nature of the regional and global political and military environments, and the possibility that the local protagonists may one day find themselves in a situation where they no longer have control over their own affairs. The Israelis realize that their critical economic problems can be satisfactorily addressed only with outside assistance. Similarly, some Arabs understand their vulnerability to emerging revolutionary trends and the ominous results which might accompany unprecedented oil wealth. The latter has caused what one Arab newspaper editor called "a potential Iran and a potential Afghanistan for nearly every state in the region . . . neither of which, may I add, is particularly appealing to most of us."

The involvement of outside powers has long provided a virtual immunity from total military defeat for both the Arabs and Israelis. The protagonists each have believed that time is working in their favor, a belief which has contributed to their reluctance to make concessions. Many Israelis currently argue that in another twenty-five years Arab oil largely will have been replaced by other energy sources; consequently, Western relations with Arab states will have assumed less importance. Arabs counter that in twenty-five years Arab oil wealth will be even more crucial as a factor in Arab-Western relations than oil is today. Arabs argue that Israel cannot maintain its current rate of inflation, political turmoil, and heavy dependency upon one external ally. Palestinians insist that an analysis of the past ten years shows clearly that time is working for the Palestinian cause and against the Israelis. Religious values, doctrines, and historical events have further clouded many of the fundamental issues that must be answered if there is to be a comprehensive settlement. The violent events of 1956, 1967, the War of Attrition, and 1973 are constant reminders of the depth of hostilities and the ever-pending danger of large-scale violence.

Those who praise or condemn the Camp David process agree that it did achieve the significant side-effect, perhaps unintended, of bringing the Palestinian issue to the forefront of consideration by the protagonists and the world community. Our discussions with Israelis and Arabs emphasized that a resolution of the Palestinian question was the *sine qua non* for the peacemaking process. Resolution of the disputes in Lebanon or the Golan Heights, for example, were seen as dependent upon agreement on the future status of the West Bank and the Gaza and on implementation of the right to self-determination of the Palestinian people. This question of the Palestinian right to self-determination is inextricably tied to the question of security for the Palestinians, Israelis, and other protagonists in the conflict. The *1979 Middle East sample* listed the most important specific issues needing immediate attention as:

- the need to gain (for the Palestinians), protect, and guarantee their sovereignty and security

- the need to control the size and function of outside parties' involvement in the region

- the need to improve the long-term economic viability of the region

This book deals primarily with the first of these concerns, security. A subsequent and more detailed publication by the author will address outside parties' involvement. The specific purpose of this volume is to provide a comparative view of how the six protagonists in the conflict privately view common problems and possible alternatives for their resolution. Attempts are made to advise the reader of the general background of quoted authorities, since attribution is not possible for reasons previously explained.

Perceptions

One of the most serious errors that outsiders make in their analysis of the Arab-Israeli conflict is the attempt to apply their own system of logic or reasoning when assessing the motivations of the protagonists. An Israeli historian argued that "for every 100 Arabs you give me I will give you 100 reasons why an enemy is undertaking a particular action . . . and if you give me 100 Israelis, I will probably give you 200 reasons. . . ." Central to an understanding of these divergent interpretations of accepted facts is the role of perceptions.

Perceptions are one's awareness and understanding of an event, actor, situation, or process. Such understanding may be heavily influenced by experience and historical considerations, cultural or socio-economic backgrounds, personality traits of policy-makers, ideologies, propaganda, bureaucratic politics, and a host of irrational factors. The more prolonged a conflict becomes, the more entrenched and suspicious are the perceptions of the protagonists.

The perceived power of an adversary is often a decisive factor in the formulation of a country's policy. Sometimes perceptions reflect a feeling of weakness, such as the perceptions held by Israelis, Palestinians, and other Arabs of their particular vulnerability in the face of a heavily armed adversary. A basic question that confronts Israeli and Arab policy-makers today is how to interpret the intentions and capabilities of their adversaries, and how to design policies that will minimize risk and maximize the achievement of important goals. Complicating this process is the fact that some goals seem to be less important as political, military, and economic conditions change.

Outsiders sometimes find it difficult to understand how the protagonists really view one another. An Israeli social scientist argued that "perceptions are as important as reality if decision-makers operate on the basis that their perceptions are reality." Actions and policies are made on the understanding of perceived reality. This perceived reality may or may not be based on data or events which an objective party would call factual. The following composite chart was drawn from remarks made by Arab and Israeli officials concerning their views of each other, expressed during discussions held in the spring of 1979.

This brief summary of Arab and Israeli perceptions about one another demonstrates how evidence supporting a predisposition is often given greater weight than it deserves while the opposite evidence is ignored or discounted. Perceptions are often translated into expectations. Since evidence is oftentimes distorted by policy-makers to conform with their pre-

ARAB AND ISRAELI PERCEPTIONS 1979

	ISRAEL VIEWS EGYPT, JORDAN, SYRIA	EGYPT, JORDAN, SYRIA VIEW ISRAEL
ECONOMICS	• dependent on oil-rich Arabs and others for essential needs	• dependent upon USA (public and private sectors) and world Jewish community for fiscal solvency and weapons
	• doubtful they can achieve development of infrastructure to accomplish modernization and self-sufficiency	• rampant inflation (over 120 percent) due to heavy military and social expenditures; unlikely to change in foreseeable future
POLITICS	• autocratic political systems with no arrangements for leadership transition	• precarious coalition system plagued by serious political infighting
	• no political freedoms (right to dissent, freedom of press, etc.)	• dormant problem of growing Arab minority in Israel; also problems with West Bank/Gaza populace under occupation
	• intra-Arab conflict and interference in each other's internal affairs	• inability to keep confidential information or prevent rampant dissent
	• web of alliances and involvement with great powers	• attempts by non-Israeli Jews to influence policy; complete dependence on USA
	• opportunistic and vindictive	• aggressive and expansionist
RELIGION	• government and policies of state are intertwined with Moslem religion	• government and policies of state are intertwined with Jewish religion
	• lack of tolerance for other religions	• lack of tolerance for other religions
LABOR	• largely unskilled and undermotivated	• overskilled with growing reliance upon West Bank and Gaza labor for construction and other blue collar jobs
DOCTRINE	• PLO Covenant calls for the elimination of an Israeli state; PLO supported by Arab World	• Eretz Israel policies try to eliminate Palestinian presence and deny right to self-determination to the Palestinian people

dispositions, it is not irrational for policy-makers to adjust incoming information to fit more closely with existing beliefs and images. A classic example is the 1973 Israeli estimate that the Arabs would not attack Israel because they could not defeat Israel in a decisive military sense. The Arabs, however, recognized that no further progress in resolving the conflict was likely to be made through negotiations, as Israel was content with the status quo. Although the Arabs recognized Israel's military superiority, they understood that neither superpower would allow a complete military defeat of either side. The Arabs believed that they could redeem their self-esteem by a favorable showing against Israel. Their goal was to score some quick advantages over the Israelis before the latter could fully mobilize and offset gains. Weapon losses for both sides would be made up by the respective guarantor powers. The immediate Arab objective was not the destruction of Israel. The Arab and Israeli perceptions were quite different, although each well understood the same basic military facts.

One of the paradoxes of international politics is that decisions which require the most serious consideration of alternative interpretations often carry with them the greatest pressure for conformity to stereotyped images. An interesting example may be seen in the responses recently given by government officials to the following question: *Why has Iraq added 1,400 mobile tank transporters to its arsenal since the 1973 war?* The major reasons cited were the following:

>*In Tel Aviv:* The build-up is part of an Arab effort to prepare for an offensive attack against Israel by the *Eastern Front* (Iraq, Syria, Jordan, and Saudi Arabia).
>
>*In Ankara:* The build-up is primarily a response to the Iraqi government's substantial ethnic and religious domestic problems and the serious tensions with neighboring Iran.
>
>*In Damascus:* The build-up is part of the Iraqi attempt to strengthen its claim to leadership of the Arab world; to threaten the Israelis with the combined military strength of the Arab people; and to provide necessary mobility for dealing with Iran as well as Iraq's own internal problems.
>
>*In Washington:* The build-up is part of a continuing Soviet effort to influence the region through major supply programs of sophisticated weaponry. It is also a potential threat to Iraq's neighbors and Israel.

Regional experts believe that Iranians would view the noticeable improvement of Iraqi military mobility as potentially threatening. A Western defense official explained that "this argument was used by the previous government more than once in discussions about Iran's weapon needs.... It is assumed by diplomatic analysts that the revolutionary government of Ayatollah Khomeini would share this view." This case is a typical example

Iraq

of how an event might appear to be self-evident and unambiguous to an objective party, but carry different connotations to policy-makers because of their predispositions. Other policy-makers holding different perspectives either perceive the new information as supporting an altogether different, sometimes contradictory, explanation or ignore it altogether.

Facts are always available to support any argument one wishes to make or decision one wishes to defend. For example, Palestinians refer to statements made by Israeli Prime Minister Menachem Begin and members of his cabinet to show Israeli intransigence and the nature of the threats to the future well-being of the Palestinian people.[1] Similarly, Israeli officials point to Articles 15, 19, 21, or 23 of the PLO Covenant[2] as demonstrating Palestinian intransigence and the nature of threats to the existence of the state of Israel. Jordan's King Hussein summarized the problem in a public statement as follows: "If Israel has the right to say that the whole of Palestine is an Israeli land, we have the right to say that every inch of the Palestinian soil is Arab and that the whole of Palestine belongs to the Arabs."[3]

The degree of a decision-maker's personal involvement in terms of time, reputation, position, and responsibility can affect the way he perceives an event and the lessons he draws from it. A policy-maker's perception of data or an event is influenced not only by his predisposition and past personal involvement, but also by the matters of primary concern at the time he receives the information. For example, the downfall of the Shah of Iran resulted in the serious curtailment of oil for Western markets, gas for the Soviet Union, an end of the Iranian oil supplies to Israel, and a revolutionary Islamic fervor that threatened to spill over throughout the area. This had an effect upon Israeli, Arab, and Western perceptions of the Sadat peace initiatives and the Egyptian-Israeli peace process.

Policy-makers tend to overestimate the degree to which others are acting in response to what they themselves do. A message may be clear to the policy-maker doing the sending, but it may not be clear to the person receiving it. Even a gesture of good faith may be rejected as being a facade for ulterior motives and sinister intentions. It is easier to search for information that is consistent with and supportive of one's own goals and attitudes than to investigate other methods of approach to a problem. As we have suggested, it is standard practice for policy-makers to discredit both new sources of information and interpretation of data that is inconsistent with their predispositions. For example, many Western readers would reject out of hand any scenarios for settlement of the West Bank and Gaza that would allow for an independent Palestinian state, even one that expressed its willingness to coexist peacefully with Israel. Others would oppose any plan that called for a limited autonomy for the Palestinians, with defense and foreign affairs matters remaining in the hands of the Israelis. For various other readers, one or another of these two options might seem a perfectly acceptable compromise. The critical problem underlying the intransigence remains the protagonists' understanding or misunderstanding of the ultimate intentions of their adversaries. If either side continues to believe the worst ultimate intentions of their adversaries, then peace will not be achieved.

A Palestinian writer noted that "a large part of the whole problem is our mutual reluctance to listen to each other . . . yes, I understand that the Israelis fear for their physical security . . . but they must see that we Palestinians do too . . . and in fact more so, since we have suffered since 1948 much worse than the Israelis have [suffered] . . . in fact, we have suffered the loss of our land, the lives of many of our people, and so much else." Palestinian casualty figures since 1965, conservatively estimated at 40,000 dead, far exceed those of Israel and the Arab states. A PLO official dejectedly commented that "it reminds me of the stupid overkill arguments of the Russians and the Americans with nuclear weapons: if you're dead once or fifty times . . . does it matter? . . . So too, this killing of women, children: we must not look at who has lost more children — killing one child is too much — but rather why the killing is going on and what can all of us do to achieve a just settlement whereby all our children — mine, Mr. Peres' [Israeli Labor Party leader], Mr. Sadat's [Egyptian President] — all of them can live. That is what we must think about."

Threats

The most important understanding that we must grasp in seeking to analyze security considerations is the nature of perceived threats. An assessment of another's intentions and capabilities helps define the parameters of anticipated threats. These threats may seem unrealistic or exaggerated to an outside observer but they remain quite real to a threatened nation's policy-makers and/or a majority of its people. Underlying the Arab and Israeli intransigence over making concessions is the very real problem of perceived threats. A Syrian diplomat, for example, argued that "what poses a set of problems is that we know Israeli goals call for the territorial expansion of Israel . . . so the intentions are there despite public statements and Western propaganda to the contrary . . . the real problem is whether or not the Israelis will attack . . . a possibility which we Arabs must consider to be very real. . . ."

Similarly, most Israelis fear an attack from the Arab *Eastern Front*, a name given by the Israelis to the loose and informal grouping of Syria, Iraq, Jordan, and Saudi Arabia. Most Israelis share the view of a retired senior military officer who stated:

> This *Eastern Front* is a very real threat to Israel because its combined military strength makes it a more formidable oppo-

Arab-Israeli Conflict Area

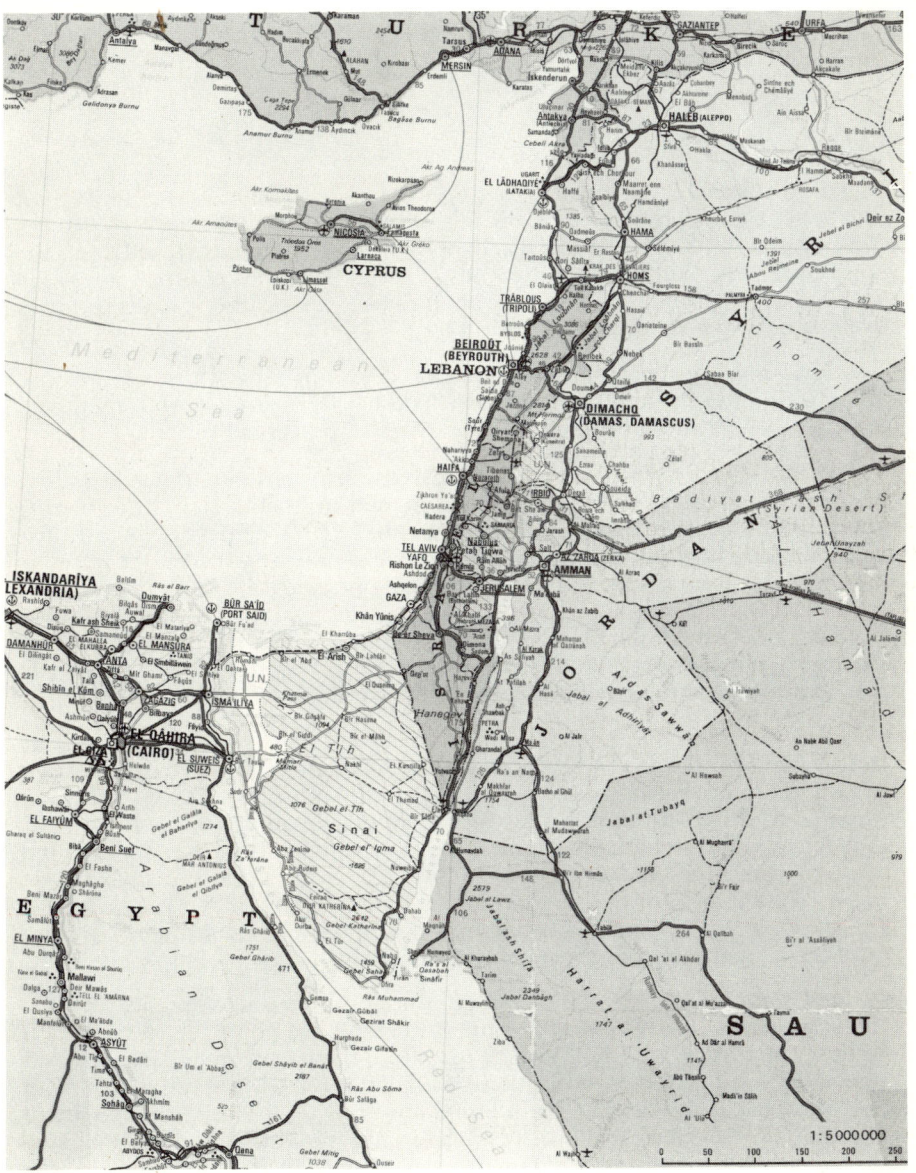

nent than Egypt ... and of course we can never discount the possibility that Egypt would renounce the Treaty and open a second front against us too.... But most of all we understand that the ultimate intentions of our Arab neighbors are by and far the same as they have been ... perhaps they are slightly more realistic now but that is hard to prove.

Assessing Capabilities

To assess perceived threats requires a system that facilitates analysis of the human and physical capabilities as well as the intentions of others. Discussions with Arab and Israeli policy-makers demonstrated that the various factors that are used to analyze the capabilities of other states are quite similar, although the degree of emphasis varies among Arab states as well as between the Arab states and Israel.

In analyzing the other protagonists' capabilities, both the Arabs and Israelis employ the following criteria. These criteria are worth remembering as we enter the second chapter's review of perceived threats.

• *Mobilization.* Although the questions most frequently asked deal with the quantity of different types of armed units and their equipment, each of the protagonists is deeply preoccupied with the question of military reserves. The limited geographical distance separating the major population centers of the six protagonists, and the sophistication of their weapons, necessitates lightning-like military maneuvers. Mobilization of reserves thus assumes an important influence over the course of any direct hostilities. A critical factor is the possible duration of a conflict — which is directly related to the question of weapons, mobilization time, and reserves.

• *Caliber.* An Israeli parliamentarian argued that there is a tendency in the region "to talk about 400 planes versus 600 planes or how many missiles one state or another possesses.... One cannot compare surface-to-surface missiles to air-to-air missiles, or aging training fighters to sophisticated modern aircraft, or helicopter gunships to reconnaissance craft ... it's like comparing oranges to watermelons." Questions which are frequently monitored include assessment of the morale and training of the regular (and reserve) forces, availability of spare parts, and the age, maintenance procedures, and operating condition of military equipment.

• *Human Resources.* The most commonly discussed elements concern the stamina, dedication, and resourcefulness of the populace to support a military operation and their ability to endure the hardships, shortages, and increased productivity requirements for sustaining the operation. An Arab political figure noted that "from our point of view, it is essential to judge whether the political and military leadership of a state is capable of sustained pressure and can remain in firm control of the situation ... the sophistication of Israeli military equipment means that a great sacrifice would be exacted in another war ... will the people tire?" Similarly, numerous Israelis have argued that a protracted war of attrition along several borders would exhaust the Israeli spirit and give question to how long Israel could sustain loss of life in a protracted violent struggle.

• *Support Capability.* One of the most important judgments to be made concerns the existence of a suitable infrastructure that can help to sustain an operation over extended periods of time. "The essential element in such an evaluation is the expected assistance from outside sources, which in the end means everything," argued a Syrian scholar. An Israeli defense correspondent agreed with this statement, but went a step further:

> Lacking the natural resources and quantity of ammunition and other basic supplies that one needs to wage a prolonged, full-scale war, both the Arabs and ourselves [Israelis] realize that above all else, we must not be mistaken in our estimate of how far allies and other third parties will go to lend assistance ... a small mistake in judging our own support sources or those of an enemy could likely mean the end of everything.

It is important to reemphasize that the six protagonists in the Arab-Israeli conflict are all highly dependent upon outside assistance for their continued day-to-day operations. Massive assistance from East, West, and other Middle Eastern states pours daily into the basic economies of Egypt, Jordan, Lebanon, Israel, Syria, as well as the West Bank and the PLO. The ability of any of these protagonists to wage war depends upon their estimation of the guarantees or assurances of support they have received or expect to receive for resupply and other indirect assistance from outside parties. It also includes an estimation of the probability and extent of such assistance to the adversary.

None of these elements by itself presents a totally accurate picture of an adversary's capabilities. For instance, cumulative Arab spending on weaponry (which since 1977 has reached an estimated $35 to $45 billion) is sometimes said to preclude the possibility for the survival of Israel in an all-out Arab-Israeli war. An Israeli statement noted that the Arabs today have 500,000 more men under arms and three times the conventional artillery of the combined NATO.[4] By 1980, it continues, the airpower of the Arab states will equal the combined Warsaw Pact forces and constitute twice the airpower of NATO and three times that of the People's Republic of China. However, a senior Israeli defense official noted:

> Having the capability means so much more than simply having the weapons. . . . Who do they [the Arabs] have to fly and maintain that equipment? . . . Where would they get spare parts and supplies? . . . Let's face it, they are as afraid of other Arabs using that equipment on each other as they are of us [Israel]. . . . If this

conflict were measured by the quantity of men under arms or aircraft ratios, we Israelis would have given up 30 years ago.

Assessing Intentions

Assessing intentions is even more difficult than judging capabilities as the former requires an analysis of psychological factors, ideological convictions, and an allowance for irrationality. The problems inherent in an assessment of intentions can be seen, for example, in an Israeli argument that the PLO must amend its Covenant and renounce terrorism before Israel will deal with the PLO. Other Israelis argue that a PLO amendment of the Covenant would serve only as what one senior Israeli diplomatic official called a "veneer applied to the reality, since the Palestinians will always want to destroy Israel." Like a West Bank official, many Palestinians who privately reject terrorism believe that "it is the only possible language which an Israeli like [Prime Minister] Begin understands. . . . When we [Palestinians] did not employ such tactics, everybody brushed us under the rug and pretended that our problem was one of a few unsettled *refugees*. . . . We all know their [Israeli] intentions. . . . They want to eliminate us as a people from the land that was ours." The Palestinians also ask why they should renounce their Covenant when Mr. Begin's "covenant" [Eretz Israel doctrine] is still publicly enunciated. An Egyptian official noted that it is difficult to bridge the barriers which exist between two people when "they both seem to believe with some historical justification that the ultimate intentions of the other calls for their own destruction."

Arab and Israeli policy-makers identified five basic factors that must be analyzed in attempting to understand the intentions of an adversary. They are:

• *Factual precedent and knowledge of the leadership's strengths and weaknesses.* A great deal of attention is paid to the patterns of leadership and authority in each of the protagonists' capitals. International opinion has clearly acknowledged that both the Arabs and Israelis have launched offensive attacks over the three and a half decades of the conflict. "There is little question," summarized a senior Arab journalist, "that our history in this dispute shows that both sides are capable and willing to launch an attack, or cause an incident, over a broad range of causes."

Arab and Israeli scholars and analysts have become experts on the styles, personalities, and records of the regional leaders. These experts carefully monitor statements and internal political nuances of Presidents Assad and Sadat, Prime Minister Begin, PLO Chairman Arafat, and King Hussein, along with a wider group of other regional leaders, including military commanders and cabinet officials. Israelis and Palestinians pay particular attention to the writings of the other's influential advisers, defense thinkers, and policy planning experts — searching for discovery or confirmation of new attitudes and policies. More often than not, one finds Hebrew articles and books in PLO offices, and Arabic articles and books in Israeli offices.

• *Change in the perceived balance of power.* The signing of special agreements with outside powers often affects the perceptions of intentions by other protagonists. The Soviet agreement with Syria in the fall of 1979 to forgive a large debt for armaments, and the proposed leasing of military facilities in Egypt to the United States seemed to some to alter the balance of power. Similarly, Syrian and Iraqi efforts during the early months of 1979 to bring about a merger of their foreign and military establishments was seen by the Israelis as a signal of a dangerous shift in the regional balance of power. This announced collaboration between two key Arab states provided the Israelis with what they called *collaborative evidence* that Israeli fears of an attack from the *Eastern Front* were well-founded. The subsequent disintegration of the collaborative efforts between Iraq and Syria in late 1979 received less formal public attention in Israel.

It should be noted that some Arab policy-makers believed that the Egyptian-Israeli Peace Treaty also denoted a collaborative effort which fit into what one Arab official called "Israel's plans to divide and subjugate the Arab world." Few regions of the earth boast such a delicate balance of power. Policy-makers are sensitive to shifts in this balance. Assessing intentions includes the search for such shifts in the political, economic, and military aspects of the regional power balance.

• *Undertaking new actions or making policy statements that indicate a change of policy.* There is a tendency to view even minor changes in the status quo as an indication of a shift in an adversary's policies. This is particularly true when suspicions of hostile intentions are taken for granted, such as in the Arab-Israeli conflict. A renewal or expanded agreement concluded with other states is often seen as an indication of increased hostile intent, as are discussions of possible alliances or cooperative agreements. The movement of troops and military equipment and the deployment of new surface-to-air missile batteries around population, industrial, and military areas are also viewed as representing an increased threat. A senior Israeli military official argued that "the stationing of an Iraqi batallion on Jordanian soil would be an act of hostility.... Such a move could only be seen by we Israelis as a further indication that the Arabs intend to launch an attack on us." Similarly, an Arab official asserted that "there is great concern over discussions to station the American Sixth Fleet at Haifa, which the Israelis have offered many times.... This would be a very difficult thing for the Arab world to accept regarding the true intentions of Israel and its allies."

• *Rising domestic difficulties.* Traditionally, governments seek to alleviate grave domestic predicaments by reinforcing the external threats that confront the state. In 1979, many Israelis believed that the Aleppo massacre of sixty-two Syrian army cadets by Moslem extremists would cause President Assad to take a harder line against Israel and the peacemaking process. Similarly, many Arabs believe that Prime Minister Begin's hard line against political leaders on the West Bank in the fall of 1979 was due to the critical state of economic affairs in Israel including an inflation rate exceeding 120 percent.

• *Estimates of intelligence activities.* It has been argued that few areas of the world have experienced the quantity of intelligence activities to the degree they have been practiced in the Middle East. "The intelligence gathering," noted an Arab military official, "is often as strong between Arab states as it is between Arabs and the Israelis." Information gleaned from professional and private channels is carefully assimilated by each of the six protagonists. An Israeli defense official believed that "in the final analysis, what really matters is our own eyes and ears and not what we hear from other sources.... Decisions, in the final analysis, must be based by and large on this information." Assessing intentions is a subjective process. A key policy-maker in the region summed up the situation this way: "We must remember that above all we must decide whether an action is a response to domestic pressures or reflects an attempt to confuse or lull us to sleep...or signals a new departure in policy.... A mistake can be fatal."

Each of the protagonists agrees that taking steps for peace will be considered dangerous, but they ask, how dangerous are the alternatives?

Special Concerns

A senior Palestinian political official argued that "outsiders cannot understand our [Arab] perception of threats until you know how we think and approach problems...." It is worth noting some of the basic procedural objections that Arabs and Israelis see as having hindered the peacemaking process. Numerous Arab officials decried the recent peacemaking process as being insensitive to their concerns. A Syrian official noted that "people in the West approach Middle East negotiations as if they were domestic labor disputes.... It is time that Westerners begin to realize that we are all Semitic peoples with our own cultural biases and history. I think I am calling for more sensitivity about our norms and thinking and not continuing to try to make us conform to your procedures and standards." The apparent lack of urgency often clashes with Western impatience for accommodation. An Arab negotiator recently chastized the American approach as being "obsessed with the need to see instant results." An Israeli parliamentarian stated that "many of us feel that some of the best proposals for settlement of specific problems might have been more favorably received had they been presented in different circumstances using different procedures. . . ." The complete lack of trust in the intentions of others precludes the possibility of a major policy position shift, as it would be seen as an act of unnecessary vulnerability and naivete.

The first special concern is the difference between the Arab and Israeli approaches to negotiation. A senior Jordanian cabinet official noted that "this conflict settlement process is not a river with forest and food but a desert with infrequent oases. . . . If we Arabs cannot see the end of the journey's destination, then we will not move." The lesson implied in this analogy helps to explain the original reluctance of other Arabs to join Egypt in the Camp David process. It is difficult to persuade Arabs that they should jump aboard the autonomy bandwagon for five years. The question is, what happens in five years? The Arabs do not accept the automatic definition used in the West of negotiation — an exercise in concession-making. Arabs argue that in 1980 they are devoid of 80 percent of what was Palestine fifty years ago. Thus, when they call for a permanent peace based on the 1967 borders, it is already a major concession, not an opening offer in a concession-making deal.

In a similar vein, historical conditions have compelled the Jewish people to think in understandably defensive terms and to review options and base decisions on a limited time-frame analysis. Mr. Begin has argued that there is no need to compete in hasty "concessionism."[5] He stressed that Jews must understand that they are living in their homeland and not in exile or in a ghetto. Decisions must not be made in haste or panic. An Arab diplomat stationed in Damascus noted that "everyone should remember that Arabs are fighting to regain something they have lost, including territory and pride, while the Israelis are fighting to preserve what they have gained. Time is perceived differently." Most Israelis privately agree that time is more likely to be against Israel than the Arabs. Some argue that history demonstrates the difficulty of retaining a military occupation over a large number of people for a prolonged period. Can three million Jews keep two million Palestinians under military occupation? For now, most Israelis agree that the answer is in the affirmative. What of the future? It is seen as certainly very difficult and perhaps very dangerous by most Israelis with whom the Task Force met.

The second concern involves the very process of negotiation itself. Each of the protagonists is seen as having established a set of intractable preconditions on specific issues that must be accepted by their adversary before they will enter the peacemaking process. In addition, the Israelis have approached the negotiations in the same manner as would a lawyer reviewing the *letter of the word* in a contract. The Arabs have approached the negotiations with a philosophy that does not accept the automatic primacy of concessions and accommodations. Whereas a Western negotiator might advocate splitting the difference between the bargaining positions of his adversary and himself in order to reach a settlement, many Arabs[6] would traditionally invoke a doctrine of true worth. A Western diplomat and student of Middle East affairs explained that doctrine as follows: "Typically, an Arab would rather sit with an empty apartment for a year to establish the worth of his property than to rent it for far less than what he feels it is worth." More importantly, the Arab people believe that they have already paid a high enough price to compensate the Jewish people for the European atrocities of the 1940s.

A third concern is language. Verbal threats and a high level of linguistic violence exudes from both Arab and Israeli capitals. A ranking Arab official recently asked how anyone could deal with "a man like [Prime Minister] Begin who utters such a continuous stream of contempt, hatred, and obstinacy in everything he says and does." The Saudi royalty was shocked by President Sadat's descriptions of the royal family following the Baghdad meeting of the rejectionist states which condemned Egypt for making peace with Israel. The tactical use of extreme language is a much-used tool in the Arab-Israeli conflict. There is also a proclivity to express positions and ideas in the most antagonistic and uncompromising fashion. Such an expression invites the hostile reception that most often greets Arab and Israeli statements. Both parties, Arabs and Israelis, point to public statements as indications of the true intentions of their adversaries. Privately, many Arabs and Israelis note that much of the extreme rhetoric is designed for political (domestic and international) consumption.

A fourth concern that both Arabs and Israelis identified in private discussions is the tendency to reject quickly options for resolving specific problems without adequate study or discussion. For example, the protagonists have not yet systematically considered the costs and benefits of various scenarios being suggested for the future of the West Bank and Gaza. These include options for a partially autonomous Palestinian entity under some limited Israeli rule, a West Bank federated with Jordan with provisions for demilitarized or limited armament zones, a neutral Palestinian state on the West Bank and Gaza based on models like Austria and Switzerland, or an independent state. The basic prerequisite that is accepted by all Arabs, and privately by a growing number of Israelis, is the right of the Palestinians to exercise self-determination. Accordingly, the fears that are held over the prospects of a full settlement could be somewhat allayed if some visions of the future were discussed which reconciled Palestinian self-determination with the mutual security needs of each of the six protagonists.

Notwithstanding the unwillingness to analyze options in depth, each of the protagonists demands immediate answers to very specific questions. "At a time when neither the Israelis, including the Israeli peace movement, nor the Arabs have carefully thought through where the whole process is going, it seems difficult to expect answers to specific questions," declared a respected Middle East newspaper editor.

A study of the root causes and history of this conflict demonstrates that treatment of the conflict as a bilateral affair (for example, between Israel and Egypt or Israelis and Palestinians) is insufficient. Nor is it a trilateral affair including the United States. The conflict is clearly a multilateral affair made up of six distinct protagonists. None of these protagonists is monolithic. For example, the political leadership among the Palestinians, Lebanese, or Israelis is splintered along ideological, social, religious, and economic lines. A senior Jordanian official noted that since Camp David, the population of the region lives in an atmosphere of "heightened insecurity brought about by the various bilateral attempts to solve what are essentially regional and multilateral problems. The result is redoubled regional insecurity and further delays to the process of reaching agreement."

Whether the current peacemaking process being advocated by Egypt, Israel, and the United States will succeed in the long run is speculation and not the subject of this publication. However, it is important to note that there are several substantive and procedural problems that have hindered the peacemaking process. A distinguished Middle East jurist argued the problem this way: "We are all guilty of not listening and in fact we do not even care to listen. . . . The conflict will not be resolved until each of us decides to pay a little attention to the hazards without and with peace . . . which each of us perceives to exist. . . and to search a little deeper for the true intentions of other peoples, not their regime's stated policies."

Israeli Deputy Prime Minister Yigael Yadin noted that beyond the often discussed physical security dimensions of the conflict are other concerns of great importance. He continued:

> Less immediately obvious, however, are the potential psychological and social hazards of peace. How does a society which had fought four wars in 30 years and of necessity developed security as its highest value learn to cope with peace? How do two former enemies overcome decades of mutual negative stereotypes and avoid cultural misunderstandings?[7]

Asked to respond to this quotation, a Syrian diplomat remarked that "the psychological hazards of war and peace are not unique to either side." The perceptions of threats and the limitations of the peacemaking process in the past give rise to what an Egyptian scholar called "an uninviting area which must be explored if there is to be real peace, but an area that requires the willingness of each party to better understand what really causes fears among the others." Questions about the future of the conflict were best summarized by an African diplomat stationed in the Middle East. He asked: "Is the sense one gets from private discussions really true? . . . Is the old conflict being outgrown? . . . And if it is, when will we see public actions confirming private opinions?" An overwhelming number of senior Arabs and Israelis agreed that the next generation will be more willing to make peace. Arabs point to the composition of the Israeli Peace Now movement—mostly young people, many from the army. Officials in Cairo and Jerusalem note that it was the military, not the diplomats and politicians, who pushed hardest for agreements in the Egyptian-Israeli peace process. Many believe that this represents a good trend—if it is not too late.

This exercise of reviewing the nature of perceptions, threats, and the peacemaking process is meant to set the stage for the difficult process that follows. It is extremely hard for anyone to be, or to be seen as, impartial in the Arab-Israeli conflict. The perceptions that each of us has formed favor the tendency to view actions as something other than what they are. Each of us is guided by idiosyncratic perceptions. If such perceptions could be brought closer to reality, where some common ground exists, then insofar as the members of the Task Force have learned, the basic public positions of the six protagonists might be brought closer to their private views. The purpose of the next chapter is to review the perceptions of threats held by each of the protagonists.

The general unhappiness of Arabs and Israelis concerning the status quo is related to a strongly held set of convictions that the ultimate goal of the adversary is its physical destruction, or the undermining of societal and political norms and institutions. The combination of these two elements has been largely responsible for the growing uneasiness over the large failures and small successes of the Arab-Israeli peacemaking process. This uneasiness is fueled by each protagonist's perception that an adversary possesses the intentions and capabilities to inflict unacceptable damage. Each protagonist's public policy position reflects these perceptions. The insecurity which is produced from acceptance of these perceptions encourages a more intractable policy-making process. In addition to the public policies, there is a second dimension to the nature of perceptions in the Arab-Israeli conflict. Privately, Israelis and Arabs agree that the status quo is not acceptable and that some concessions will have to be made. Making concessions, however, depends upon perceptions of some good intentions on the part of the adversary. It must be grounded in the belief that each protagonist seeks to live in peace.

Many Israelis said that Arabs would never consider making concessions. Similarly, most Arabs believed that the Israelis would not willingly make concessions over the occupied territories. Yet, the overwhelming majority of Arabs and Israelis in the *sample* privately argued that both sides would eventually make some concessions. Arabs and Israelis privately agreed that the most urgent problem to be resolved is Palestinian self-determination and the future status of the West Bank and Gaza. Both argued that some form of Palestinian entity would have to evolve in order to resolve the Palestinian question. Privately, the Task Force held long discussions with Arabs and Israelis, including Israeli Arabs, about possible scenarios of the future for the region if there was a comprehensive peace. These ranged from the idea of a *Benelux-type union* to a region neutral in great power politics and military ventures. Several specific, more immediate ideas were suggested and are examined in Chapter Four.

The Task Force analyzed the perceived threats and security requirements presented by the six protagonists. In addition, the Task Force made efforts to assess confidence-building strategies that could help alter the perceptions of threat. Two basic conclusions resulted from the assessment. The first is a belief that each protagonist's gradual display of true intentions to live in peace would feed the other protagonists' hopes and private beliefs that peace is indeed possible. The second is the apparent need to suggest and institute confidence-building measures that would be mutually reinforcing. These confidence-building measures could be unilateral or bilateral in nature, and could be implemented by the protagonists themselves or include an objective third party. A Jordanian official noted, "As long as we each choose to offer only unmovable positions, there can be no progress . . . but unless the enemy does something to show us that we should change our perceptions, we won't."

Small changes in reality can generate a much wider shift in perceptions. The *private* views in the region, as expressed to the Task Force in 1979, are far more conciliatory, and demonstrate greater willingness to experiment with new options, than has been the case in the past. If the protagonists' perceptions could be brought closer to the factual reality as perceived by objective parties, where some common ground exists, then greater progress might be expected in the peacemaking process. We first must ask if it is true that a majority of the populace of each of the six protagonists desires peace and is willing to live within secure and recognized borders with each other, including the Palestinians (whether it be in confederation with Jordan, or whatever form is decided by the Palestinian people and other peoples directly concerned). If this is true, then we must ask, what is preventing the protagonists from achieving a full settlement and peace? The answer can be found in the perceptions of threat still held by the protagonists for one another.

2
Perceptions of Threats

Each of the six protagonists in the Arab-Israeli conflict has particular fears that are based upon clearly defined threats and precedents. Certain fears are shared by both Arabs and Israelis. This chapter provides a comparative review of how each of the protagonists perceives some of the major threats which currently exist in the conflict. There is no attempt to refute or support any one of the listed threats. Some Middle East policy-makers strongly supported this exercise of collecting private views of perceived threats and presenting a composite picture. A Jordanian scholar was among those who favored the idea. He stated that "the time has come for an impartial party to identify and present the basic worries or fears which privately are held by each of the parties in this conflict.... It would be helpful for each party to see how others listed their private concerns.... It is difficult for people in the West and elsewhere to see that security is a multifaceted thing and that each of us has legitimate fears."

Each of the listed threats in this chapter is examined along three dimensions. The first identifies the nature of what is perceived as threatened and attempts to distinguish which segment of the population perceives the threat. For example, a threat against one's survival and physical safety is a more serious threat than one against prestige, natural resources, or political authority. It is also important to distinguish what segment of the population perceives the threat. The second dimension concerns the credibility of the threatening party. Is the party capable of carrying out the threat? Precedents form an important dimension in such an analysis. Is the threatening party willing to take the risks inherent in carrying out the threat, or is the threat largely a bluff or weakly supported action that might be rescinded in the face of any demonstrative response? The third dimension concerns the estimation of costs and benefits for the threatening party to carry out a particular action. Would the costs of implementing the threat be greater than what is to be gained?

Each of the listed threats in this chapter meets three basic criteria: First, each must be listed as a threat by more than half of those Arabs or Israelis who participated in the 1978 and 1979 Middle East Task Force discussions. Second, it must be reflected as a legitimate concern in the public record (statements and documents) during 1978 and 1979. Finally, it must correspond to events which happened during that period or which were reported to have happened.

The reader is reminded that the threats presented in this chapter are those expressed by the governmental and non-governmental professionals who talked with the Task Force members in Jordan, Syria, the West Bank, Gaza, Lebanon, Egypt, and Israel. The material presented does not represent the views of the author or Task Force, but rather summarizes as succinctly as possible the views expressed privately by those living in the region. Understanding some of these perceived threats will not be easy for the reader. It is important, however, to try to understand what is seen as threatened and ask, *why*? In the next chapters we will analyze suggestions for meeting the threats.

Israel

Prior to the 1979 Egyptian-Israeli Peace Treaty, Israel had never achieved agreement on permanent borders with any of its neighbors. Its frontiers in existence since 1948 followed as a consequence of war. Despite the peace treaty with Egypt, the majority of Israelis today still adhere to the view that defensible borders without peace are preferable to peace without defensible borders. In an October 1976 *Foreign Affairs* article, Yigal Allon wrote that the Arab states seek to "isolate, strangle, and erase Israel from the world's map."[1] The Israeli public embraced the concept that Israel was saved in October, 1973, largely because the enemy had been at a distance when the war began, and there was sufficient time for mobilization to stop the several front attacks.

Today, Israel is in a quandary. Lacking the support of world public opinion and having achieved peace with Egypt (thus effecting the isolation of Egypt from the Arab world—a long-term goal of some Israelis), it faces unrelenting pressure for more concessions, particularly over the West Bank, Gaza, and Jerusalem. Israel's traditional benefactor, the United States, is now responsible for much of that pressure. The facts confronting Israel are not pleasant. Israeli officials note that defense spending and government debt service consumes some 60 percent of the state budget. The balance of payments deficit was expected to reach $4.5 billion for the 1979 fiscal year. Inflation exceeded 120 percent. The estimated 1978 GNP was $10.5 billion, of which defense spending was said to have accounted for some 28 percent.

Since 1973, the United States has pumped more than $10 billion worth of aid into Israel, more than half of it in military equipment, including the latest and most sophisticated weapons in the American arsenal.[2] A respected Western analyst said that compared to 1973, today Israel is 60

Israel

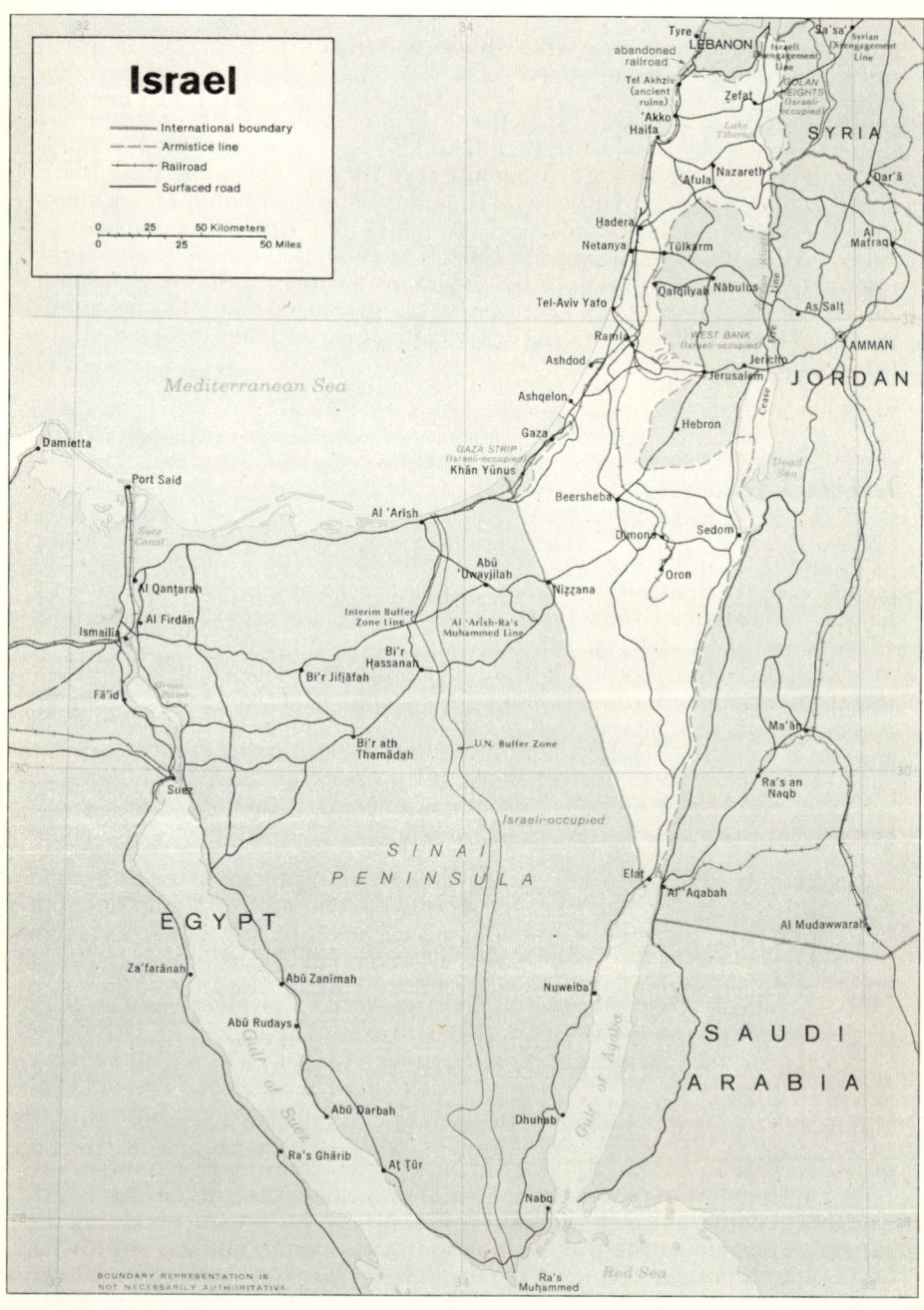

percent stronger in terms of armaments and Egypt 10 percent weaker. In the opinion of many American and European officials, Israel will never be proportionately stronger than it is now and, therefore, may never again be in a better position to make peace.

Twelve years is a relatively short span of time in the Middle East. But it is sufficient time for a people to grow accustomed to having a larger country. "The added territory [seized in the 1967 war]," noted a senior Israeli defense official, "has given us a feeling of security that we have not known before. It is probably hard for an outsider to understand how such a small piece of land has affected us so greatly, but it has." He added, "For some, security is an intellectual construct, but for Jews, security means life."

A 1978 poll noted that 90 percent of all Israelis believed that there would be another war within the next eight years. A similarly high percentage believed that the Arab objective remains to drive Jews into the sea. The polltaker, Louis Guttman of the Institute for Applied Social Research in Jerusalem, noted that "it is significant that the same 80 percent does not think that anything can be done to change this."[3] General Rafael Eytan, as Chief-of-Staff in 1978, said that the Arabs were currently using "other means in their aim of eliminating Israel." When asked by an Israeli reporter whether this included their participation in negotiations, he replied, "everything they're doing."[4]

The peace treaty with Egypt has begun to convince Israelis that peace might be possible, eventually. But a recently retired Israeli military officer noted, "Nobody has fears for their security like we do . . . nobody."

Israeli Perceptions of Threat

- *An attack from the* Eastern Front *(Syria, Iraq, Jordan, Saudi Arabia)*

Many Arabs believe that Israel is again becoming complacent with the status quo. Israeli intelligence estimates conclude that, although it is unlikely that the Arabs today could defeat Israel in another surprise war, they could score modest tactical victories—such as seizing Jericho and blocking the road to Jerusalem or detaching the finger of Galilee known as the Hula Valley, which is only five miles across at its base. (See map on page 48.) This conclusion could serve as a motivating force for new negotiations and American pressures upon Israel for altering the status quo. A tank crossing of the Jordan River could reach Tel Aviv in less than twelve hours. Currently, private estimates of the partial-mobilization time needed for Israel to deflect an attack range from four to eighteen hours. (A precise figure depends upon circumstances.) Full mobilization can be undertaken within 16-48 hours, considerably less than the official figure of 72 hours. Privately,

Golan Heights and Vicinity (including the Hula Valley)

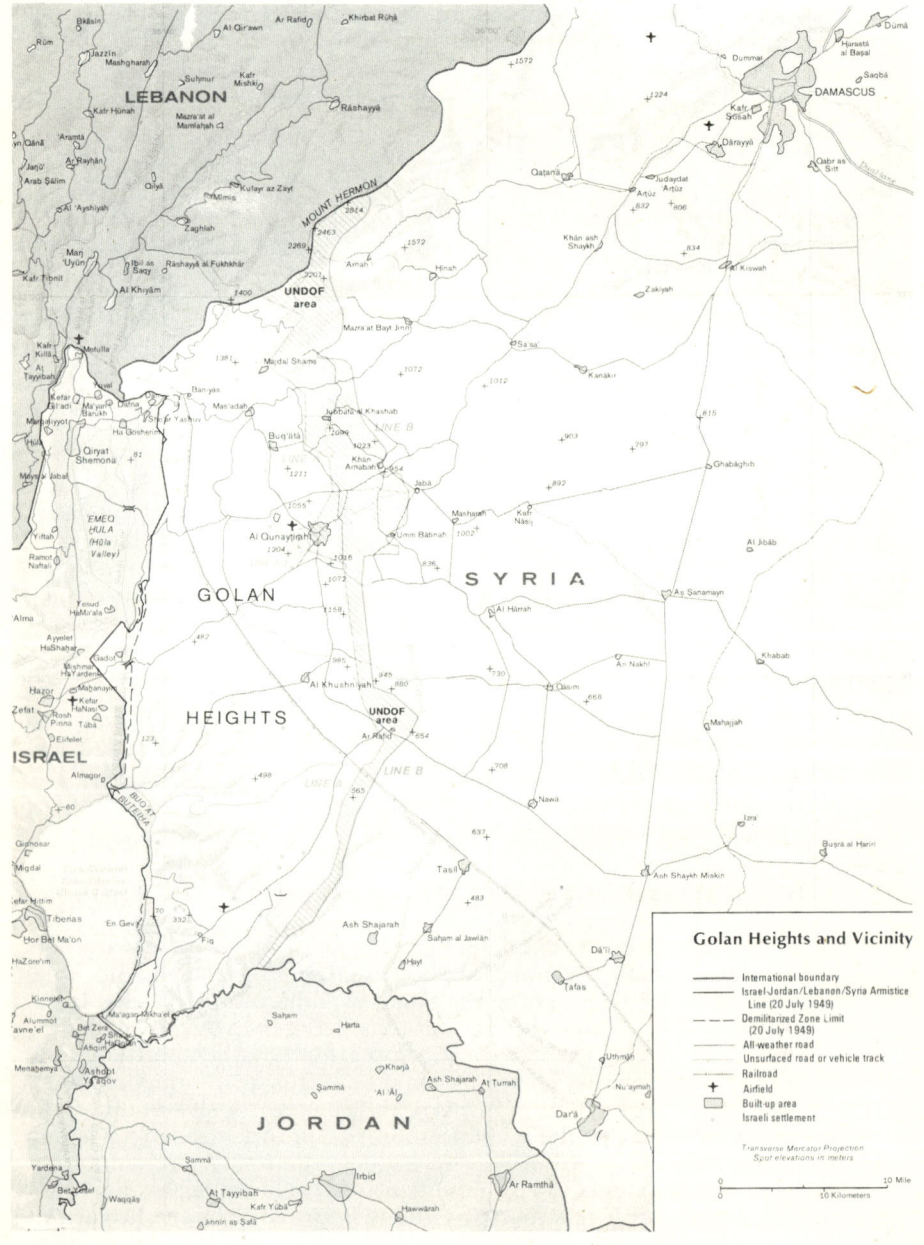

Western strategic thinkers have estimated that a fully mobilized Israel could withstand an attack by forces outnumbering them by 3:1. According to the 1979/80 edition of *The Military Balance* (London, IISS), the total armed forces are: Jordan (67,200); Iraq (222,000); Syria (227,500); and Israel (165,600 up to 400,000 when mobilized). Since 1973, Israel and the three key *Eastern Front* countries have spent nearly the same amount ($12 to $15 billion) on military costs, according to composite public figures. The total amount of Israeli defense spending is not known precisely; 1973-78 estimates range from a low of $16 billion to a high of $20 billion. The U.S. Arms Control and Disarmament Agency report, *World Military Expenditures and Arms Transfers 1968-77* (October 1979), estimates the figure at $16.5 billion. There is some disagreement in Israel as to whether Saudi Arabia should be added to the list of countries belonging to the *Eastern Front*. Saudi Arabia's geographical proximity and recent arms procurements have given new impetus to consider Saudi Arabia a potential threat. The Saudi army is said to have 44,500 troops (IISS). Saudi Arabia is more often than not omitted from Israeli discussions of the *Eastern Front*. Its inclusion in this discussion is to present to the reader the hardest-line Israeli arguments.

Since the 1973 war, the Moslem nations of the region are said to have spent some $48 billion on arms.[5] A review of other published data indicates that this figure is closer to $60 billion. Jordan has doubled its combat aircraft and deployed its first surface-to-air missile batteries. Iraq and Syria have doubled their ground and air forces. The number of Iraqi helicopters capable of anti-tank warfare has risen dramatically. Syria now possesses surface-to-surface missiles capable of hitting targets anywhere in Israel. Both Syria and Iraq have received T-72 Soviet tanks, which are rated superior to the American-made tanks as well as the Centurions that form the bulk of Israel's arsenal. Israel, however, is building and deploying the Chariot tank which is rated equal to the T-72 Russian tank.

According to published figures, the Iraqi-Syrian-Jordanian front along Israel's northern and eastern borders would have 500,000 troops; 4,500 tanks and some 800 combat planes (compared to 650 for Israel). The Syrians have "better arms than in 1973 when they came close to overrunning Israel's northern towns," said Defense Minister Weizman.[6] Israelis have expressed fears over the potential use of the arsenal that remains in Iran, including 500 aircraft of equal quality to Israel's air force. The Israeli Chief-of-Staff has argued that a joint *Eastern Front* is twice as strong as the Egyptian front.[7] Russian T-72 battle tanks together with Scud missiles, 122mm and 150mm self-propelled guns, and TU-22 medium-range bombers have been introduced into the arsenals of these countries. The reopening of the Iraqi-Syrian railroad and introduction of 1,400 Iraqi mobile tank transports add the important element of mobility to Arab fighting capability. If one includes Saudi matériel, the imbalance appears even greater.

The quantity of weapons in itself does not present an accurate picture of fighting capability. Armaments added to combat aircraft are an important determinant of fighting capability. For example, Israeli A-4E Skyhawk planes can fire Maverick TV-guided air-to-surface missiles from a range of 22 kilometers. The Israeli Luz-1 missile (air-to-surface) has a range reported at 80 kilometers which would allow Israelis to hit important land targets without risking entry of enemy airspace.

The Israelis believe that Egypt could be dragged into another Arab-Israeli war. Egyptian Premier Mustapha Khalil told his Parliament that "if Syria made an attempt to liberate the Golan Heights by force, this should be considered a defensive war and in that event the joint Arab Defence Pact [of which Egypt is a member] could be invoked."[8] This possibility raised considerable concerns in Israel. In particular, questions were raised about the relative importance of the peace treaty vis-à-vis this Arab Defence Pact. Israeli strategists agree that despite the composite weapons imbalance, Israel has a clear, even decisive, edge over the *Eastern Front* countries in terms of accuracy, firepower, tactics, and training.

A respected Israeli general noted, "Outsiders simply do not believe that these four countries will attack Israel without Egypt. Yes, they know that they cannot obliterate us yet, but they also know that they could defeat Israel in phases . . . you know, the attitude that 'if we can't take Haifa, then let's take something a little closer and easier, and get Haifa later.' " Another Israeli General who is held in high regard in Israel added, "What would be worse would be a wide-spread, coordinated attack on all of our borders. Perhaps they [Arabs] do not today have the coordination or political will to work together, but when that day comes, it will be a realization of the nightmare every Jew dreams could happen."

- *Establishment of a Palestinian state on the West Bank and Gaza*

Most Israelis recognize that the Palestinian people and the majority of Arab, socialist, and third world nations are committed to see an independent Palestinian state established on the West Bank and in Gaza. Even traditionally pro-Israeli countries like the United States are expressing their interest for some form of self-determination for the Palestinian people, which Israelis see as leading to an independent state. The Palestinian people appear to be committed to this goal.

Mr. Begin has frequently noted that such a state would become a "lackey of the Soviet Union sniffing around for Middle East oil." Past Israeli polls showed 90 percent of the Israeli populace were publicly opposed to the establishment of a fully independent and armed Palestinian state.[9] Israelis cite statistics such as the following:

- There are just eight miles between the West Bank hills above Tel Aviv and the waterline [sea]. (See maps on pages 52-53.)

- Soviet artillery already in the hands of the PLO have a maximum range of an M-46 medium-range field gun, 10,000 meters — which would place every Israeli citizen within direct firing range from a Palestinian West Bank state.

The Israelis argue that even if the Palestinians under PLO leadership were to take control over this new state, they could not prevent Palestinian fringe-groups from carrying out acts of terrorism. A prominent Israeli dove said, "Even if it wished, a moderate Palestinian government in Nablus could not suppress the extremist who wanted Haifa or Jaffa." The most critical arguments for the Israelis are those which relate to the military realities. For example, a senior government official noted privately, "We know foreign troops would be invited to stage maneuvers on Palestinian territory or even be stationed on Palestinian territory under some defense pact. Such actions would threaten Israeli security."

Israelis claim that most Arabs would also fear a heavily armed, aggressive Palestinian state. On the eve of the signing of the Egyptian-Israeli Peace Treaty, an Israeli Cabinet minister spoke of a conversation he and other Israeli ministers had with a senior U.S. official. They said, "He told us that Egypt, Jordan, Saudi Arabia, and even Syria were against the establishment of a Palestinian state, no matter what they said publicly."[10]

The goal of an independent Palestinian state has been espoused by the Arabs in one form or another since 1948. Israelis believe that the security and very existence of the Jewish state of Israel is at stake. Most Israelis, including many members of the Israeli peace movement, fear the implications of a sovereign Palestinian state on the future viability of Israel. The quandary for most Israelis is how to accommodate the need to give the Palestinians an entity of their own without granting full sovereignty. Many fear the two are not reconcilable.

- *Arab population growth in Israel*

Many Israelis believe that the addition of more than a million Arabs in Gaza and the West Bank to the population of Israel would seriously jeopardize the Jewish nature of the state. There are some 6,000 Jews currently living on the West Bank. Prime Minister Levi Eshkol summarized the conquest of the Arab lands in 1967 with their million Arab residents: "The dowry is gorgeous, but the bride is so homely."[11] The Israeli response after 1967 was not to annex the areas, excepting Arab Jerusalem, but to establish a military governing authority over the occupied territories with limited political and economic powers given to the inhabitants.

It is estimated that the total Arab population within the area controlled by Israel today is 1.7 million.[12] Deputy Prime Minister Yigael Yadin argued,

Israeli Maps Showing Geo-Strategic Dangers

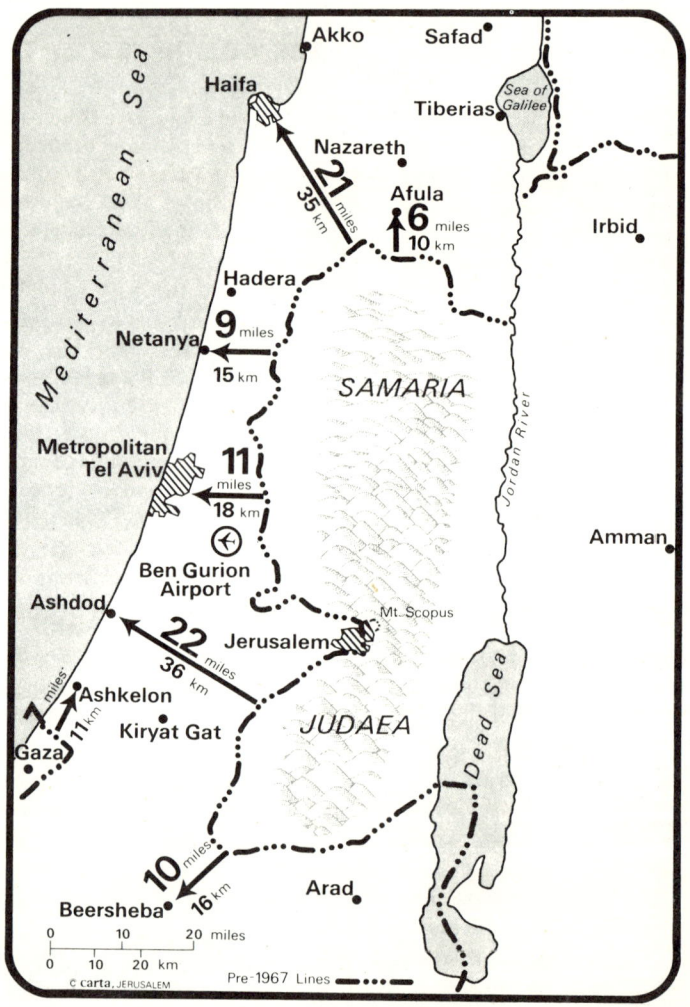

NATURAL BOUNDARIES

Prior to 1967, there was no natural boundary between Jordan and Israel (or between the Gaza district and Israel), such as the Jordan River, which serves today as a clear physical barrier against both military attack and terrorist infiltration. Instead, the pre-1967 armistice line skirted the western foothills of the central mountain range of Judaea-Samaria — stretching more than 2½ times the length of today's cease-fire line in the same sector. Thus, all communication between the north and south of Israel was forced to make a wide detour around the Judaea-Samaria bulge, and Israel's narrow coastal strip was hopelessly vulnerable. A Palestinian state can only be established in Judaea-Samaria and Gaza by reinstating these totally intolerable conditions.

CONTROL OVER ISRAEL'S AIRSPACE

Anti-aircraft missiles would control almost all of Israel's airspace, and would thus be a constant threat to the country's main communications link with the rest of the world. In time of war, such missiles could totally paralyze the aerial activity which is so vital for Israel's defence, and for the re-supply of its armed forces.

ARTILLERY THREAT TO CIVILIAN CENTRES

The range and destructive capacity of the artillery in Arab arsenals has more than doubled since 1967. Thus, over 90% of Israel's civilian population and virtually all of its industrial infrastructure would today be vulnerable to massive bombardment from beyond the pre-1967 armistice lines, with inestimable human suffering and casualties.

Reprinted from *A PLO State - mortal danger*, Israel Information Centre, 1/78.

"If we go on forever controlling the whole of the West Bank, we won't be able to remain a state that is both democratic and Jewish."[13]

Equally significant to the Israeli leaders is the declining number of immigrants as well as the sizeable emigration of young Israelis, particularly to the United States. A prominent Israeli scholar revealed that "private government figures show that there are nearly 400,000 Israeli citizens living in the eastern United States, including many of our best young minds." According to the *1979 American Jewish Yearbook*, the Jewish population of Israel increased by 1.8 percent in 1978, while the non-Jewish rate increased by 3.5 percent. The *Yearbook* quotes the balance between immigration and emigration as a 4,000 rise in population in 1978.

Composite figures of published data indicate that Israeli Arabs living in pre-1967 Israel now number some 500,000 of whom 78 percent are Moslem. This population has a rate of natural increase of some 36.2 per thousand and a median age of 15.5, making them one of the youngest populations in the world.[14] There has been some debate in Israel over whether there should be integration or segregation of the Israeli Arabs. Either alternative can be seen as threatening some of the basic norms of the Jewish state. These Israeli Arab communities conduct business and teach in schools in the Arabic language; Hebrew is a second language. Overall, given current growth rates, Israeli Jews should double their numbers every forty-one years, while Palestinian Arabs inside Israel should double every nineteen years.

The results of a recent poll sponsored by the Ford Foundation taken among Arabs within Israel's 1967 borders were discomforting to Israeli policy-makers. Half of Israel's Arab minority responded that they did not recognize Israel's right to exist as an independent state and 75 percent favored an independent Palestinian state on the West Bank.[15] The designer of the study, Dr. Sami Smouha of Haifa University, noted that 48 percent of those polled described themselves as Palestinians.[16] Some 87 percent of Israel's Arabs supported a return to the pre-June 1967 borders.[17] All of this led Professor Smouha to conclude that sooner or later the Israeli government will have to include the problems of Israel's Arabs on the agenda of the peace process. There are approximately 500,000 Arabs currently residing in pre-1967 Israel.

Jewish mayors in Galilee denounced the emerging radicalism among Galilean Arabs and called on the government to respond vigorously by settling another 300,000 Jews in the region in the next five years.[18] Since the 1967 war, the Jewish majority in Galilee has dropped from 56 to 52 percent. Israeli Northern Command head, General Aluf Avigdor Ben-Gal, reportedly told Knesset members that the Galilee Arabs were a "cancer in Israel."[19] His remarks sparked a bitter debate over the minority problem in Israel.

Finally, if the 1.5 million Arabs now within Israeli-controlled areas were mobilized into an effective resistance, it is conceivable that they could raise internal havoc and create an important wartime diversion of crucial Israeli forces from the fronts. A former high-ranking Israeli official said, "This is the classic case of damned if you do, damned if you don't. We don't know the answer, but we do know that the threat from within is very real."

Israelis publicly recognize that some resistance from the Arabs, particularly on the West Bank and Gaza, has been constant since 1967. Privately, Israeli officials acknowledge that the birthrate and the immigration/emigration statistics are most worrisome to them.

The Jewish character of Israel and the democratic values which Israel's founders sought to instill as an inherent part of the character of the state are seen as most directly threatened. Some argue that the very security and existence of the state of Israel is at stake. Most Jewish Israelis share the fear of losing the Jewish character and values; many express concern over the evident growing discontent among Israeli Arabs.

Recent polls and statements emanating from Israeli Arabs as well as those in the the occupied lands demonstrate that the Arab political will to express its disapproval is growing more direct and aggressive. Those under occupation know the risks of rising up against the authorities. However, the process can be a gradual one, presenting a *fait accompli*. "I will tell you personally that one day the Jewish state of Israel may discover that it has a clear majority of Moslem Arab citizens," noted a Hebrew University administrator.

The threat posed by the large Arab population within Israel is often given as the reason why Israel has not annexed the West Bank and Gaza and is perhaps the most difficult problem that the Israelis must confront. An Israeli analyst, Yehoshafat Harkabi, once chief of the Israeli Army Intelligence, paraphrased the Arabs, saying, "Now we [Arabs] don't have to destroy Israel, but make it unviable, produce the conditions by which Israel will destroy itself. . . ."[20]

Israeli concern over the issue of the *right of return* is related to population fears. A senior official painted the scenario, "What if they [the Palestinians] decided to subvert us and in a peace agreement many thousands asked to come back to Jaffa, Haifa, and the rest. . . . It would mean so many more Arabs and they reproduce so quickly . . . This could indicate another way to destroy us." This *right of return* issue is considered by many Israeli officials to represent the ultimate test of Palestinian intentions about living in peace with Israel. A Knesset member argued, "I can never believe that the PLO would agree to relinquish the right to return to our [pre-1967] borders. . . ." When asked what would happen if the PLO were to agree to such an item, he responded, "I might quit my seat [in the Knesset] because it would

signify that everything I have fought for was based on a mistaken premise
. . . but don't worry, because it will never happen."

- *An alteration of Israel's special relationship with the United States*

U.S. Senator Patrick Moynihan argued that "you cannot simply change [policy] because the Saudi King, Prince or whatever, has said, 'Well, we'll let you have another million barrels of oil a day as a Fourth of July present . . .' to repeat — the American foreign policy is not for sale. . . Americans would walk to work before we sell out another democratic power for oil."[21]

Israelis admit that it is this kind of support along with billions of dollars in financial assistance raised privately by Jewish organizations throughout the world that help to maintain the financial viability of the state of Israel. Israelis fear that a lessened sense of urgency about the threats to Israel's security, or pressure from U.S. public opinion reacting to the dictates of OPEC, could jeopardize that flow of funds.

In Israel recent trends are viewed as indicative of a significant change, not an erosion, of U.S. policy. Former Foreign Minister Moshe Dayan attributes the change to a real concern in the United States about the "problems of its economy, energy and the price of oil."[22] Others attribute the change to the Egyptian-Israeli Peace Treaty, which has encouraged a willingness among many in the United States to deal in terms of parity between Egypt and Israel. Polls show an increasing tendency in U.S. public opinion to be more critical of Israel, especially of its policies regarding the West Bank and Gaza. Aircraft on order by Egypt include 42 F-5E, 8 F-5F, 35 F-4E, 14 Mirage 5 and 12 C-130 H transports, and most recently the sophisticated F-16 and F-15. The announcement by the United States that it was selling up to 300 M-60 tanks to Jordan as replacement for its M-48 model was a shock to the Israelis. So was the announcement that West Germany was selling 500 Leopard tanks, some missiles, and some fighter-bomber Tornados to Iraq. The announced sale of French AMX-30 tanks and Mirage 3 jets to Saudi Arabia, in addition to 45 F-15 fighters and 150 M-60 tanks already on order from the United States, has further raised Israeli fears.

The Americans reportedly informed Israel that the nuclear reactor promised by President Richard Nixon would be delivered only if Israel agreed to comprehensive supervision of all of its nuclear facilities. Israel has refused this kind of surveillance in the past. These trends are seen as results of a U.S. decision to be more even-handed in the Arab-Israeli conflict. In February 1979, Defense Minister Ezer Weizman told U.S. Defense Secretary Harold Brown that Israel planned to reduce its military requirements by 25 percent over the next ten years. Yet, in the early fall, Defense Minister Weizman visited Washington with a shopping list of aid requirements that far exceeded previous requests. The Dean of the Economics Department at Jerusalem's Hebrew University estimates that one-fifth of Israel's gross national product goes for defense spending, and added, "Actually, in real terms, it's probably closer to 30 percent of all that we produce."[23]

Some Israeli journalists argue that many Americans believe that a solution to the Palestinian problem would solve the primary cause of the conflict. Some Israelis fear that this attitude could lessen the sense of urgency and importance that underlies the massive aid to Israel. The other fear is based on the threats by OPEC and the PLO to take radical measures against the energy-hungry Western nations. An influential Saudi official once remarked that he would not be surprised if the Palestinians sank one or two super tankers in the Strait of Hormuz (See map on page 58.) to force the world to do something about their plight. Many Israelis fear that in a time of severe oil crisis, American support for Israel could be largely eroded.

Israeli-American relations have been characterized by a close bond of friendship, although there have been periods when Israelis have perceived their influence to be waning. The Egyptian-American relationship worries the Israelis insofar as it could mean that America will no longer see Israel as its sole, reliable partner in the region. All Israelis realize that Israel's economic well-being and security depend upon the continued close cooperation between the United States and Israel. However, most Israelis understand that this relationship could change to the detriment of Israel. Many American advocates of the peace process believe that once peace is achieved, Israel will need less foreign aid. As Israel reduces her arms expenditures, it could open new markets that would become available after peace is reached and diplomatic relations have been established with many new states. Israelis are not so certain that the change would be in Israel's best interests. Dramatic upheavals in Iran and Afghanistan have reinforced the Israeli belief that Israel represents the only stable and dependable Western ally in the Middle East region. They argue that the U.S. aid given each year (which amounts to nearly $3500 for every man, woman, and child in Israel) is a fair price to pay for keeping America's only reliable ally in the region strong. Many Israelis also argue that more investment money from America and elsewhere would pour into Israel if there was peace in the region — giving new wealth, employment, and strength to Israel. A Knesset member argued, "You cannot tell me that Israel will fail if there is peace.... I know many wealthy men who would invest heavily here if we had peace. Don't fall victim to those crying wolf. We will be stronger in peace than in war."

The old belief that the Jewish lobby never lost a vote on Capitol Hill was shattered over the issue of selling F-15 fighters to Saudi Arabia. Former Foreign Minister Moshe Dayan said Israel is viewed as "a state in need of charity and as financially dependent upon foreigners, unable to withstand political pressures.... It [this attitude] is very dangerous because it encourages outsiders to apply pressure on Israel."[24]

Persian Gulf Area (including Strait of Hormuz)

- *Terrorism as a current security threat*

Since 1965, some 650 people have been killed in terrorist attacks in Israel. This figure has been disputed by non-Israeli sources as being nearly three times the actual number killed, less so if the fatality figure includes fedayeen killed making the attacks, and anti-Israeli raids conducted outside Israel. Figures of fatalities in southern Lebanon caused by Israeli preemptive raids likewise vary greatly, but certainly are substantially higher than those cited above. Since 1975, there have been some 2,000 individual acts of aggression involving artillery, Katyusha rockets, mortar, and other attacks mounted against Israel from Lebanese territory alone.[25] Israelis note that about 80 percent of terrorists who try to enter Israel are killed or captured before they have a chance to inflict damage.[26] Captured arms include RDX explosives sold to Saudi Arabia and 105mm howitzers supplied to Lebanon by the United States.

Israelis say that threats to the daily physical security of Israeli citizens and tourists, economic stability, and the psychological well-being of the populace are the imminent values that are harmed in these terrorist attacks. Terrorist warfare offers little immediate benefit to those employing it, but it does gradually affect the morale of the victim population. Most Israelis know that the fedayeen are attacking out of a belief that they are fighting to regain their homeland, and death is an acceptable sacrifice.

Israelis believe that acts of terrorism, although fairly well-controlled, will continue into the foreseeable future. Said an Israeli retired military officer, "We are told that if the Palestinians get a homeland, we will be free of this terrorism. How can you guarantee this to us? My family and I, we want to know how you can promise us that there will never again be a terrorist attack on Israel.... Can you promise that? Can Carter or Kreisky? Can Arafat?"

Comments

Israel has other security concerns as well, including attempts by Libya and Iraq to procure a nuclear capability. There has been considerable concern in Israel over Syria's intentions in Lebanon. An Arab League Peacekeeping Force composed primarily of Syrian troops (some 30,000 out of a force of 32,000 troops) has been in control of much of Lebanon since 1976. Many Israelis do not believe that the Syrians will leave Lebanon when and if a peace is arranged between Lebanese Moslems and Christians. Others believe that the Syrian regime is using its Lebanese involvement as a tool for retaining influence and keeping alive the threat of another war with Israel. Most recently Israelis have expressed a heightened fear of a low-level war of attrition by Syria.

Israel's increased dependency upon foreign energy sources (and ultimately a 15-year guarantee from the United States for its oil needs as part of the arrangements for the Egyptian-Israeli Peace Treaty) is another worry. Israelis note that the Arabs could also wreak havoc with the Israeli economy if they drilled a few major water wells into the western slopes of what is called *Samaria*. If the water level dropped below that of the Mediterranean, sea-water could seep in and foul the entire water supply in the same way as has happened in northern Cyprus. According to Israeli sources, one-third of the water reaching Israeli kitchens and farms originates in the West Bank. Desalination is still too expensive for commercial ventures. An official in the Israeli Ministry of Agriculture said that "the choices to seriously increase the water supply for irrigation on the West Bank are twofold: drawing Jordan water at the expense of the East Bank (Jordan), or boring wells into the water slopes of the West Bank at the expense of Israel. It's obvious," he said, "what we can and would like to do while we are in control and I guess it's clear what they would want to do too." Another study expands on the water problems which are a legitimate security concern in this region:

> Israel is also vulnerable to hostile actions against its water supply, as critical elements in its water system are close to the borders. These include the Banias and Hasbani springs in the Golan Heights, which if restored to Syrian control could be diverted into the Litani River in Lebanon and the Yarmouk River in Jordan, or [could be] contaminated at the source; the northern Jordan River through which these tributaries supply 62 percent of the water in Lake Kinneret (Tiberias); the Lake itself, which supplies one-third of Israel's water via the National Water Carrier; the main pumping station of the conduit at Zalmon; the first 30 miles of the Carrier itself, which are an open canal; and several secondary reservoirs and storage areas along this span.[27]

How broadly one defines security is extremely important. A retired Israeli diplomat in Tel Aviv posed the following question:

> What do we Israelis want to include under that word *security*? Can we be promised complete freedom always from terrorism? No. Is Switzerland or Fiji completely free of terrorist attacks? No. What we need is to find some formulas that will guarantee us as much a right to live a peaceful life as is guaranteed to any other human being on this planet. That is what we mean by security. Is that asking too much?

Basically, one of the most critical underlying fears is that Israel has grown too dependent upon outside powers for its economic and military needs. Israeli government leaders have warned that Israel must reduce her dependency upon outside powers or one day suffer the consequences of being pressured into actions that would seriously endanger the future viability of a Jewish state of Israel.

Jordan

The Armistice Agreement signed in Rhodes in 1949 established the lines which endured between Israel and Jordan until 1967. The Armistice lines were never recognized as final borders since the Armistice itself was established as a transitional stage which was to be followed by a permanent peace. Between 1949 and 1951, Jordan made several attempts to reach a permanent settlement with Israel. After the 1967 war, the Israelis declared the Armistice null and void.

When Jordan defines its position regarding frontiers with Israel, it cannot use previously existing international boundaries except for the section between the Dead Sea and Elat, which has not been a subject of controversy, and some of the area south of Lake Tiberias, where the Jordan and Yarmuk rivers constitute a clear border. (See map on page 62.) The most critical area is the line inside the territory of the former mandate of Palestine (west of the Jordan River).

Long before any Egyptian leader had expressed a willingness to make peace with Israel, King Hussein had offered peace and recognition of Israel in exchange for withdrawal from territories captured in the 1967 war. In 1974, when Secretary of State Henry Kissinger was arranging a partial withdrawal and military separations in the Sinai and Golan, King Hussein urged similar procedures for the West Bank. Nothing was done. King Hussein notes that United States policy-makers now admit that they made a "tragic mistake."[28]

The political realities have changed greatly since 1974. Jordan no longer represents the Palestinians. In 1974, a decision was made at the Rabat Arab summit meeting to recognize the PLO as the sole representative of the Palestinian people; today the PLO has gained that recognition from 117 states in all parts of the world. Jordan, however, remains a key player in the peacemaking process, as evidenced by the vital role it played in the 1979 Baghdad meetings. Jordan also serves as an important bridge for Palestinians to enter the occupied territories of the West Bank. More than 60 percent of the Jordanian population is Palestinian, including key members of the cabinet and influential business leaders. Long-term stability for Jordan is in many ways directly related to settlement of the Palestinian issue. The Jordanians currently perceive several distinct threats, and the most frequently mentioned are discussed in the following section.

Jordanian Perceptions of Threat

- *A preemptive Israeli attack*

Jordanians believe that an uprising on the West Bank or unusual military activity by Syria and Iraq could trigger an Israeli preemptive attack

Jordan

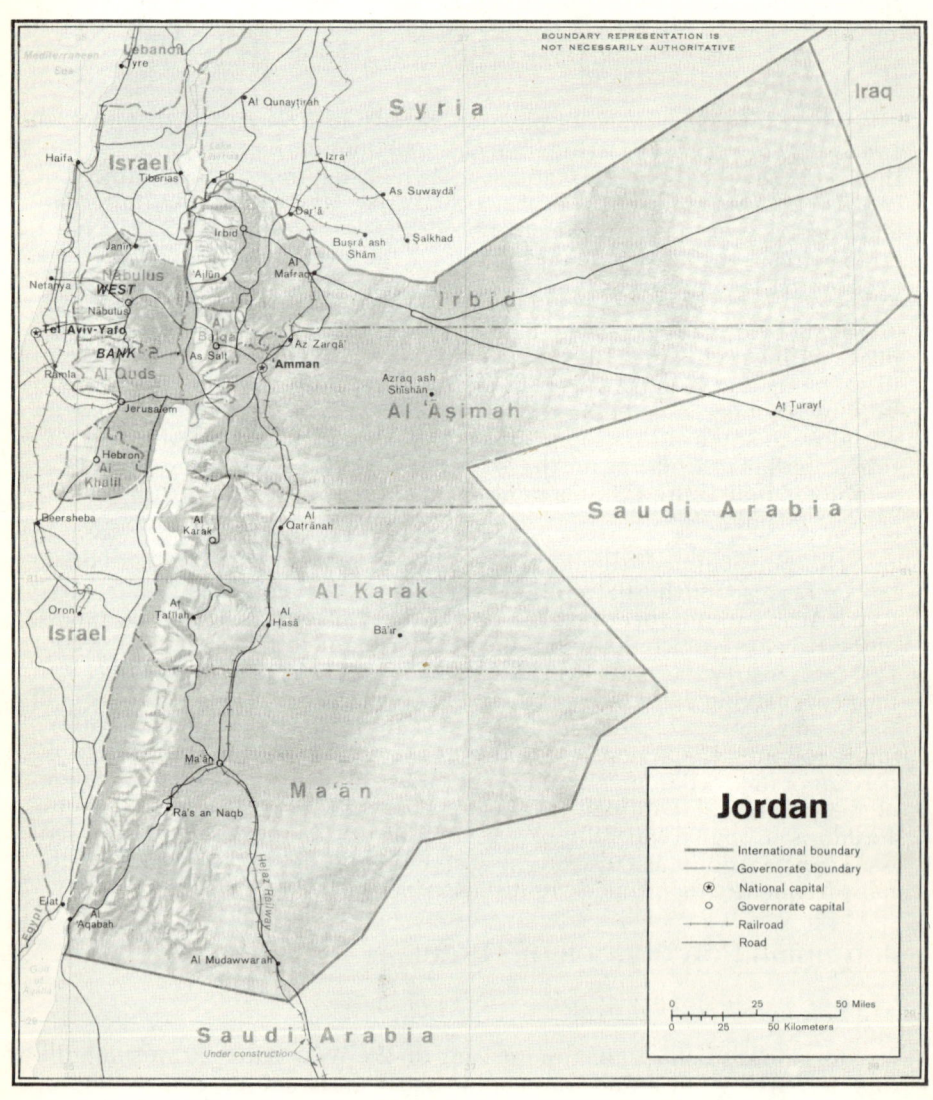

and ensuing war. An essential element of Israeli foreign policy is the use of preemptive attacks, as evidenced in the late 1970s in Lebanon. Israelis often consider such attacks as retaliatory actions in reprisal to Arab terrorist attacks against Israel. Jordanians believe they would be caught in the middle of a new war and would have to enter it. King Hussein made a series of observations in 1975 that showed he regarded this situation as possible. He stated that if Israel's objective is to hit the Syrian army, then it can do so only by going through Jordan. If its objective is to threaten the oil-producing countries, then Jordan is in its way. If its objective is to alter the ground situation—by destroying a defensive line in an area that would threaten all the Arab world — then obviously Jordan must be its target. The King noted that it appears that if there is another war, then Jordan this time is going to be in the center of it. For these reasons, Jordanians feel threatened and vulnerable. The King has argued that Jordanians must take measures to brace themselves for what might happen.

Jordanians see the stability of their government and the continued existence of the state of Jordan as being threatened. "Although I cannot imagine Israel wishing to occupy Amman," noted a Jordanian official, "I can envision an attack which would cripple our economy and bring extensive devastation which would take years [from which] to recover." Some Jordanians argue that the Israelis ultimately desire to set their frontiers in the mountains east of the Jordan River for *security* reasons.

The Israelis have made it clear, most recently in Lebanon, that they would not hesitate to launch preemptive raids against any neighboring state if Israel felt that its security was being threatened. A Jordanian diplomatic official noted that "within hours after we would again[29] allow raids on Israel from Jordanian territory, we would be the recipient of swift attacks ... nobody really knows how extensive or explosive they might become...."

Israel would face the possibility of fighting a full-scale war, perhaps on several fronts. Israeli military strategy is prepared for such a contingency. Jordanians know that their armed forces are highly regarded as fighters by the Israeli Defence Forces. A senior Jordanian official remarked, "We are certain that they do not want to engage us in battle for no reason but they define preemptive attack in such a broad way that anything is possible." In general, one hears speculation on this possibility from a wide range of Jordanians, among both the leadership and the public. Jordanians believe that Israel has the capability to launch such an attack and many believe that the intentions are there to match.

- *Forced emigration of Palestinians from the occupied territories*

Jordan still retains a profound interest in the future of the territory of the West Bank which was seized from Jordan during the 1967 war. Although the Jordanians are no longer recognized by the Arab world as the representative of the Palestinian people, nor do they claim to be, they are extremely concerned about the West Bank, which had been under Jordanian rule since it was seized during the 1948 war and put into union with East Jordan. The Jordanians, like other Arabs, fear that the national cohesiveness and viability of the residents of the West Bank and Gaza and their determination to continue their struggle to end occupation are being threatened by protracted Israeli actions in the territories.

Jordanians note that some estimates place the reduction of the Arab population in Jerusalem and the West Bank at 32 percent since 1967. Jordanian figures show that 22,000 Arab youths left the West Bank for Jordan and the Gulf in 1978. There is less land for the Arabs as Israeli settlements continue to be built in the West Bank, where they now occupy an estimated 27 percent of the total area. Israeli officials argue that settlements physically take less than one percent of the lands of Judea and Samaria, the remainder of the area being needed for military purposes and future settlement growth. In addition, Arab mayors on the West Bank have protested the drilling of wells in the settlements which deny nearby Arab inhabitants the water necessary to irrigate their farms. Educational opportunities are limited and employment of university graduates on the West Bank is severely restricted. The Jordanians have paid some $1.1 billion to municipalities for office rents, pensions, salaries, and schools on the West Bank between 1967 and 1978 to offset what they see as *Israeli attempts to force migration.* Israeli U.N. Ambassador Yehuda Blum dismissed claims that Arab inhabitants were subjected to continuous pressure to emigrate by citing figures designed to show there had been economic growth.[30] A Jordanian diplomat responded, "Look carefully at his remarks and you will see that they [Israelis] respond to apples with oranges. . . . They made a clever try to answer the question of why Arabs are being forced to emigrate but did not address the specific question. . . . Instead, they talk selectively of economic growth."

Jordanians believe that the high growth rate of the Arab population in the West Bank, Gaza, and Israel, coupled with the slower growth rate of Jews (due to a lower birth rate and a recent near balance between emigration and immigration) has driven Israel to seek ways to reduce the number of young and educated Arabs in the occupied territories. Jordanians argue that since 1967, the Israelis have deported many of the brightest, most articulate, and best educated Palestinians from the West Bank and Gaza. A West Bank political leader noted that the "Israelis have tried to make life uncomfortable enough for all of our populace to the point where a better life is sought by the progressive and educated people, but not so bad as to cause widespread dissent."

The Jordanian press labeled Israeli policies acts of economic sabotage, cultural deprivation, and psychological warfare. This harassment is seen by Jordanians as a required Israeli response to counteract the increasing population imbalance and unrest among the Arab people in the territories.

Confirmed reports by international, impartial parties of beatings of children in refugee camps by some Israeli soldiers is an example of this.

The Israelis are seen to have suffered little from these actions, which are gradual and often subtle. Jordanians believe that the benefits to Israel for removing the educated populace from the occupied territories is clear: the people remaining will be more governable for many more years, which is precisely what the Israelis desire. A retired Jordanian government official in Jerusalem felt that "we Arabs should not be surprised, should we? Let us recall that occupying powers throughout history have done what is being done to us by Israel. The difference is one of degree. . . . I suppose in that sense we Arabs should be thankful — deportation is better than execution although some of my Palestinian friends here might disagree in principle." Jordanians frequently remind outsiders that deportation of individuals from occupied territories is prohibited by the Fourth Geneva Convention, to which Israel adheres.

- *Arab vulnerability to radicalism and external influences*

Jordanian officials privately worry that the unity and common destiny of the Arab people is being undermined in their time of greatest prosperity. The rift between Egypt and the other Arabs that became serious during 1979 has caused great discomfort in Amman. The growing number of other disputes between Moslem states over questions of ideology, religious sectarianism, economics, territory, and politics demonstrate the seriousness of the problem. A Jordanian scholar argued:

> The ability of the Arab nation to gain its rightful place as a world actor of the most important sort diminishes. . . . We must look at our situation in 30 years when exporting oil can no longer be our source of strength or primary income. Every conflict that separates us for one or two or three years will have long-reaching implications for the Arab people. The time we lose now is the most crucial time . . . yet we squander it so easily.

Jordanians label the divisions and disunities within the Arab world as one of the Arabs' greatest weaknesses and one of Israel's greatest strengths. The inability of the Arabs to arrive at a common bargaining strategy and position has allowed the Israelis to pursue successfully a policy of divide and conquer, noted a number of Jordanians. Others argued that, together with current Israeli intransigence, the divisions within the Arab world were a major stumbling block to a successful settlement.

Senior government officials believe that there is little choice for Arabs but to become more radical as they see a continued lack of progress being made on the West Bank/Gaza and Jerusalem issues. Hundreds of thousands of Palestinians currently live and work in Saudi Arabia, Jordan, Kuwait,

Lebanon, and the Gulf States. Financial aid from the Soviet Union and radical Arab states is readily available to those attempting to increase the radicalism of the populace and undermine non-leftist governments. Officials recall Jordan's difficult and violent conflict in the early 1970s with the PLO, and note that the PLO has publicly stated that it could topple any Arab government which rejected its cause. Jordanian support for a Palestinian solution is deeply-rooted. Officials believe that the danger to the Arab world and the Western world increases day by day the longer this problem is prolonged.

Jordanian leadership is, consequently, fearful of threats to traditional values or the stability of the region. A Cabinet official argued that "we [Arabs] continue to play the game which the radical elements wish to see us play.... Don't forget that most Arab radical elements are now a different breed from Communist radicals, but in ten years that will likely change if frustrations continue to be compounded." Others argue that the very stability of the West hangs in the balance. Even a temporary blocking of the Strait of Hormuz could bring the Western world to the brink of serious disruption as some 60 percent of the vital flow of oil used by the United States, Western Europe, and Japan could be stopped. (See map on page 58.) It should be noted that sinking one or several ships would not prevent continued use of the Strait. Gulf strategists argue that the only real threat is the laying of mines by a party that is capable of hindering minesweeping efforts.

Concerted efforts to increase the radicalism among university students and other Arabs continue throughout the region. "The driving force," said a Jordanian college student, "is fed primarily by our frustrations of the Israeli intransigence over the peace process." The longer the Palestinian question remains unresolved, the faster this radicalizing process will develop. "A Marxist Moslem is a contradiction in terms," said an Amman civic official, "But a tired and frustrated Moslem is an expedient person.... Expediency can be dangerous."

- *Permanent loss of the Arab sector and the character of Jerusalem*

Jordanians feel a particular responsibility for leading the struggle to regain East Jerusalem, which had been under Jordanian control from 1948 to 1967 and which represents an important religious and historical Arab land. East Jerusalem was seized in the 1967 war and later annexed by Israel. Since the 1960s, Israel has embarked on what some Jordanian officials called "the fattening of Jerusalem." Jordanian officials point to General Ariel Sharon's *Planning Jerusalem* (prepared by the Israeli Ministry of the Interior and the Municipality of Jerusalem). Sharon's book shows plans for an Israeli Metropolitan Jerusalem stretching from a point about 10 kilometers north of Ramallah, south to an area almost halfway between Hebron and Bethlehem (See map on page 67.) and extending eastward toward Jericho. Other "fattening plans" (Shaked, Israel Land Administration

Jerusalem

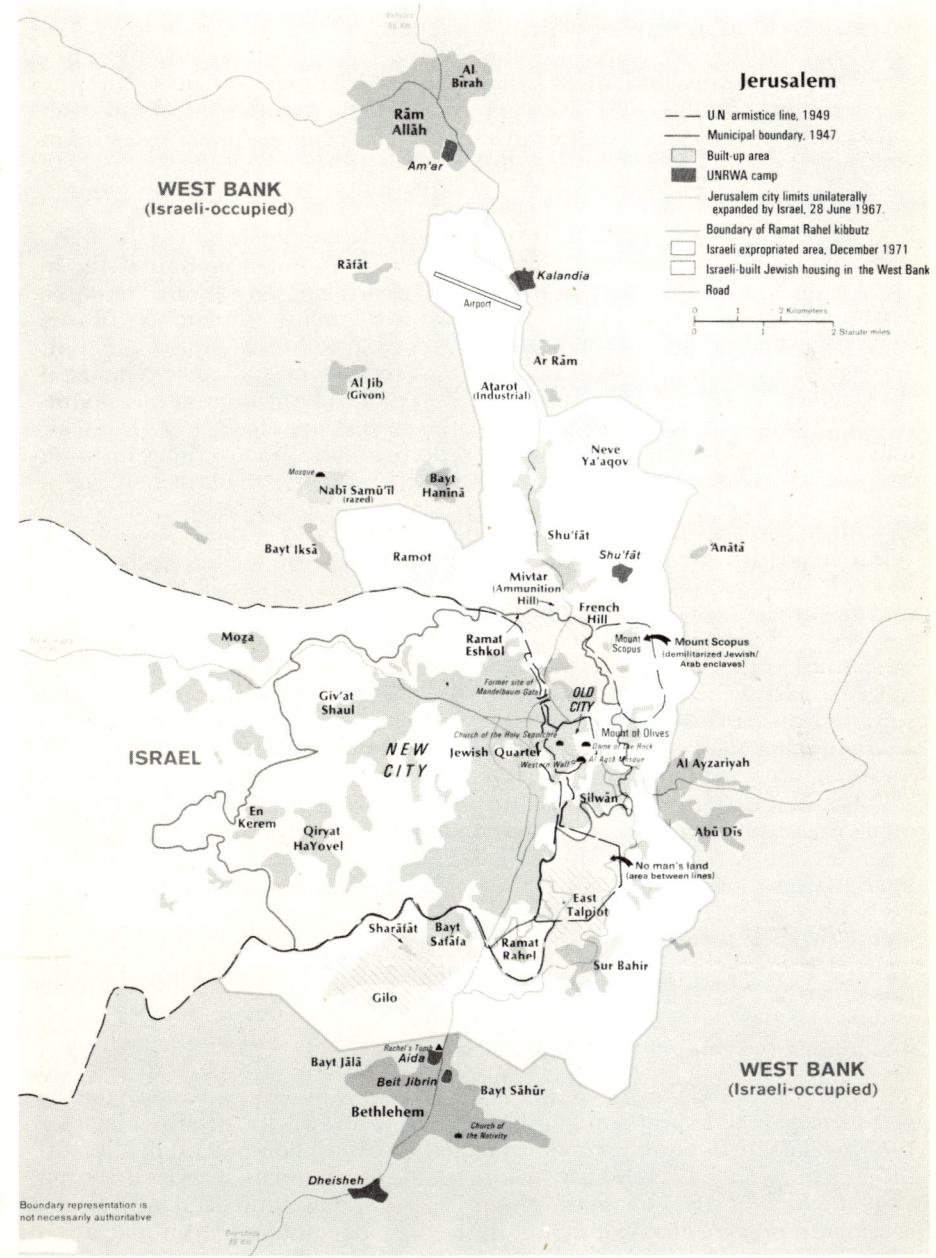

Green Booklet, Ministry of Housing Plan) emphasized similar goals. Benvenisti's *Jerusalem, The Torn City* is often quoted:

> The metropolitan area of Jerusalem beyond the annexed area in which the proposed settlements were planned, covers some 95 square miles. It includes the towns of Ramallah, al-Bira, Bethlehem, Beit Sahur, Beit Jala, Beit Zayit, Beitunya and more than 20 small villages.[31]

Jordanians note that the former Rabin Labor government in 1975 considered an enlarged Jerusalem to extend from north of Ramallah to Hebron in the south, Latroun in the west, and near Jericho in the east. Jordanians point to the most recent Israeli statements by members of the governing Likhud and the opposition Labor party which emphasize that Jerusalem is non-negotiable and argue that Jerusalem shall never again be divided between Arabs and Israelis and that all of Jerusalem must remain under Israeli sovereignty. It is clear to the Jordanians that for the foreseeable future, the Israelis have the money, political will, and military force to carry out these policies of annexation and the *fattening* of Jerusalem.

All Arabs see two central values being threatened — the Arab right to retain its historical area of Jerusalem (East Jerusalem), including the Moslem religious sites, and the right of the Arab people to live in their homes and keep their property. The Jordanians are particularly concerned about this loss of Jerusalem and believe that if immediate steps are not taken, irreparable damage will be done to the character of Arab Jerusalem. "Every day that passes," said a member of the Royal Family, "makes this issue less soluble and more critical to all the Arab people." The Arab people are adamant that East Jerusalem cannot be under Israeli sovereignty.

The inability of the Arab world and international public opinion to apply pressure on Israel to stop construction of new settlements has created a perceived low-risk situation for the Israelis. "They [Israelis] see that they have little to lose by annexing Jerusalem . . . that is, for the short run. Perhaps this is a reason why they do not support a comprehensive settlement," argued a Jordanian graduate student. The escalation by Israel of constructing new settlements after Camp David is frequently mentioned in this regard.

- *A limited Israeli attack to create a new crisis*

Many Jordanians believe that if the United States applied strong-arm pressure against Israel, for example demanding an Israeli withdrawal to the 1967 borders by threatening a sharp reduction of military and financial aid, the Israelis would launch an attack to create a new crisis. The Jordanians believe that the Israelis would count on receiving additional American support to prevent the Arabs from inflicting a defeat upon Israel.

Israel is seen to have little, if any, choice but to create an immediate crisis, should the United States government ever threaten to curtail its crucial military and economic aid. There is no country capable of replacing American financial support, nor is there a bloc of countries willing to give such sophisticated military assistance and widespread economic aid. Although Israeli leaders publicly state that Israel will resist any firm American pressures, most privately agree that in the final analysis, if the United States acted "as the dog wagging the tail rather than having the tail wag the dog," Israel would be forced to make concessions. The thought is disturbing to Israelis. It is seen by Jordanians as the only possible way other than war to force Israel to make concessions essential for a comprehensive peace.

The Israeli people and their political parties have historically rallied behind their government when outside pressures were being applied. In March 1979, when President Jimmy Carter attempted to pressure the Begin government, opposition factions from all sides came to the immediate support of the Israeli government. A Jordanian official pointed to opposition leader Peres' statement that "although we remain divided on what is the best solution for the future, I am fully behind Mr. Begin's resistance to American pressure."[32]

The Jordanians believe that the Israelis have a *crisis mentality* which would override fears of a negative backlash in United States public opinion. This concern over public opinion is said to have deterred former Prime Minister Golda Meir from launching a preemptive attack in 1973 against Arab forces that shortly thereafter were waging battle against Israel. Many Jordanians believe that if the United States were to elect a conservative President and a Congress whose majority of members did not rely heavily upon Jewish contributions, considerable pressure upon Israel to make concessions would be possible. The threat of attack is based on what Jordanians say is "knowing how the Israelis think and act" and "what they would do if the United States threatened to withdraw its support." Some Jordanians believe that American public opinion will eventually tire of escalating energy costs and crises and reduce its support of Israel. Jordanian officials have privately warned that the Arabs have yet to use their influence over the West to the full extent — oil and petrodollars. The day of reckoning, they believe, is not far off. "The purpose of pressuring the United States," noted a high official, "is not to help us destroy Israel. Israel is here to stay and every Arab knows it. But rather it is to make Israel realize that a nation of three million cannot continue to fight 100 million Arabs. . . . We are today willing to accept Israel. . . . If this continues twenty years we will no longer be able to say that most Arabs are willing to permanently accept Israel as a state in our region. . . . That is why we want pressure."

Many Jordanians argue that as a desperation effort to save Israel's special relationship with the United States, there would be little fear given to risking another limited war. This threat of an Israeli-instigated limited attack is deemed to be possible now, but not probable. It is possible that certain factors could result in an American determination to try to force a settlement upon Israel. A Jordanian businessman summarized the problem: "Without strong United States assistance, Israel is another state like Kenya or Nepal. Every Israeli knows that as a fact. So do we [Arabs]. . . . So we must assume they would do anything to maintain that special relationship."

Comments

Jordan's leadership and populace fear other threats in addition to the cases presented here. Jordan, for example, is highly vulnerable to efforts which could destroy high-value water resources. In the summer of 1969, Jordan's main aqueduct, which supplies water to nearly half the area of the East Bank, was temporarily put out of action by an Israeli bombing (as part of Israeli efforts to force Jordan to curb Palestinian guerilla attacks). Today Jordan is discussing with Iraq the possibility of drawing water (for drinking and irrigation purposes) from the Euphrates River through a proposed canal,[33] and the building of a large dam with U.S. assistance.

Prior to any agreement of a comprehensive peace, Jordan is concerned about its aid from other Arab states. Its current aid is considerably more than Jordan was reported to have received under previous Arab agreements dating from 1967 to 1974. Jordanian leaders also expressed fears over the introduction of nuclear weapons into the region's arsenals, by such nations as Israel and Iraq. Jordanians also worry about the long-term economic viability of the region. A government official concluded a discussion with the following: "In brief, I must tell you that Jordan internally is secure . . . but Jordan wonders about what is happening elsewhere. . . . The threats to Jordan are as real and dangerous as they are to every government in this region."

Syria

Syria today finds itself in the position of being the major confrontation state with Israel, a position indisputably held by Egypt from 1948 to 1978. The separate peace treaty signed between Egypt and Israel came as a blow to the Syrians, who consistently advocated the need for Arab solidarity in dealing with the Israelis. Today Syria is a major ally of the Palestine Liberation Organization and has been responsible for maintaining order in most of Lebanon with some 30,000 of its troops stationed in that country. It is beset with domestic uncertainties between the governing minority Alawite religious sect and the majority Sunni population; and it remains involved in a serious rivalry with Iraq.

Syria

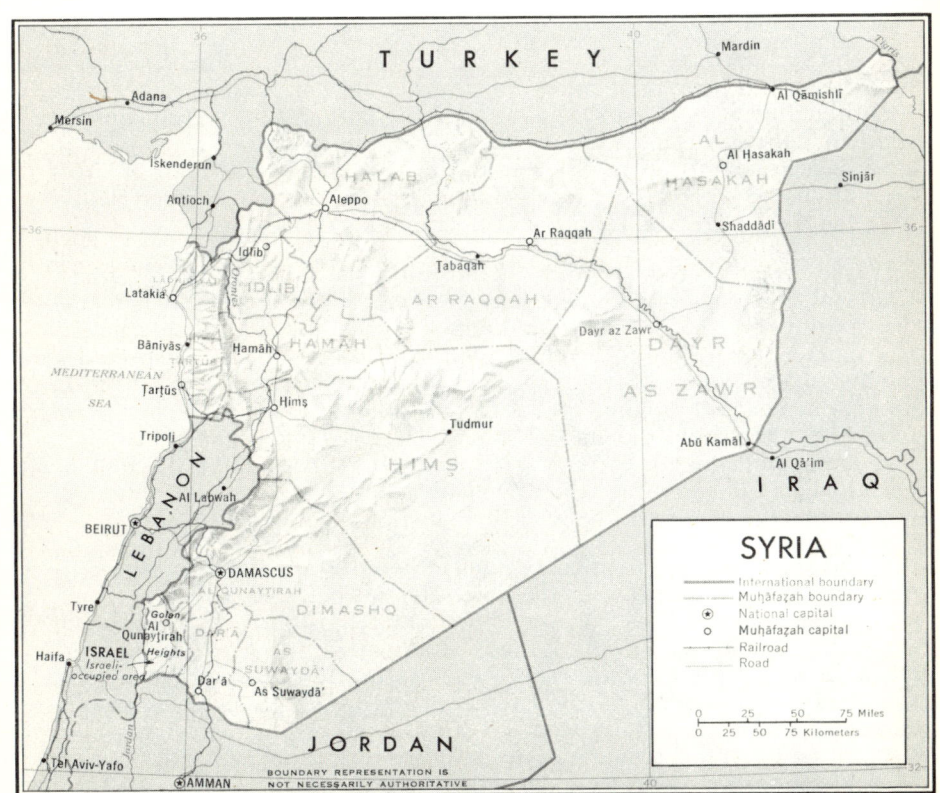

The sudden rise in militant Sunni fundamentalism in Syria is attributed by Arab observers to two factors: a genuine return to traditional religious values; and a latent unhappiness over the imbalance between the Sunnis and the Alawites who represent 10 percent of the Syrian population and yet hold a disproportionate share of the top military, political, and governmental offices.

President Assad's work to improve relations with the majority Sunni sect, which makes up more than 65 percent of Syria's population of eight million, has been somewhat successful although the tensions and periodic eruptions of violence demonstrate that the conflict is deep-rooted. Religious friction has also emerged between Christian villagers and the Sunnis. The event which shocked the world, however, was the massacre of scores of young army cadets at the Artillery School near Alleppo in June, 1979, by a fanatically religious army captain. He was a member of the *Moslem Brotherhood*, a militant body that seeks to defend the traditional Sunni strain of Islam. The massacre resulted in a strict government crackdown on Sunni extremists.

The Syrians have taken a strong public stand in furthering the Palestinian cause and have reaffirmed that they would not make an agreement with Israel over the Golan Heights until the Palestinians were given the right to self-determination. In early 1979, Syria and Iraq attempted to establish collaboration in defense and foreign affairs matters, but this long-discussed plan was not successful, in part due to the continued rivalry between the Syrian and Iraqi Baath Socialist Parties.

The Syrians receive significant military assistance from the Soviet Union, although the government has been careful to maintain its independence from Moscow. In 1979 Syria banned several dozen leftist journalists who had written for the government-controlled press and were suspected of having pro-Soviet views. A respected Syrian scholar, now teaching in another Arab country, noted that scores of leftist teachers and writers were forced from their jobs during 1979 alone. The Syrian government receives token financial assistance from the United States, although the aid could be curtailed in 1980/81. Since the Soviet invasion of Afghanistan, there are indications that the Syrian-Soviet link has tightened.

The Syrian government cooperates fully with United Nations personnel who staff the buffer zone on the Golan Heights between Syria and Israel. (See map on page 73.) A Syrian merchant noted that "our fears are as much over subversion by the Soviets or Americans or other Arabs, particularly the Iraqis, as they are about the Israelis. . . . We all know the Israeli intentions, so it makes it easier to know how to deal with them. . . ." Other Arabs are currently studying the improved relations between the Soviet Union and Syria to see if it indicates a major departure in Syrian foreign policy—from tactical friendship to strategic dependency on the Soviets.

Golan Heights (including UNDOF area)

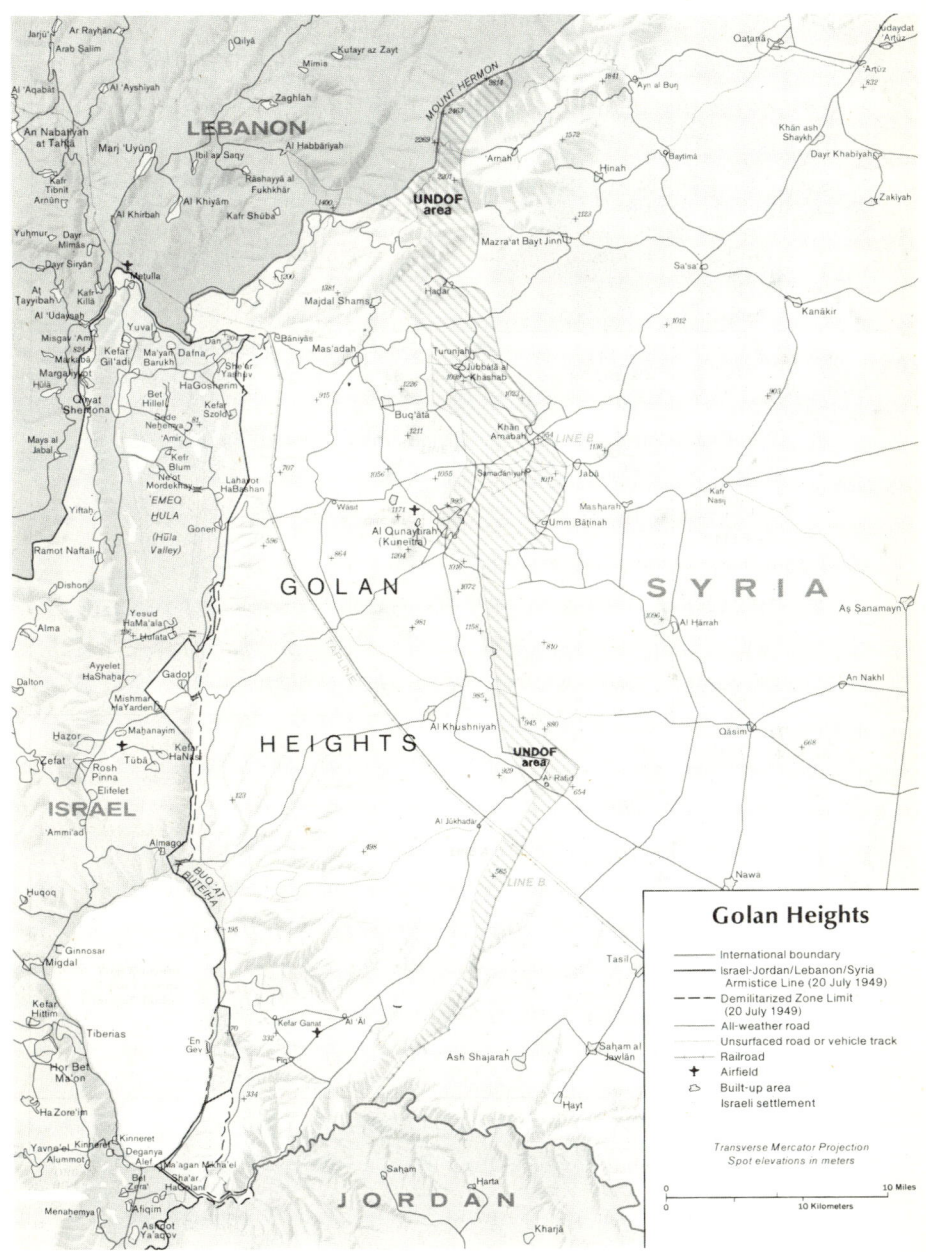

Syrian Perceptions of Threat

- *An Israeli attack*

Syrians list five plausible reasons which might cause Israel to attack Syria:

- Response to a perceived Arab threat, which might result from unusual military maneuvers or other factors — for example, the stationing of Iraqi divisions on Syrian soil, which Israel could argue is meant to launch a surprise Arab attack against Israel.

- Escalation of the Lebanese war into a situation where Syrian peacekeeping troops and Israeli troops would clash directly — for example, a Syrian crossing of the so-called "red line" along the Litani River.

- Enactment of aggressive expansionist aims to further the territorial desires of the Zionist state.

- Provocation of a crisis to maintain high-level American assistance, if that should be threatened in a get-tough stance of a new American administration.

- A direct attempt to exploit internal problems within Syria (such as a clash between religious groups) with the goal of overthrowing the government and establishing a conservative government more friendly to Israel. This could be extended to include exploiting a problem between Iraq and Syria.

The Israelis have made known their willingness to use preemptive attacks when they deem it necessary. The Syrians believe the Israelis are willing to use their superior military strength to enact changes in the region and would not be shy of interfering in a domestic difficulty if assured of some chance of installing a government more to their liking. A senior Syrian diplomat noted that President Assad has frequently stated that "Syria, not Israel, needed security guarantees against a likely aggression." The very security and economic viability of the state would be threatened by an Israeli attack. A Syrian professor who considers himself a moderate Arab said that "every Syrian knows that he lives under the sword of the Israelis and that the sword could fall at any moment." A government official in Damascus posed a question during an informal conversation:

> Why don't you ask the Israelis when you are there again who is afraid of whom and why? If Begin used a nuclear weapon in the next war to destroy Damascus, would the big powers risk a nuclear ... what do you call it ... holocaust? ... What would the Americans do? Ultimately, who is the offensive force with the upper hand ... we Syrians? Ask the Israelis that question some day....

Syrians point to Israeli actions and government statements, the build-up of their offensive weapons capability, leaks about their military plans, and policy debates in the Knesset as further indications of aggressive Israeli intentions and threat. A Syrian diplomatic officer, discussing various members of Mr. Begin's Cabinet, opened a desk drawer and withdrew a folder of clippings. He passed a copy of a *Newsweek* article that quoted Israeli General Sharon. Underlined in red was the following:

> The next one [Arab-Israeli war] . . . will be quick as lightning and so devastating that it will take the Arabs ten years to recover. They will be so groggy that they won't even have the incentive to apply another oil embargo. That's when we will solve the Palestinian problem. . . .[34]

When the Syrian diplomatic officer was asked to respond to General Sharon's statement, his comment was simple: "The major Israeli goals seem always to be to buy time. . . . Perhaps a war a decade, which we are averaging during these years from 1948, is not so bad for them. But one day they will not win the war." Syrians refer to statements like General Sharon's as evidence of ultimate Israeli intentions. A senior official argued, "You can't believe what they tell you privately about wanting peace—you must look at their statements and see what they intend to do."

Most Syrians believe that Israel could not be strategically defeated in another war at this time. A Syrian military officer noted that "speaking personally, I cannot imagine what they would do with Damascus if they captured it. . . . I guess it means an attack would have other purposes like destroying our military organization and equipment, defeating our egos, or destroying us completely."

Perhaps the best summary was given by a small businessman in Damascus who had served in the army and dealt frequently with Western tourists: "Americans always ask me why Syria is so aggressive to Israel. They tell me that if we weren't so aggressive, that Israel would make peace with us and give us back the Golan. . . . I say to them a simple thing—every coin has two sides, have you ever turned the coin over?"

- *Israeli retention of the Golan Heights*

According to a senior government official in Damascus, the pre-1967 population of the Golan Heights area now occupied by Israel was around 120,000. Of that number, some 9,400 remain in their homes in the occupied lands. Several hundred more were allowed to return to their villages near the newly drawn disengagement line that resulted from the 1974 Disengagement Agreement between Israel and Syria.

The Syrian refugees from the 1967 war in the Golan today live primarily in and around Damascus. They reportedly receive six dollars of government assistance per month. Meanwhile, Israel has continued to strengthen the extensive network of settlements it has constructed in the Golan, numbering at least twenty-six by Syrian estimates.[35] (See map on page 77.)

Prime Minister Begin and the Israeli government have repeatedly stated that the Golan is vital for Israeli security and that the settlements cannot be foresaken. The Syrians frequently quote Mr. Begin:

> We shall never withdraw from the Golan Heights. There is no such thing as giving up security in return for peace. There is no peace without security. Without the Golan Heights, there is no security.[36]

The opposition Labor Party leadership has also stated that Israel would not withdraw from the Golan Heights to any significant extent and would abandon only a small part of it if peace were signed with Syria. The Syrians argue that Israeli financial investments in the settlements and kibbutzim lend credence to Israeli public statements. Syrians do note that Israel does not claim the Golan as Biblical land belonging to Israel, nor do they cite historical or legal reasons for annexing the Golan, unlike the West Bank, Gaza, and Jerusalem. "The arguments used for keeping occupied Golan are always security and economic arguments," noted a Syrian military official.

An Egyptian official remarked that "understandably, the Syrian refugees, the entire Syrian population and its leadership are deeply hostile to this continued and intransigent occupation of Syrian sovereign territory. . . . How else would you expect them to feel . . . content and snug?"

Israeli settlement policies and government statements demonstrate to the Syrians that Israel has no intention of negotiating a settlement over the Golan in the foreseeable future. The Syrians understand that the Israelis are content with the status quo. Syrians believe that the Israelis' ability to continue expanding their settlements in the occupied territories despite worldwide opposition has reinforced their willingness to retain the occupied lands.

Syrians argue that there will be no settlement of the Arab-Israeli conflict until their land is returned and there will be no negotiations on the Golan until the Palestinian issue is resolved. The Syrians view the future for settlement as unfavorable.

- *Israeli cultural and economic penetration into the Arab world*

"Israeli actions and goals and their materialistic, Western-influenced, moral-less society will one day pose a more important threat to all of the Arab world than their combat aircraft and missiles," argued a Syrian government officer. He continued, "I am talking about Zionism and about

Jewish Settlements in Israeli-occupied Golan Heights

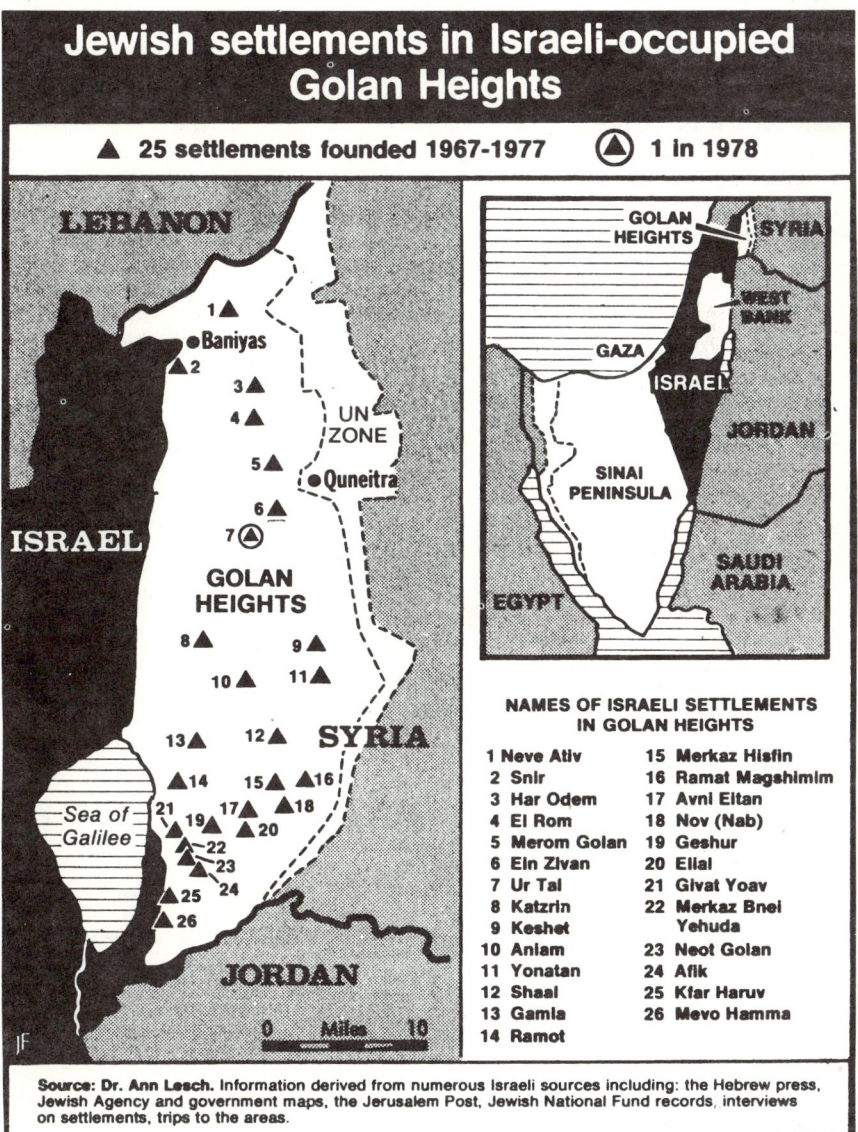

Joan Forbes in the *Christian Science Monitor* © 1978

Reprinted with permission.

Western society. It is not the people as individuals but the way of life, the values or lack of them, like lack of respect for authority. This is what I mean."

The Syrians, like many other Arabs, fear the ability of Israeli society to permeate traditional Arab religious norms, values, cultural and institutional structures, and economy. To many Syrians, Israel represents an advanced technical society with few natural resources — a threat to the surrounding Moslem states. A Syrian economist stated that "it is a setting that is perfect for the establishment of a colonialist relationship. Look what they [Israelis] have done with the West Bank and Gaza." Ironically, the Palestinians appear to be least afraid of this aspect of Arab-Israeli relations.

A *New York Times* article quoted a Syrian official as saying, "Israel needs Arab markets and manpower and wants to turn the Arab society into a consumer market for Israeli goods produced by Arab workers."[37]

The Syrians repeatedly point to the publicly expressed Egyptian concerns over Israeli efforts to accelerate the pace of normalizing relations after the peace treaty was signed. Israeli ideas for immediate cooperation came in all fields—education, agriculture, industry, cultural activities, and trade affairs. The Egyptians constantly had to act as a braking influence on the Israelis. A Syrian professor noted:

> Did you see that within 48 hours of signing the peace treaty that a hundred specific Israeli plans were suggested in great detail for joint economic, health, education, and agricultural ventures? . . . They must have spent months deciding how to penetrate the Egyptian economy. . . . They cannot understand that we Arabs have a concern about the Israelis penetrating our societies . . . it can only be dangerous. Many of us feel that this is the new plan for Zionism . . . a gradual effort, but very threatening.

Other Syrians have been publicly quoted as saying that if the Egyptians went through with the plan for economic cooperation with Israel, "their economy would be tied to Zionism and they would lose their independence."[38]

The Egyptian-Israeli case is being watched very closely by the Syrians and other Arabs. The pressures being applied by Israeli groups as well as their government to accelerate establishment of joint ventures with Egypt in every aspect of society reaffirms their perceived threat.

These Syrian fears for the erosion of the values and institutional structures upon which Arab life and society are built are shared by many in the Arab world. A religious official noted that "it is the quiet, small efforts that perhaps represent the greatest threat to us because we are not aware sometimes that it is happening. But they [Israelis] know that it will weaken us internally, which is what they desire." Syrians believe that the Israelis see themselves as an outpost of the Western advanced world in a backward and traditionalist region. "Their efforts to influence and dominate we Arabs are seen in almost every Israeli action," noted a Syrian diplomat. Hard-line statements which denigrate the Arabs' capability and norms are widely noticed after their publication in the Israeli or Western press. Syrians believe that the Zionist Israeli state sees as part of its mission the need to modernize and influence the *backward Arabs*.

A Syrian youth working in a restaurant "to improve my English and French and to earn wages," said, "We respect the good things which Western society has contributed to the world like medicine and communication things, but we also fear the bad things which come with your society. Israel represents, in a way, both and sits on our doorstep. We can see the good things and the bad. We fear that Israel will share the bad and keep the good from us."

Comments

The Syrians are also concerned about the reports of nuclear weapon development by two of her neighbors, Israel and Iraq, both of which she distrusts. President Assad warned the rejectionist state summit of another fear that "we may see the day when, with the wheel of time, Egypt will join Israel to attack Syria."[39]

A senior Syrian diplomatic official noted that the Syrians are concerned about what they call the *growing alliance between the United States, Israel, and Egypt.* Syrian leadership is also concerned about the area's economic viability. The most pressing problem for the Syrians is the continuing delay by Israel in resolving the Palestinian issue. In May, 1979, a Syrian merchant remarked, "Settle the Palestinian question and the whole conflict will lose its energy . . . all of us Syrians feel that way privately." He then added, "Of course there will be a period for a shakedown within the Arab world as many people have built careers on the old war with Israel." There are some Syrians who believe that the latter represents a significant threat to the viability of the present Syrian regime as well as to other regimes in the region. Finally, Syrians and other Arabs express concern over the Israeli involvement in fostering armed resistance by minority groups in the region against the established regimes.

Lebanon

More than 65,000 Lebanese have been killed since the Civil War erupted in 1975. The Lebanese war has been characterized by three levels of conflict: inter-religious fighting between Christians and Moslems; intra-religious fighting between Phalangist and Franjiehist Christians and Sunni and Shiia Moslems; and Palestinian-Israeli and Palestinian-Lebanese fighting caused by the presence of external forces, including the fighting forces and leadership of the Palestine Liberation Organization. In addition, there have been some 2,300 Christian militiamen in the south who are financed and supplied by Israel; 350,000 Palestinians; a 30,000-man Arab League Peacekeeping Force (primarily Syrian); and a 6,000-man United Nations peacekeeping force in the south, the United Nations Interim Force in Lebanon (UNIFIL).

The devastation of the country is well known. The ancient port city of Tyre today has fewer than 10,000 inhabitants. Four years ago it was a thriving metropolitan city of nearly 80,000. United States figures show that as many Lebanese were killed by Israeli retaliatory bombing and shelling raids during the first eight months of 1979 as Israelis died in Israel from all terrorist acts committed during the past twelve years.[40] PLO leader Yasir Arafat said, "It seems that Lebanese and Palestinian blood is cheap. . . . Will it become dearer if it is mixed with oil?"[41]

During the years 1948-75, the Lebanese leadership kept Lebanon's involvement in the Arab-Israeli conflict at a very low level. The Lebanese Civil War in 1975/76 reversed this situation by destroying Lebanese political authority and its military capability. The near total breakdown of authority and ensuing Civil War resulted in the introduction of the Arab League Peacekeeping Force. Many Lebanese believe that Syria initially intervened in Lebanon to prevent the Palestinians and leftist Moslems from achieving victory over the Christians and establishing a radical state from which Palestinians could launch attacks against Israel and so destabilize Syria's own frontier with Israel.

In March, 1978, following a Palestinian attack outside Tel Aviv that took many civilian lives, the Israeli army invaded southern Lebanon up to the Litani River. (See map on page 82.) The Arab world feared that Israel would try to annex southern Lebanon. The international community, seeking a way to defuse the crisis from further escalation (such as a confrontation between Israeli troops south of the Litani River and 30,000 Syrian troops north of the Litani River), established a United Nations peacekeeping force, UNIFIL.[42] This peacekeeping force was envisioned as a two-stage operation. In its first stage, UNIFIL was to confirm the withdrawal of Israeli forces from Lebanese territory to the international border. In the second stage UNIFIL would establish its forces to supervise the cessation of hostilities,

Lebanon

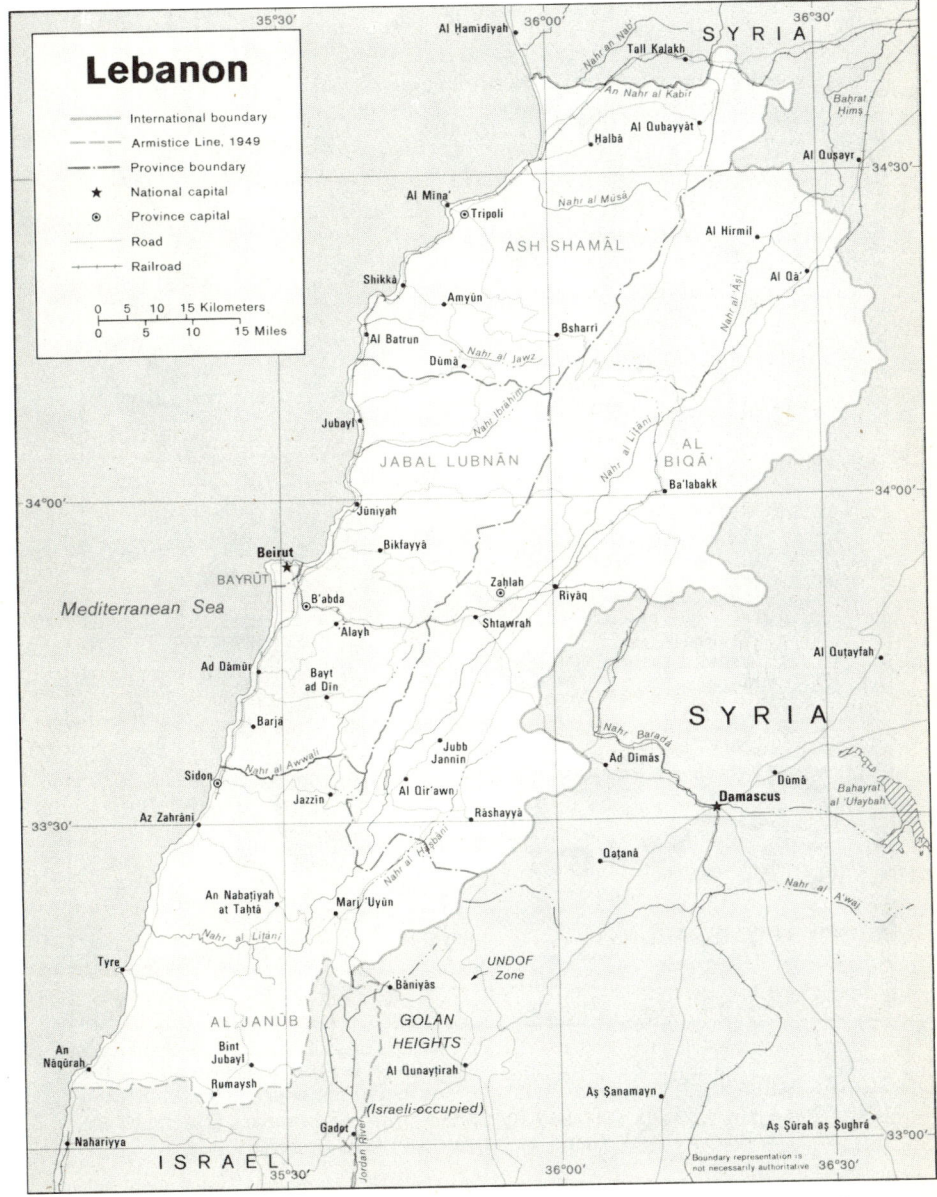

Southern Lebanon after Israeli Invasion, March 1978

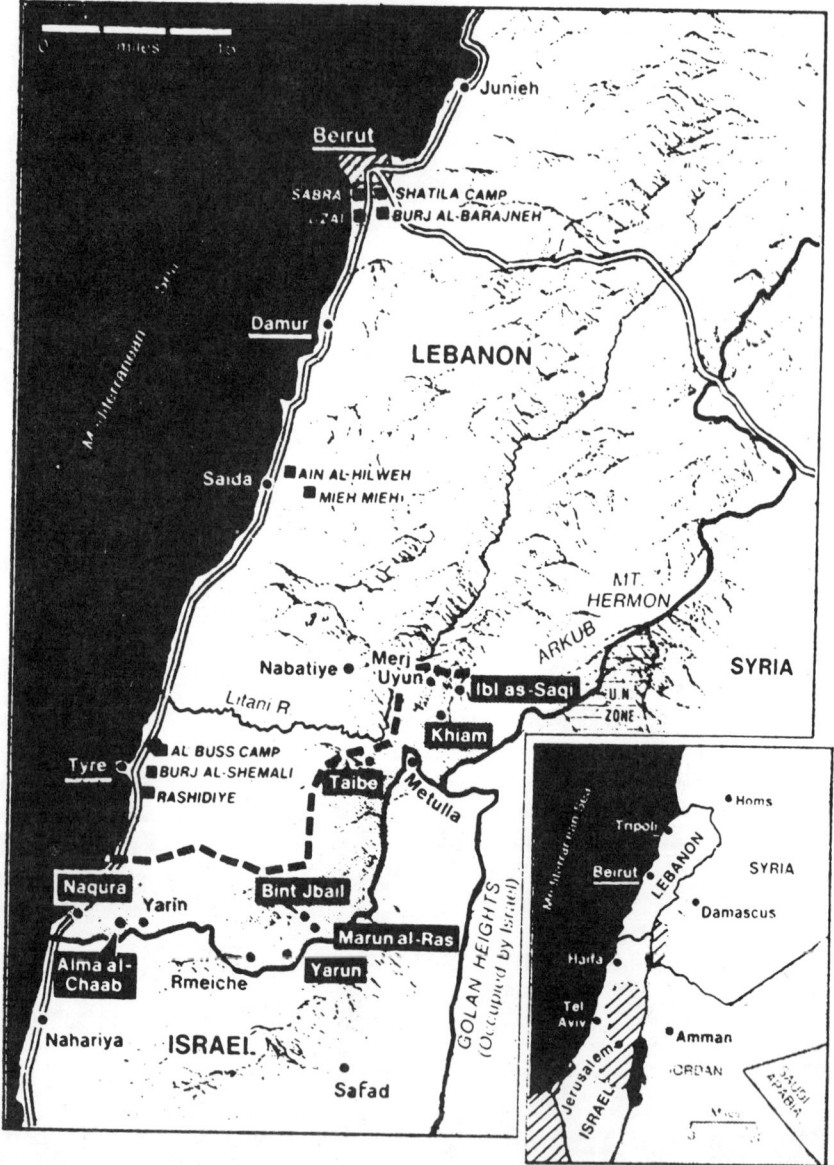

Israelis established "security belt" in southern Lebanon after capturing Palestinian strongholds (marked by panels). Israeli gunboats attacked Tyre, and jets struck there, at Damur and also in Beirut area.

© 1978 by the New York Times Company
Reprinted by permission.

ensure the peaceful character of the area of operations, control movement, and take all measures which were necessary to restore Lebanese sovereignty and authority over the area.

The Israelis, however, did not believe that UNIFIL could effectively prevent Palestinian raids on Israel. Accordingly, during the Israeli withdrawal, they created a narrow zone between the UNIFIL forces and the Israeli border, which they turned over to Major Saad Haddad, a Christian militiaman. Since there was a considerable Palestinian commando force entrenched in the enclave surrounding the port city of Tyre and in other pockets north of the Litani River, infiltration and raids upon Israel did continue, although on a much reduced scale.

Since the spring of 1978, the Palestinians and Major Haddad's Christian militia have exchanged heavy fire daily. Israel began a policy of reprisal raids into Lebanon for terrorist attacks conducted within Israel. The intensity and nature of these raids escalated and have been condemned by the international community, including the United States and other traditional allies of Israel. A distinguished Lebanese ambassador protested at the United Nations. He said that his protest of these retaliatory and preemptive Israeli attacks on Lebanon was made in the spirit of protest against the apparent expectation that Lebanese are to die in silence and permit the destruction of their country . . . the one country in the Middle East that has refused to share in the destruction of others.

The discussion of the nature and strength of Israeli raids into Lebanon has become the major topic of conversation among Lebanese. One senior Lebanese official addressed the problem of Israeli retaliations in this way:

> Israel does not want the United States to talk to the PLO as they fear this will lead to a Palestinian state. Bombing Lebanon undercuts the PLO moderates who want the PLO to make some changes so the American dialogue can happen. It reinforces the extremists. It is ironic but true that Israeli actions inadvertently reinforce the PLO extremists. So we suffer for these political games.

Lebanese Perceptions of Threat

• *Continued death and destruction*

There are few signs to indicate that the Palestinians or Israelis are willing to change their goals or tactics. This means that Lebanon will remain the staging ground for the major violence between these two protagonists. Lebanese believe that the death and destruction will continue for the foreseeable future. The Palestinian-Israeli conflict has promoted

Lebanese domestic political in-fighting, as evidenced by the recent waves of killing between Christian forces. These are attributed to disagreements over a Christian leader's endorsement of the need for the Syrian peacekeeping presence in Lebanon. The daily bombings, shellings, extortions at the village level, and acts of terrorism continue unabated.

In the late 1960s, the Palestinians used Jordan as their staging ground against the Israelis. Since their bloody expulsion from Jordan in 1970, the PLO has used Lebanon as its staging area for such attacks. This use of Lebanon brought widespread retaliatory destruction by the Israelis upon Lebanon and has promoted conflicts within the Lebanese leadership. All Lebanese currently fear for the physical security and the long-term political viability of a unified state of Lebanon if this destructive situation continues.

The Palestinians feel they have no choice but to continue to use Lebanon as their base of operations. Egypt, Jordan, and Syria are not possible staging grounds for continued PLO attacks on the Israelis, since those governments have sealed their borders to prevent such raids. The Israelis believe that their doctrine of preemptive retaliation must be maintained as a way to protect Israel, and to demonstrate Israeli determination to punish anyone who attempts to inflict harm upon Israel. The Palestinian goals are clear to the Lebanese and Israelis—continue fighting until they win recognition for Palestinian rights to self-determination and achieve the ultimate goal of establishing a Palestinian state. The Lebanese people do not see how their domestic situation can be made right and peace be achieved until the Palestinian-Israeli situation is first resolved.

The Lebanese feel that they are clearly the losers in this struggle. They believe their first goal must be to seek a solution to the Palestinian problem. Following that, they feel they must focus on a plan for rebuilding the political, economic, and moral structures of their once prosperous society—a task in which they express their self-confidence. In the meantime, dozens of women, children, and men die each week in raids and shellings by Major Haddad, the Israelis, or extremist Arab groups.

- *Israeli annexation* (de jure *or* de facto) *of Lebanon south of the Litani River*

The Israelis have made it known that they will not tolerate terrorist raids upon Israel staged from southern Lebanon. Their invasion in March, 1978,[43] demonstrated their willingness to launch a full-scale occupying attack. Their establishment of a zone for right-wing Christian militiamen in April/May, 1978, and their support for this effort since that time, demonstrate their continued interest in this area. Lebanese believe that the Israelis have the military capability and could easily have the political will to seize and annex southern Lebanon. The restraining factors are the United Nations force (UNIFIL), world public opinion, United States response, and the possibility of provoking another general Middle East war.

Lebanese cite the 1978 invasion and subsequent involvement of Israelis in the southern areas of Lebanon, which include Israeli military personnel, tanks, and use of land to stage raids north of the Litani River on Palestinian strongholds, as precedents for such an Israeli attempt to seize and possibly annex southern Lebanon. Lebanese believe that the political, economic, and moral viability of Lebanon is at stake. In addition, many Lebanese, especially the Shiia Moslems of the south, would likely be driven from their homeland. Several times since March, 1978, the Israelis have threatened to reoccupy the south of Lebanon should the terrorist attacks continue. Although the majority of Israeli public opinion would not favor such annexation, many Lebanese feel it might be done out of political expediency. It is agreed that Israel would lose face in the international community, although a Lebanese journalist noted that in the final analysis "it is only [saving] face with the American public opinion that counts for the Israelis." Few Lebanese believe that the United States could sit back and watch such an annexation take place. Israel has never claimed the lands above the old international border with Lebanon. Lebanon is the only protagonist state that has no territorial claims on Israel. However, many Lebanese believe that Israel desires the valuable land and important water resources of the Litani River, in addition to any added sense of security it would get from annexing southern Lebanon.

Although common sense tells the Lebanese that an Israeli annexation could not happen, they do not trust Israeli motives. Lebanese look at the on-going precedent of the Golan, the West Bank, and Gaza. A retired Moslem politican known for his moderate views said:

> If the Israelis decide to refuse ever allowing a Palestinian state in the region then we must face the consequences here in Lebanon ... the permanent destruction of Lebanon as we knew it before 1975. The Israelis do so much in the name of security that we are not at all sure that annexing the south of our land might not be considered one day an essential security requirement by the Israeli government. What could we do? And would you believe that the Americans would really prevent it from taking place?

His colleague with more radical views added, "Then we shall see once and for all who is right and who is wrong about the real motivations of Zionist Israel."

- *Syrian annexation* (de jure *or* de facto) *of Lebanon north of the Litani River*

Most Lebanese believe that Syria has never made clear its ultimate intentions for occupying much of Lebanon under the rubric of the Arab League Peacekeeping Force. The Syrians, since 1976, have fought at different times against the Palestinians, Lebanese Christians, and Lebanese Moslems. Most Lebanese believe that they did this to maintain or re-establish order or to achieve limited political goals. Some Lebanese Christians saw these Syrian actions as part of an effort to extinguish pockets of non-Moslem Arabs in the Arab world. Some Lebanese Moslems viewed Syrian efforts as an attempt to gain ultimate influence over the PLO. Syrian threats to withdraw the peacekeeping forces in the winter of 1980 were viewed by some Lebanese as an attempt to further increase Syrian influence over the PLO. According to these arguments, a withdrawal of the Syrian forces would precipitate renewed hostilities, possible Israeli intervention, and would create a dangerous situation for the PLO.

The force of 30,000 Syrian troops has been by far the strongest military force within Lebanon. The Syrians have sought to avoid confrontation with the Israelis except for several aerial dogfights in 1979. They have cooperated with UNIFIL, and have not opposed attempts to rebuild the Lebanese army or equip it with American weapons. When the Arab League threatened not to renew its Arab League Peacekeeping Force in Lebanon, due to political disagreements and operational needs for troops by some other contributing countries in their own capitals, the Syrians made it clear that they would remain regardless. However, subsequent developments have cast some doubt on that assertion.

Many Lebanese are quick to point out that there had been, for many years, talk in Syria of re-establishing *Greater Syria*, which at one time included all the lands that are now part of Lebanon. Fundamentalist Moslems view such a plan as a positive measure toward the long-desired Arab unity. The traditional struggle for leadership in the Arab world between Baghdad, Cairo, and Damascus has not abated. Since Cairo is currently removed from that leadership struggle, this merger, if achieved by Syria, would be seen as an attempt to strengthen its claim to that leadership.

Many Lebanese Christians believe that the political independence and economic viability of Lebanon is threatened by the presence of Syrian troops. Some Moslems share this fear that Syrian interests might be translated into a permanent arrangement to unite Lebanon with Syria.

Many Lebanese officials believe that the Syrians cannot withdraw under the current situation without being responsible for a renewed general bloodbath throughout Lebanon. Others argue that the Syrians have made a large sacrifice by keeping their troops in Lebanon. President Assad stated that the Syrian presence is "at the expense of our economy and of our daily bread...." He estimated Syria's cost of "$2 million a day — an unusually heavy burden for a poor nation that for decades has imported twice as much annually as it exports and has a per capita income of about $400 a year."[44] Other Lebanese note that Saudi Arabia and other Arab states have contributed much of the estimated $1 billion a year cost for this operation. A senior Arab diplomat said that "it is generally believed in the West that the rich Arabs are footing the bill for this largely Syrian operation. I can tell you that the Arab League contribution does not cover the full costs and this is hurting Syria. Also remember that these 30,000 troops belong on the Golan and in case of a renewal of hostilities with Israel or anyone else, they must be withdrawn from Lebanon."

From an economic and pan-Arabic ideological view which espouses Arab unity, such an annexation by Syria would be seen as a positive step. However, an attempt to undertake it would risk confrontation with Israel, the United States, and other states, including possibly some Arabs. It would meet with bloody resistance from the Christian community and perhaps others. It could also further destabilize Syria's internal politics.

Many Christians do not trust Syrian intentions. A respected Christian religious leader noted this spring:

> We all know in our hearts that Syria sees her destined role and possible long-term economic viability in terms of an Arab union. What country in the region has better resources, industrious people, and the will to succeed than Lebanon? It is quite clear what they [Syrians] want. At the very least they are determined to influence our next political structure. Everyone in Lebanon will agree with that.

Comments

All Lebanese agree that central to these concerns is the need to resolve the Palestinian issue. The Lebanese believe that Lebanon will regain its past prosperity and peacefulness. They are concerned, however, over the protracted nature of the Palestinian-Israeli conflict, noting that time, more than any other factor, will hinder the healing process in Lebanon. With each passing day, more death and destruction occurs. Each event carries repercussions in the moral, economic, and political dimensions of the society. The youth are growing up in the midst of this violence, watching family members and friends suffer the consequences of something that was not essentially their problem. Some Lebanese would welcome Palestinians living in Lebanon to remain and become part of Lebanese society if they decided not to leave for a newly created Palestinian state. However, many Christian Lebanese fear that if large numbers of Palestinians were allowed to remain permanently in Lebanon, it would affect the delicate population balance between Moslems and Christians. Shiia Lebanese in the south also fear competition for jobs from the Palestinians in their areas. This question of the Palestinian refugees in Lebanon is particularly difficult, since most of them came from pre-1967 Israel—areas like Galilee, Haifa, and Jaffa.

The interference in domestic politics continues unabated. Attempts by outside parties, including the United States, France, Iraq, the PLO, USSR,

Libya, and others, to influence Lebanese political factions have escalated dramatically since 1975. A respected Lebanese religious leader now living outside the region summarized the problem this way:

> If we were left to ourselves, the problems would be settled. Already there are informal meetings between Christians of different sects, Shiite and Sunni Moslems, and Druze people regarding how we can restructure a unified Lebanon and rebuild ourselves. But this can never happen while every outside party considers Beirut his Middle East base of operations.

Finally, many Lebanese have fearfully assessed the long-term implications of President Assad's remarks that, according to his Baath Party principles, Arab unity comes first — from Mauritania [sic] to Iraq, President Assad stated that one day, perhaps, Arabs will have to fight each other to create Arab unity — just as was done in the American Civil War. Lebanese concern over their position in the Arab-Israeli confliet is clearly extended to intra-Arab conflicts as well. Thus, for some, the possibility of a neutral Lebanon is an appealing option for consideration.

Palestinians

Central to efforts to achieve a comprehensive settlement of the Arab-Israeli conflict remains the need to resolve the Palestinian component of the conflict. A PLO official summarized the error he felt Palestinians made during the period 1948 to 1968 as a reluctance of Palestinians to *sell their cause:*

> We Palestinians historically approached politics as what ought to be, will be. We never asked what can be and how do we achieve it. Our self-righteousness gave us nothing to negotiate about, and few cared about our just cause. In the 1960s, we finally realized that we had to use so-called terrorist violence and armed warfare rather than seek political negotiations because there was nothing to negotiate about. We learned that offering our cause was not enough....

A great deal has been written about the historical, religious, and political dimensions of the conflict between the Palestinians and the Israelis since the 1940s. What seems to have happened to the Palestinians during the past two decades might be described as an awakening of their ethnic and national consciousness and the development of a nationalist political movement. Palestinians attribute this change to the single-minded determination of the Palestine Liberation Organization, established in May, 1964. Today, with recognition given in most capitals of the world to the principle

West Bank

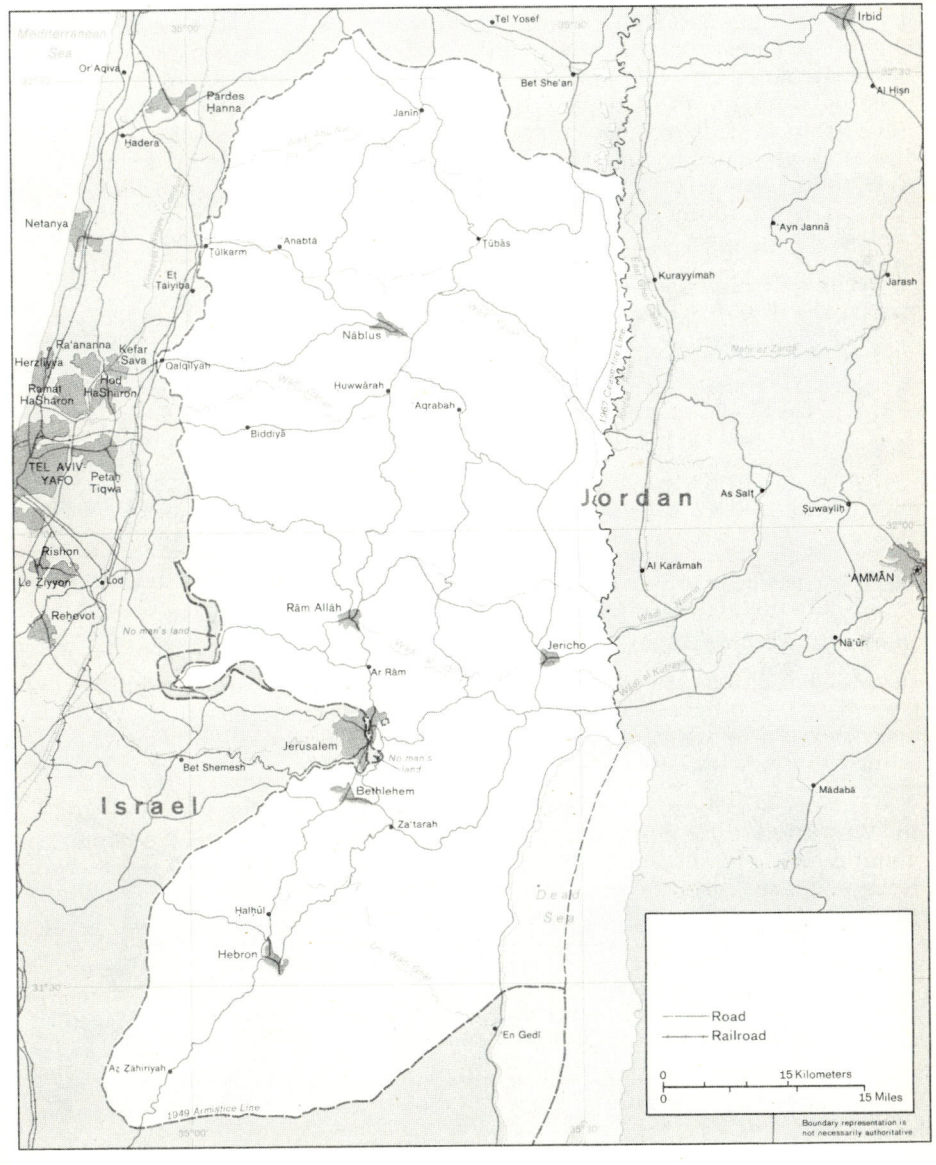

of the right of Palestinian self-determination, their dream of nationalism has never been closer to reality.

The Palestinian struggle has been extremely bitter, waged not only with Israelis but with others. A senior Palestinian figure on the West Bank noted that "outsiders should look at the death statistics to see that as many if not more Palestinians have been killed by other Arabs since 1948 as by the Jews." He noted the course of events over thirty years when Arabs fought to destroy Israel, not to recognize the Palestinians' right to exist. He added, "The Arabs kept their silence for so many years. Iraqis assassinated us. . . . Jordanians fought us. . . . All the Arabs at one time or another let us down. We were for 25 years very much on our own. But now that is past and our struggle is becoming an all-Arab struggle. . . . In fact, it is becoming accepted as a struggle of justice by 90 percent of the world now."

It is with this background in mind that an attempt is made to summarize the threats which Palestinians, within and without the PLO, feel are the most important. A West Bank mayor said:

> Don't forget that we can't be threatened much more than we have been since 1948 or 1967. What more can someone threaten us—to kill us like the Jews in the late 1940s?—to send us to some South Seas island and forget us?—to take away our identity and make us, what do you Americans say, put us in the melting pot? There were twenty-five years when our identity was nearly taken away, but those days are gone. Do you know much about animals? When blood is smelled among a weak victim, the strong pounce on him to devour the weak one. This time the blood is not ours. It is the blood of those who try to deny us the right to self-determination.

He added after a pause, "I am not talking here about the Israeli people but some people in it [Israel] and others elsewhere in Washington and New York and other places who deny us our right to self-determination. . . . We are willing to live with Israel in permanent peace."

Faculty members at the Palestinian university, Bir Zeit University on the West Bank, were asked why they believed the Israelis were so adamant about refusing to allow a Palestinian state. They answered that there were three primary reasons:

> • A Palestinian state would bring the skeleton out of the closet for the Israelis. "This would bring home the arguments about loss of property, the refugees who had to leave their homes, and so many other issues which the Israelis do not want to address," said one professor educated in the West.

> • A Palestinian state on the West Bank and Gaza would meet with strong opposition on the basis of religious and ideological arguments.

- A Palestinian state would be seen to pose security threats to Israel.

One faculty member commented, "Even if they [Israelis] went along with withdrawal from West Bank areas and allowed a Palestinian state, the minute Russian tanks or missiles or Iraqi soldiers stepped foot into the area, they would swoop down and reoccupy us.... Is there any doubt of this?" Security for the Israelis, they believed, was a political as much as a military doctrine. A professor added, "If one thinks of security only as a military term, he must remain a colonialist." A former West Bank leader (during the Jordanian rule in the mid-1960s) said that "we Palestinians must remember that the Israelis have a *fortress mentality*." He quoted King Hussein in reference to the Israelis as "still living from day to day without vision." The Palestinian continued, "We try to remind our Israeli friends that they are experts at winning wars and losing the peace that could follow.... Isn't learning how to make peace better than fighting the last war again?" The threats which were discussed most often by the Palestinians follow.

Palestinian Perceptions of Threat

- *Denial of Palestinian right to self-determination*

The Israelis have been explicit about their intentions to prevent self-determination and in particular any aspect of such a process that might lead to the establishment of a Palestinian state. The Palestinians argue that the failure of the autonomy talks to produce any results was foreseen. Said a West Bank mayor, "How can representatives of three foreign governments, Egypt, Israel, and the United States, determine the future of any other people?" Opposition to the autonomy talks is deeply embedded among the Palestinians as they see these talks resulting in a dead end which would perpetuate a new form of Israeli ultimate rule over the West Bank and Gaza. Several Palestinians were reminded of the Austrian decision after the war not to accept Russian offers for a partial Russian withdrawal into specific security (restricted military) locations. The Austrian people rejected this offer and waited until the Russians agreed to leave Austria altogether as part of the general agreement, resulting in their full independence in 1955.

The Palestinians recognize the Israelis' ability to maintain control over the occupied territories for the foreseeable future. They see a reversal of U.S. policy as the key to influencing the Israelis, believing that the Israelis will never choose to leave the West Bank and Gaza. Palestinians believe that, although most of the world community has condemned the occupation and the expanding settlements and has called for a return to the 1967 borders, the rhetorical support has not been translated into practical support, such as pressure on Israel to make concessions. The Israeli experience since 1948 was regularly cited as one continuous example of how the Israelis have worked to deny the Palestinians the right to self-determination and their homeland. Palestinians argue that the growing Palestinian willingness to negotiate while minimizing violence will be lost if delays continue to occur. They also argue that continued postponement of the right to self-determination will further radicalize and frustrate the Palestinians, causing renewed violence and perhaps a resumption of attacks on non-Israeli targets in Europe or America. Palestinians agree that Israeli strength has, for the short run, enabled the Israelis to maintain their occupation despite the protests of their allies and the world community. A Palestinian who has had contact with Israeli doves on these matters said:

> Apparently, all Israelis agree that for the short term, they cannot lose by following current policies . . . but there is disagreement about the long term . . . and what if the Arabs decided to really use their oil weapon? Would the result be the Americans forcing Israel to do things? . . . They [Israelis] feel that Israel is strong now and so this is the time to do something to get this Palestinian issue going in a way that would be best for Israel. But the hardliners just do not have the foresight to understand that this might be their best chance.

Some Israelis currently believe that delaying settlement of this Palestinian issue by a decade or two favors their cause. Palestinians find it difficult to see how Israelis can honestly think this way. Said a PLO official, "We have here a time bomb for Israel. Instead of trying to defuse it, the Israelis have decided to sit on it. That is their choice, and one day will be their loss."

Most Palestinians believe that the Israelis have no intentions of allowing any change in the status of the occupied territories during the next decade. This belief causes Palestinian frustration and resentment. Said a PLO spokesman:

> They [Israelis] ask us to change our Covenant which rejects compromise and denies Israel's right to exist. We ask them to change their policy which rejects compromise and denies the Palestinian people the right to exist as a nation. Now are we both wrong or both right? Does it matter? I think what matters is that the problem will not be solved unless we both have the desire to see it solved. Time is not an irrelevant factor. It is clearly in our favor over the long period of time. Yet we are willing to go to the negotiating table. . . .

- *Israeli efforts to change the character and economy of the West Bank and Gaza*

The Palestinians argue that Israel is attempting to alter the very character of the occupied territories through its policies of establishing Jewish settlements; deporting Arabs; restricting the development of the economy by discouraging outside investment in industry and placing severe restrictions on everything from export of foodstuffs to Israel and other countries to drilling for water on Arab lands; discouraging creation of jobs which would keep young, educated Palestinians in the territories; and other practices which harass and complicate the daily life of the Arab people in the occupied territories.

The International Labor Organization noted that between 1970 and 1978 there had been a drop of 6,000 employed people in the occupied territories, while the active population there increased by 34,600 people and the number of Palestinian workers in Israel rose from 20,000 to 70,000.[45] In May of 1979, Mr. Matitiyahu Drobless, co-chairman of the World Zionist Organization's settlements department, announced that over the next five years 58,000 families would settle in twenty new settlements in Judea and Samaria, perhaps as many as 200,000 people in all. He said the current figures showed 6,000 Jews in the territories and one million Arabs.[46] The *Jerusalem Post* estimated that 50,000 Jews live in new developments in the expanded city of Jerusalem. The housing expansion exploded in 1970 when Israel "leaped beyond the existing built-up area. . . . In East Talpiot, for instance, construction was deliberately started on the ridge furthest away from Jewish Jerusalem in order to sink stakes as quickly as possible close to the new edge of the city."[47]

Palestinians cite articles in the public press that Housing Minister David Levy was not willing to discuss the issue of his massive transfer of billions of Israeli pounds to the right-wing, expansionist Gush Emunim sect via General Ariel Sharon's Ministry (Agriculture) at the expense of social services;[48] and that Jewish settlements inside the occupied territories are financed by such groups as the United Jewish Appeal.[49] Palestinians point to figures gathered by the Jordanian government which show that 92 percent of the West Bank's imports come from Israel, while its exports to Jordan have dropped sharply, due to the Israeli freeze of the Arab banking system on the West Bank.[50] The Israeli response to the arguments that Arab youth and workers are being *encouraged* to leave the territories centers on figures for the period between 1968 and 1978 which show a rise of 85 percent on field crops on the West Bank, a doubling of citrus crops, and a 250 percent rise in vegetables and potatoes. The *Jerusalem Post* asks, "Does that suggest a policy of rural depopulation?"[51] Palestinians argue that the improved use of irrigation and fertilizer are responsible for the rise in productivity, factors that obscure a policy of depopulation. They also point out that these figures of prosperity do not reflect industry and other fields where the Israelis have disocuraged growth, intending to build a dependency of an agricultural West Bank upon Israeli markets.

The Israeli Cabinet's decision to allow individual Israeli citizens to buy land in occupied areas is cited by the Palestinians. So too is a recent announcement that 80,000 acres of land around Bethlehem owned by Arabs living in the United States, Canada, and Latin America would be handed over to an Israeli Custodian of Absentee Property. This would, in effect, make Israel the owner.[52] The International Labor Organization reports that since 1975, there has been a net migration of some 20,000 persons a year from the West Bank and Gaza.[53] One-third of the labor force of the West Bank works in Israel; and Palestinians constitute 25 percent of the Israeli workforce in the construction trades.[54]

Palestinians ask how Israelis can claim to administer autonomy in an area over which it does not now claim to exercise sovereignty. A special commission established by the United Nations visited the Middle East and reported that land seized by the Israeli authorities, either specifically for settlement purposes or for other stated reasons covered 27 percent of the West Bank.[55] Some Palestinians have argued that even the high Israeli inflation rate is meant to serve Israel's interests by financing the settlements with cheap money; and since many imports for the West Bank and Gaza are charged high customs duties, the prices for West Bankers and Gaza residents are increased. Abuses are mentioned in the U.S. State Department's *Report on Human Rights Practices in Countries Receiving U.S. Aid* and have been widely covered in the world press.[56] The mayor of a large West Bank city stated that the Jordanian-built prison in his city, meant to hold 150 prisoners, was currently holding 600 political prisoners. Stories of beatings and intimidation of children and women in refugee camps by Israeli soldiers have been substantiated by outside observers in the public press. A Jordanian defense official noted that "it is surprising to me sometimes that outsiders coming to the West Bank are surprised to see that this is a military occupation. As a military historian of sorts, I am hard pressed to give you cases of successful long-term military occupations. . . . Can you?"

The Palestinians point to the statistics, the quotations from the Israeli and Western press, statements of the residents of the occupied territories and settlement policies of the Israeli Government itself to demonstrate that the Israelis have embarked on a campaign to transform the character of the West Bank, Gaza, and its people.

The Palestinians believe that the Israelis, since 1967, have embarked on a policy to make the occupied territories dependent upon Israel. The annexation of Jerusalem is described as a possible precedent for their final goal for the West Bank and Gaza. Most Palestinians see the destruction of the Palestinian character of the West Bank and Gaza as the ultimate Israeli goal. Palestinians argue that Israeli actions speak as loud as their words, both of which claim *Judea and Samaria* as Biblical lands of *Eretz Israel*. Most Palestinians agree with a PLO official who said, "The policies are deliberate and clear: to destroy all vestiges of the Palestinian character of the land and build a Jewish structure to become part of Israel. Their [Israeli] style is direct and unmistakable as evidenced by their economic policies, their deportation and harassment of the educated young, and their settlements policy." Current Israeli policies are seen as deliberate components of a master plan to transform the territories and discourage the local Palestinians. A Palestinian professor stated:

> Did you see the article in the *New York Times* where an Israeli was quoted as saying 'If you have a headache, you don't cut off your head'? She [the Israeli quoted] added that, 'Israel has a 30-year margin before the Palestinian Arabs outnumber Jews, so let's make the best of it.' Do you see now why we Arabs say the Israelis are narrow-sighted? It's almost unbelievable.

- *Complacency in world public opinion on the Palestinian problem*

One of the major threats which Palestinians have seen in the autonomy talks following Camp David was that a limited agreement for partial autonomy under Israeli supervision would be seen by the world community as a solution to the Palestinian issue.

The only chance that most Palestinians see for realizing their goal of self-determination is to maintain the support and initiative that they have gained during the 1970s throughout the world. They see their willingness to end both terrorist attacks in Europe and acts which threatened or harmed civilians outside Israel, such as aircraft hijackings, as part of their understanding of the need to keep public opinion in sympathy with their cause of self-determination. Yet, the Palestinians have experienced fluctuations in outside support, even by other Arabs, for their fight to regain their homeland. Developments in Iran and Afghanistan in early 1980 have set back the Palestinian cause and its momentum, at least temporarily although European initiatives are anticipated.

The Palestinians feel that without even greater international support, they will be unable in the foreseeable future to reach their objective of self-determination. Palestinians recognize that public support is often distracted by other events that may arise in a different region of the world which could prompt the public to forget about the urgency of the Palestinian cause. "Commitment to any cause by an outsider runs quite shallow," said a PLO official. Loss of public support is seen by the Palestinians as an indirect and gradual threat which comes about when there is a feeling that the problem has basically been resolved or that there are more urgent problems about which one should focus. The Palestinians believe this can be true of government policy in much the same way as public opinion.

The Palestinians believe it would be extremely difficult for them to convince the Israelis of the need to seek accommodation on these issues without outside pressure from the United States and others. Said a PLO leader, "Public opinion is becoming our best ally, but it is a fickle thing, like a bird in flight. . . . We cannot risk losing sight of its beauty or fickleness."

The Palestinians have designed much of their campaign to capture the world's attention to their cause. They claim this was done initially through such violent attacks as the Munich massacre during the Olympics and various aircraft hijackings. Once world attention was secured in the mid-1970s, they decided to devote their energies to convincing the world of the justice and importance of their cause. Feeling they have accomplished this as well, they have decided in the early 1980s to enlist strong world support in the quest to realize their goal of self-determination. Palestinians note that their tactics in the 1970s were reminiscent of terrorist acts committed by Mr. Begin and Knesset Speaker Shamir. "The difference," wrote a PLO leader, "is that in the 1970s we have mass media so you can watch events during dinner. . . . If such a thing was available in the 1940s, most Americans and Europeans would have reacted as they did in the 1970s." In recent years the PLO leadership has noticeably reduced training for radical elements in Europe and elsewhere, largely due to their belief that diplomatic and political efforts have been successful and will ultimately lead to the achievement of their self-determination objectives.

Comments

The Palestinians do not feel threatened at this stage by what one official called "bullets and nasty neighbors." However, they have expressed serious concerns about security needs that would be required for a Palestinian state established on the West Bank and Gaza. They strongly object to the Western bias that only Israel will have security fears. Palestinians point to a heavily armed, advanced state of Israel sitting on a border with this new Palestinian state. They frequently ask, "What guarantee will we have from Israeli attacks of a military nature, or economic exploitation, or cultural and social penetration?" A PLO spokesman in Damascus noted:

> It is too easy to think of security in strictly a military light. . . . It is so much more than protection from missiles or rifle shots. . . . Yes, we are very concerned about the future security of a Palestinian state on the West Bank and Gaza. Would the Israelis let us live in peace and develop our resources? These are the questions to ask when you talk to Israelis about security.

The Palestinians also express their grave concerns over water resources. They note that although the new Jewish settlements on the West Bank are allowed new wells, the Arabs are not allowed to make any new wells.[57] They raise questions about the lack of proper social services. The Palestinian city of Nablus, for example, has been allowed to build only one new school since 1967, despite a high population growth. They point to the lack of freedoms. Said a prominent Palestinian political official in the spring of 1979:

> What threats do I personally fear? I will tell you. I fear that my children will know nothing better than this life we are living. I fear threats that any day someone can tell me — you, go to jail,

or, close your shop, or stop using so much water, or do not go to meetings, or maybe some day, stop speaking.... That's what I fear for me and my family.... But fears only feed our commitment to our cause.... What other people in the world are denied their basic right — self-determination — which is enshrined so well in the American Declaration of Independence?

Palestinians and other Arabs ask how the United States can deplore Soviet military occupation of Afghanistan and tolerate so readily military occupation of the West Bank and Gaza. A Palestinian writer argued that "Thomas Paine would have a field day with this double standard that violates the basic democratic principles which the United States was formed to represent.... If we asked for the destruction of Israel together with our right to self-determination, then the Americans would be just in refusing to help.... But we have made it clear that we are willing to agree to a permanent peace with full and permanent recognition of Israel."

In the meantime the PLO continues to build its infrastructure, which today includes dozens of factories in Lebanon, modern hospitals, nursing and other schools, an extensive pension system for families of those who have died in the conflict, a computer center for statistical and financial information, a scholarship program for university students, a tax collection system including five percent of the wages of Palestinians working in the Gulf and other states, and a large, democratically elected Palestine National Council (301 members). "It becomes evident," argues a retired Jordanian Cabinet member, "that the PLO is in fact a government in exile — and a government with a track record that is more impressive than perhaps 75 member states of the United Nations, in terms of its services, efficiency, and, I would even say, democracy."

Egypt

Following the conclusion of the Egyptian-Israeli Peace Treaty of March 26, 1979, the Egyptians were confronted with the consequences of a serious rift within the Arab world. The resulting isolation of Egypt from the Arab world has caused considerable concern among the bureaucratic and well-educated sectors of the Egyptian society. Forty million Egyptians (representing the largest grouping of Arabs) now look for immediate action on the innumerable inadequacies of the Egyptian economy, health care, education, and living conditions. Today, Egypt's isolation strongly colors Egyptians' perceptions of threat, not the least of which is a concern over the continued health and security of their President. Discussions held in Cairo in the spring of 1979 revealed that the Egyptian people perceive two major external threats: an Israeli attempt to reoccupy the Sinai and Soviet domination of the Middle East.

Egypt

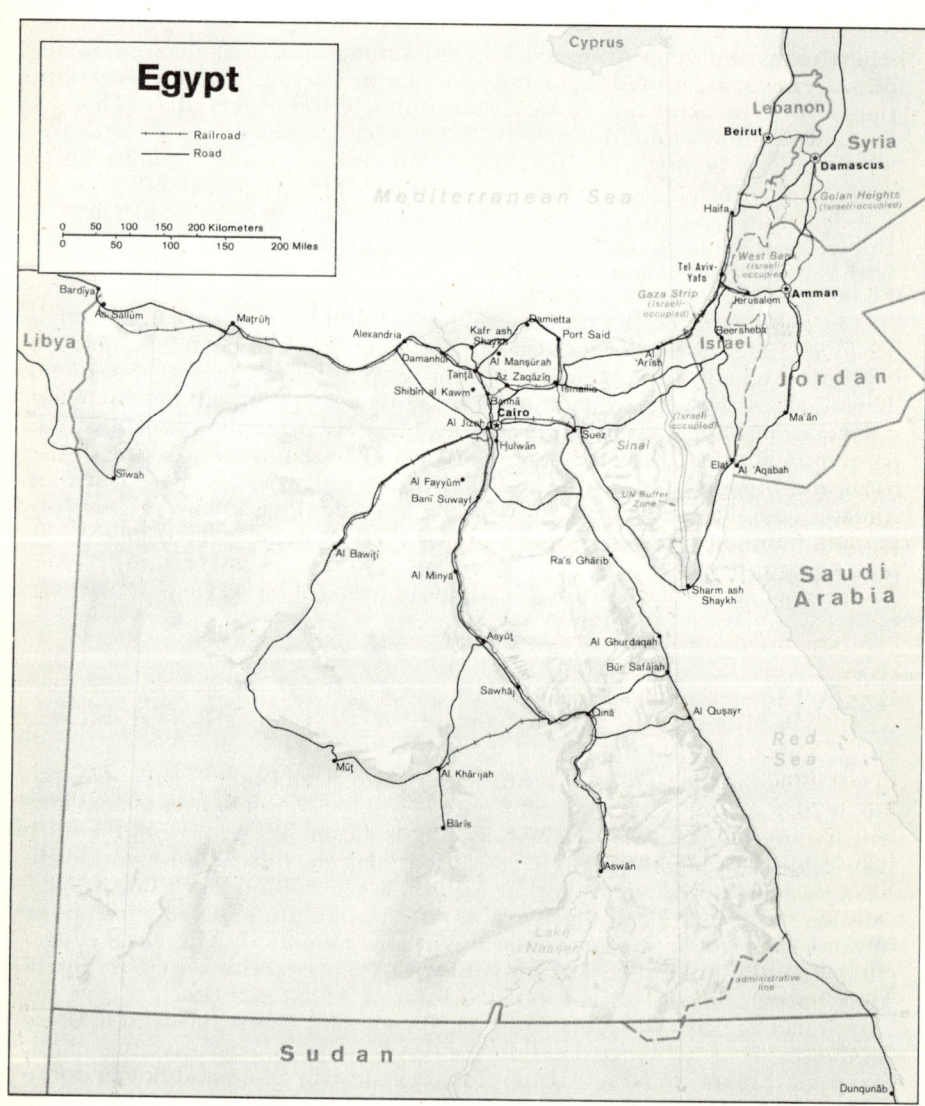

Egyptian Perceptions of Threat

- *An Israeli attempt to reoccupy the Sinai*

The peace treaty is being tested. Some Egyptians believe that if another Arab-Israeli war were to break out, the Israelis would again try to seize the Sinai and would not wish to give it up another time. Many Egyptians believe that it would be difficult for Egypt to remain outside a war between fellow Arabs and Israelis.

Egyptians believe that Israel could regain large parts of the Sinai in another war. In addition to the added territory, Israel would regain valuable oil and airfields. Her military strength, knowledge of the terrain, and desire to have strategic depth and access to the oilfields are important factors which might pressure an Israeli decision to reoccupy the Sinai. It is often noted that Labor Party members in Israel have said that they would not have given up settlements like Yamit; or that influential Knesset members like Moshe Arens, who chairs the Defence and Foreign Affairs Committee, opposed the peace treaty; or that many prominent Israelis have stated that Israel should have extracted a higher price for the return of the oilfields.

Since Egypt's population and industry are almost entirely concentrated in the northeast quadrant of the country, bounded by Alexandria, Cairo, Suez, and Port Said, it would again present a situation where the very survival of Egypt could be threatened. Some Egyptians privately fear that Israel might one day try to reoccupy the Sinai. They do believe, however, that solving the Palestinian issue, coupled with the passage of time during which peaceful relations are strengthened, will reduce the likelihood of war.

Israeli leaders have clearly stated that they have military plans for reoccupying the Sinai, should that become necessary. Defence Minister Ezer Weizman publicly said that "if there is a change in Egyptian positions, we will simply enter Sinai a fourth time."[58] An Egyptian official notes, "We are well aware that many Israelis would like the Sinai back. We are willing to continue with the peace process. But both of us know that peace can be tenuous." Egyptians agree that a process of confidence-building is required and that the peace process must be expanded to include the other protagonists. "The threat is most real," noted a senior official in Cairo, "until the Palestinian question is resolved and trust is generated from relations established as a result of the treaty . . . we have taken a risk for peace now and we must wait to see if we shall succeed. . . . This cannot be stressed enough to those who believe the Camp David achievements are enough. They are not."

- *Soviet domination of the Middle East*

Egyptian officials cite evidence of growing threats to the stability of the region, including the Soviet Friendship Treaty recently signed with South

Yemen; the presence of Soviet advisers and sophisticated military equipment (including MIG-25s and T-72 tanks) in Syria, South Yemen, Libya, Iraq, as well as Afghanistan and Ethiopia; the strong presence of the Soviet navy in the region, including a missile-carrying nuclear submarine in Aden harbor; and the presence of Cubans and East Germans in the region, largely as pilots and advisers. An Egyptian military officer stressed that "the Russians are too clever for this to be a series of hit and miss attempts to win friends. They know what they are doing."

To some Egyptians, the Soviets unquestionably have the ability to carry out their designs, which some believe include threats to the vital Western oil shipping routes. The only potential counterbalance is the United States, but some Egyptians still believe that political restraints and lack of political will render the United States unable to challenge Soviet objectives. The Egyptian leadership perceives this threat as a challenge to the very lifeline of the West and a threat to the security of every anticommunist Middle Eastern state. An Egyptian defense analyst summarized: "This is not paranoia about communism.... We know the Russians rather well.... We are getting to know the Americans, too, and both of them have problems of different sorts ... if one refuses to act as a true superpower, it is an open invitation to the other to take more risks than they otherwise would."

Egyptians see the developments in the region as part of a planned Soviet effort to exert domineering influence over the area and to set back the interests of the Western world, and specifically to achieve superiority over the United States in this region. The continuation of the protracted Arab-Israeli conflict is seen as fueling the progress of this Soviet plan. According to this view if a settlement were reached, there would be a heightened resistance to such Soviet military influence by the Arab states. Egyptians believe that some of the Arabs who currently serve as friends to the U.S.S.R. are doing so out of necessity to gain weapons and other resources while they remain in conflict with Israel. The Egyptians point out that Iraq, for example, continues to execute known communists, yet purchases some $2 billion worth of Russian weapons. It should also be noted that some Syrian, Palestinian, and Jordanian officials favor the limitation of great power military presence in the region, as part of a comprehensive peace.

Comments

Egyptians also fear the growing involvement of Cuban and East European personnel in Libya. Soviet missile units equipped with Scud missiles (medium-range surface-to-surface missiles) and MIG-23 and -25 fighters based in Libya, are a cause for Egyptian concern. The April 1977 Egyptian attack on Libya reportedly was caused by a series of factors, including the

Libyan stationing of Sam 2, 3, and 6 anti-aircraft batteries around the Scud missiles (which were supposedly targeted on Alexandria and other Egyptian cites); the construction of two Russian radar stations near the Egyptian border; and the reported appearance of Soviet F-class submarines in Tobruk at a time when much of the Egyptian navy was tied up in the Red Sea and Gulf of Suez.

The Egyptians express concern about the threats to the stability of their neighbor and ally, Sudan. A large number of Egyptian armored, naval, and air units are assigned to the Sudan. Also, the Egyptians apprehensively watch the efforts by Libya, Iraq, and Israel to secure a nuclear capability which would allow development of nuclear weapons. Most important perhaps is the fear that the peacemaking process will break down and lead to another costly loss of Egyptian lives and another prolonged period of destruction.

Observations

The reader may well disagree with some of the previously listed threats, or question how a protagonist could consider them to be realistic. Perceptions reflect a subjective awareness and understanding of events, actors, situations, and processes. They do not have to reflect what an objective observer would consider to be the real facts or events, for as previously shown, the same event may have as many different meanings as there are people observing it. What determines how each of the protagonists perceives current threats? The single most important factor is the historical relations of the protagonists.

The impact of four decades of bitter conflict between Jews and Arabs has greatly colored the perceptions of both peoples. Arabs and Israelis cannot forget the scope and nature of the violence and destruction that have characterized this conflict. For example, the documented atrocities that have been committed against unarmed civilians in both Arab and Jewish villages are well-remembered. Contemporary leaders in the Middle East have survived ordeals that have had a profound impact upon the way they see events and personalities. Most of the current top Israeli leadership, for example, grew up in Europe during the 1930s and the 1940s. They witnessed or experienced firsthand the atrocities of the Nazis. Palestinian leaders have grown up in refugee camps under terrible conditions or have lived under occupation, their basic rights denied. Other Arab leaders spent their early years under despotic rulers who largely served personal and/or Western interests, neglecting the welfare of their own people.

Societies have developed mechanisms for insuring cultural conformity. Information sources, a primary factor in the maintenance of conformity, are pressured to reconcile their presentations with prevailing stereotyped images. The regional media, whether government-controlled or democratic and searching for sensationalism, reinforce stereotypes. Textbooks used in many schools distort history and reinforce intransigence, which has become a hallmark in the attitudes in the conflict. The socio-economic, religious, and cultural differences between the largely Western-oriented Israeli society and the Arab world of Islamic mores have substantially influenced Arab and Israeli perceptions of one another.

No matter how unrealistic or exaggerated the perceived threats may seem, they remain quite real for the threatened nation's policy-makers and a majority of their population. Many Israelis note with disbelief that Arabs actually fear a concerted effort by Israel to penetrate and undermine their economic, social, and political institutions. Similarly, many Arabs express dismay that Israel would be fearful for its security should a small Palestinian state be established in the West Bank and Gaza. An Arab diplomat queried, "Does the existence of a small, lightly-armed Palestinian state really make a quantative and qualitative difference in the region's power equation?. . . I doubt so very much and am sure that Israeli strategists do as well." Arabs believe that Israelis realize that a small Palestinian state would not represent a threat to Israel for many reasons:

- Israel would not tolerate the military buildup of such a state;

- Israel would take preemptive military measures against the new state, as it did against Jordan in 1970 and Lebanon in 1979, should the new state allow terrorists to stage raids upon Israel from its territory;

- Palestinians are willing to discuss various formulas for special limited armament zones, international supervision, and other agreements as part of a just, comprehensive peace;

- Some other Arab states do not desire to see a heavily armed Palestinian state;

- The Palestinians are tired of four decades of war and want to have the opportunity to raise their families in peace and prosperity;

- The United States would not allow the situation to develop to Israel's military disadvantage;

- When the Israelis once and for all decide what they want for their final, just borders, and when they recognize the Palestinians' right to self-determination, discussions regarding mutual security arrangements could proceed with a high possibility for accommodation.

Many Israelis privately said that they agree with these arguments and expect that eventually an accommodation could be reached to meet mutual needs. Similarly, many Arabs privately admit that agreements could be negotiated that would prevent Israeli penetration of traditional institutions and values in Arab lands.

Unquestionably, all of the threats listed in this chapter are taken quite seriously by each of the protagonists. Until a comprehensive agreement is reached, there will be little opportunity for developing the confidence-building measures that could eventually diminish and perhaps eliminate these basic perceived threats. Each of the protagonists believes that it could be the victim of an attack. For example, while the Israelis perceive an *Eastern Front* threat to be very real, the Arabs fear an attack on the *Eastern Front* countries by Israel.

The greatest sensitivities, however, remain centered on the developments on the West Bank and Gaza, including Jerusalem. Most Arabs and Israelis privately agree that another war is likely to be caused by aspects of the Palestinian problem. Some Arabs refer to the Israeli activities in the occupied territories as *structural violence*. Arabs see the expansion of Israeli settlements and their efforts to alter the character of the occupied territories as a form of violence that is little different in its long-term implications from an armed attack on the Arab people. Similarly, most Israelis view the continuation of terrorist attacks upon civilians as little different from a fully-armed act of aggression by organized army units. The daily structural violence in the occupied territories and the terrorism are considered by the Arabs and Israelis, respectively, to be powder kegs that could explode into full-scale war.

Evaluating the nature of threats requires a careful assessment of capabilities and intentions. The first step is an assessment of the strength, caliber, human resources, and support-capability of the protagonist doing the threatening. In this conflict, each of the protagonists is sensitive to the critical role that outside parties play in strengthening them as well as the other protagonists. The second step is an assessment of intentions. An understanding of a leader's strengths and weaknesses and the detection of shifts in the domestic balance of power are the areas where perceptions play their most important role. A policy-maker's perception of the reality that surrounds him ultimately determines his understanding of the intent of a particular action, and his choice of an appropriate response.

The threats which have been presented in this chapter are indicative of the types of problems that must be addressed in the peacemaking process. Policy-makers, in formal negotiating forums, invariably dismiss as premature suggestions for exploring solutions to the perceived threats. However, the formal negotiating process should not be considered finite or limited. Formal negotiating forums are but one mechanism. An Arab political official agreed that "we must begin to break down the barriers of mistrust before either side will be willing to make the basic concessions which are necessary to successfully negotiate a comprehensive settlement."

The willingness of Arabs and Israelis to discuss their security concerns indicates that the formal process can be supplemented by the exchange of specific, constructive views of how certain types of fundamental problems might be resolved. A Palestinian lawyer offered:

> Perhaps the way to start building confidence is to realize that the other fellow cares enough to understand how you feel and what you worry about . . . that is the first step from which you can sit and talk about mutual accommodation . . . up to now you must admit that the Israelis do not give a care about Palestinians' fears and sufferings . . . of course they argue the same [about us] and it's probably true at this point for all of us. . . .

The question that most often appears in our notes from the private discussions with Arabs and Israelis is "how can we begin to believe that the others truly desire to live in peace with their neighbors?" Exploring and comparing the security concerns of each of the protagonists is a small step in the difficult process of building mutual confidence that fears are shared and that if there is a commitment by each protagonist to live in peace, the fears can be allayed and a full settlement achieved.

3
The Search for Security

A simple definition of *security* is the *relative freedom* from harmful threats. In studies of international relations, the term is usually employed to denote the physical safety of a nation, its territorial inviolability, and its national sovereignty. Although the term *security* is most often used in the Middle East in a military context, it has strong connotations of political, economic, and social stability issues as well. The common thread which runs through all of the variations is the psychological underpinning of the term *security* itself.

A people's or nation's feelings of security depend upon their assessment of external threats, their own domestic stability and capabilities, and value preferences. The depth of insecurity depends upon the perceived and the real nature of a threat, the threat's source, credibility, and duration. In addition, a nation's relative sense of security is often related to its own historical experience. A study of the histories of Russia and Israel, for example, shows that prolonged periods of insecurity have caused these nations to place what many observers see as an unjustifiably high value on protective military security measures. It is the historical and psychological background of a people or nation that determines, in great measure, the way in which security is perceived.

The term *security* has acquired many different meanings in the Arab-Israeli conflict. A senior Jordanian official, for example, decried the Israeli use of the term as follows: "The Israelis define the term in its absolute sense to mean everything. . . . Economic, legal, and political concerns have become security concerns under their definition. . . . Security means nothing when defined as everything. . . . When there is peace, there will be less confusion over the term *security*." Arabs argue that it is possible to contend that a relationship exists between military security and territorial dispositions, but not between the latter and legal institutions. They believe that the way to verify claims based on security is to relate the claims to the specific issue(s).

Asked for a response to this argument, an Israeli defense official replied:

> Some Arabs claim that there will be no worries for security once peace is agreed . . . this is nonsense and they know it . . . . If you

> read between the lines you will see that they worry about their security, which is also sometimes broadly defined by them to include protection from outside influences upon their religious and governmental structures.... Security means more than being able to repel a major military assault ... it covers the whole spectrum of what is defined as protecting the national interests....

There is no agreement over the precise definition of security within the Arab world or within Israel, let alone between the two. An Arab military official recently said that "each of the parties defines security as they see it helping them in their struggle with their enemies."

Since 1978, the author has attempted to determine what elements are common among the ways the six protagonists define security. Analysis shows that the basic extended definition of security used in the region includes relative freedom from both physical harm and outside interference in domestic matters. The term *security* as it is used in this conflict has three major components:

- The relative freedom from primary military threats (such as full-scale armed confrontation) to the physical safety of the population, property, and accepted governing institutions.

- The relative freedom from secondary military threats (short of full-scale armed confrontation) to the physical safety of the population, property, and accepted governing institutions.

- The relative freedom from non-military security threats, for example, serious shifts by outside parties in their influence on and support of a particular government, or domination by outside parties of the essential elements which constitute national sovereignty.

The degree of subjectivity inherent in each component increases as we pass from primary military to secondary military to non-military threats. The three components when taken together constitute the broadest possible definition of security.

This chapter explores Arab and Israeli views on each of these three components of the security definition. The emphasis upon relative rather than absolute freedom from threats in each of the three components is intentional. A noted international relations expert has argued that absolute security has never been enjoyed by sovereign states.[1] Palestinians frequently point to Israeli statements expressing the view that, if all acts of terrorism were halted against Israel for a specified number of years, then Israel would negotiate with the PLO. The Palestinians ask whether any state in the world has such an absolute guarantee against terrorism. Other Palestinians express the belief that, if necessary, Israel would sponsor terrorist attacks on itself, blaming the PLO or other Palestinian groups and thus evade having to recognize Palestinian rights to self-determination. Some

Arabs personally believe that Israel has done just this. Israelis privately agree that there is no such thing as absolute security, but some claim that demanding an absolute end to terrorism is necessary—to persuade the PLO leadership that Israel expects splinter groups to be controlled.

A respected Israeli scholar has remarked, "This age of interdependence has robbed us of most of the realities which justified a medieval-fortress type approach to politics and security." This emerging realization that absolute security cannot be guaranteed by any nation can be attributed to several factors: the advent of sophisticated weapons systems, which blur the distinction between offensive and defensive armaments; escalation of outside involvement in the area to include the vital security concerns of the great powers; and a growing reliance upon third parties for arms, food, energy, and finances by each of the protagonists.

Self-preservation, as it is understood by individual nations, is the core of all security considerations. This corresponds to the traditional definition of security normally used—relative freedom from primary military threats. Self-preservation seems to have two basic levels of meaning in international politics. Traditionally, it suggests respect for territorial integrity, national independence, and the relative safety of the population. The second meaning is an expanded version of the first. It includes respect for zones of influence, establishment of *cordons sanitaires*, treatment of nationals and co-religionists abroad, protection of foreign investments, and claims based on historical, religious, or ideological writings or beliefs. Whereas most Arabs traditionally have assumed the first, more globally accepted definition of self-preservation, the Israelis strongly adhere to the second. Hence, these peoples differ significantly in their perceptions of security violations, threats, and essential security requirements.

There is another dimension to the definition of security held by Arabs and Israelis in this conflict. A number of leaders in the region owe their rise to power and maintenance of their control of government to the continuation of the Arab-Israeli conflict. Thus, for some security is defined as the ability to preserve the political and economic establishment. An Arab military officer privately noted, "We are able to keep a tight reign over the press, universities and others, in the name of the common goal to defeat the Israelis if there is another war—a thought, by the way, which we think is possible. . . . [If you] take away that goal . . . the people would likely not stand for things to remain as they are today. . . . In fact, my family believes that . . . the economy of war could not continue, nor the regime." Similarly, an Israeli businessman noted that "it is difficult to imagine our leadership being able to get away with what they do if there was a real peace with our neighbors. . . . There would be such tremendous demands to do away with runaway inflation which is over 100 percent now. . . . We accept it because the people are convinced that threats continue to exist . . . so we are patient." Some Israelis argued that the conflict preserves the Israeli national character and cohesiveness of the Israeli society.

Many Arabs and Israelis privately argued that although they could possibly foresee the ability of Israelis and Arabs to agree on meeting mutual national security needs, they could not foresee compromises of the sort that would help to guarantee the stability of incumbent regimes. A retired Arab League official argued that "security for our people and nation can be agreed and secured much more readily than security for our leaders or party . . . especially when that leader has built his mode of governing upon the continued struggle with an external enemy." Many Arabs and Israelis doubted whether resolution of the Palestinian question would benefit the stability of any regime — Israeli or Arab. The threat presented by the Palestinian cause has been used as a unifying factor for both the Arab and Israeli people for many years. Removal of this threat or cause could pose a series of difficult questions and challenges to the protagonists. At the same time, continuation of the Palestinian question has had an unsettling effect on many Arab regimes and as well as on Israel.

Several Arabs and Israelis believed that the influence of their respective military establishments was so strong that any regime agreeing to a comprehensive settlement of the Arab-Israeli conflict might be toppled. A senior Arab diplomat from a rejectionist state (those opposed to the Camp David process) stated, "Why would we need all those sophisticated weapons if the conflict ended in a general peace? . . . But also, what military would be happy without its playthings? . . ." Others have pointed to President Sadat's efforts to build up the quality and quantity of Egypt's military arsenal despite its peace with Israel. An Israeli official asked, "Perhaps this is Sadat's only way of keeping his military happy after the peace with Israel?" A number of the *1979 sample* members privately questioned whether incumbent regimes in the region could in fact survive a comprehensive peace. An Arab journalist argued, "Remove the Palestinians as a *cause célèbre*, and some of these men [leaders] have nothing to stand for or stand on . . . nothing." Others argued that the great powers, and some Arab states as well, would not favor a comprehensive peace because it would reduce the degree of influence they hold over certain regimes due to their high dependency for war matériel. Most frequently mentioned was the question of the economic consequences of peace—could economies geared to war or defense remain viable if peace and security were achieved?

As this study progresses, the reader is asked to remember this parallel definition of security because it raises basic questions about the permanence of regimes in the region and their role in facilitating or obstructing the peacemaking process. It also helps to explain initial public reactions to some of the seemingly logical options presented. A Jordanian diplomat argued that "if the Palestinian question were to be resolved, and the majority of people see that real peace was at last possible, it will be interesting to see how many regimes can prevent it [resolution of the Palestinian question] by the sheer personal determination of their leaders to stay in power."

Some Arabs and Israelis agree that several political leaders, fearing for their stability, have decided to impede indirectly the peacemaking process. Security for a regime to remain in power is not necessarily equated with the security of a people or nation. The latter is the subject of this study, although the former must not be forgotten as a reality. A retired Israeli military official argued that "it is rare in history, is it not, when the needs of a particular regime outlasted the needs of a people. . . . A concerted effort by a regime is an important stumbling block to the settlement of the conflict, but in the end, the whole is greater than any of its parts." An Arab military officer had earlier argued:

> The goal of any regime is to see how it can adapt itself to new conditions, like peace. . . . If it can't adapt itself then it doesn't deserve to remain in power. . . . There have been cases where those who rose to power over an external threat were able to solidify their appeal and power by reconciliation with that enemy. . . . Did not Nixon build his political career on hatred of the Chinese and Russian communists . . . and yet did he not open Peking-American relations and pursue the SALT talks with Moscow?

A colleague agreed, "In fact these policies added greatly to his popularity in his days before Watergate, but the irony which I enjoy is that immediately after his ouster in disgrace after Watergate, Nixon was welcomed enthusiastically only by the Chinese Communists—yet, hatred of the same Chinese had been the cause of Nixon's political rise. . . . We should learn from such experiences." A number of Arabs and Israelis asked how one resolves the question of whether the leader makes events or events make a leader. That question has more than a rhetorical importance in this conflict.

The definition of security, in terms of the stability of the regime, does not appear in public statements or in discussions by individuals in the presence of their co-nationals. However, many Israelis and Arabs see the tendency to translate this fear for the stability of the regime to the definition of security as a major stumbling block to agreement and termination of the conflict. On the other hand, these same people urge that the real security concerns of the nation, not the regime, should be explored and discussed more widely.

Primary Military Security Threats

Primary military security threats are the most obvious, accepted, and well-understood. Both Arabs and Israelis perceive those threats that pose potential danger of a full-scale, armed attack as threatening physical harm and damage upon the population, property, and accepted governing institutions. The following threats, introduced in the previous chapter, belong to this security category:

- Israeli fear of an attack from the *Eastern Front* (p. 47)
- Israeli fear of establishment of a Palestinian state (p. 50)
- Jordanian fear of a preemptive Israeli attack (p. 61)
- Jordanian fear of a limited Israeli attack to create a new crisis (p. 68)
- Syrian fear of an Israeli attack (p. 74)
- Lebanese fear of continued death and destruction (p. 83)
- Egyptian fear of an Israeli attempt to reoccupy the Sinai (p. 99)

Each of the protagonists perceives these threats as the most immediate challenges that it confronts. These perceived threats elicit security considerations, including defensible and secure borders; the importance of topography, demography, and resources; the importance of timing; and the consequences of the political will and intentions of the other protagonists and outside parties. To evaluate alternative strategies to effectively deal with these perceived threats, it is necessary to conduct a careful review of the ways in which Arabs and Israelis view the concept of security.

Arab Views of Primary Military Security Threats

Despite the differences that exist among the five Arab protagonists in the conflict, the area of security requirements is one where some basic agreement is possible. Discussions with Egyptians, Jordanians, Lebanese, Palestinians, and Syrians resulted in the compilation of the following five points that represent some of the basic, shared Arab views on primary military security threats.

- *Without peace there are no secure borders*

Without a comprehensive peace settlement, particularly a resolution of the Palestinian question, no Israeli borders will be recognized and secure. Arabs argue publicly and privately that implementation of a comprehensive settlement will bring an end to military hostilities and an agreement recognizing the territorial security of Israel and the neighboring Arab states, including a Palestinian homeland. A pro-PLO political leader on the West Bank pointed out that "nowhere in the world is there a *truly safe* geographical border except perhaps in the case of Eastern Europe's borders with Western countries where barbed wire, floodlights, and armed guards keep watch." He asked the question, "Is this what Israel wants as its final border relationship with its neighbors? It is not what we want. . . . Without trust and mutual agreements with our neighbors, there can be no real peace and establishment of normal relations."

All of the Arabs with whom the Task Force members spoke noted that proposals discussed in comprehensive settlement talks must address the mutual fears and security needs of all the protagonists. Palestinians, speaking about the need for reciprocity in weapon limitations, noted that they were not speaking of numerical reciprocity with Israel, but a conceptual reciprocity of a sort that would have to be based on limited confidence and perhaps outside guarantees or supervision.

Arabs are disturbed over the unwillingness of the West to show concern about Arab security needs. A group of Palestinian intellectuals on the West Bank told the Task Force members that they were the first Western-based group to show an interest in Palestinian and Arab security concerns as well as those of Israel. One Palestinian professor noted that "Western people come here and ask us what are we willing to do to help guarantee the security of the Israelis." Another added that "the irony of such questions is the fact that Israel occupies our land and other Arab land. . . . When they do give it up, who is going to guarantee us some protection from their doing it all over again?"

Recently, more Arabs and Israelis have shown an increasing flexibility in their willingness to privately discuss measures that could allay fears, build confidence, and help to guarantee security. Many of these measures would involve objective third parties, such as United Nations observers, joint patrols, and other arrangements such as limited armament zones. Few Arabs mentioned the need to disarm Israel, although many expressed an interest in instituting restrictions that would prevent all regional nations from acquiring certain types of weapons, most notably nuclear and laser weapons. Arabs note traditional Israeli opposition to third-party roles, such as the stationing of United Nations peacekeeping forces, and ask if peace will moderate such attitudes. Arabs note that a U.N. presence need not "lack teeth" — as antitank minefields and trenches could be installed in critical areas as easily as unarmed observers and observer posts.

- *Topographical features are not absolute guarantees of greater security*

Arabs believe that in the 1980s topographical features like hilly terrain are not a guarantee for greater security in the case of a full-scale armed confrontation. Arabs frequently cite the fact that in 1973 Israel suffered several serious defeats from attacks launched at borders that it had regarded as secure, while in 1967 Israel achieved substantial victories over attacks from borders that it had long regarded as insecure.[2]

Unlike the Israelis, few Arabs make claims that certain territories, because of their topographical features, are essential for security. This difference could be due in part to the larger land areas of most Arab nations compared to the small size of Israel. It must be noted, however, that a Palestinian state would be similar in size to Israel prior to 1967. Few

Palestinians argue that a certain hill or plateau must be given to them to help protect their overall security interests. The Palestinians, like other Arabs, believe that secure borders depend on the normal relations between neighboring states that would follow a comprehensive settlement.

A respected Arab strategist who has been recognized for his planning role in the last war argued:

> The Israelis know that holding high ground instead of low ground can buy them a few more hours, but they also know that the sophistication of weapons in the region are [sic] relegating former strategic advantages into tactical advantages which can quickly be overcome. Israelis must remember that it was when they held the most territory that they came closest to defeat.

- *Sophistication of arms lessens importance of distance*

The Arabs agree that the ever-increasing sophistication of modern arms now possessed by both Israelis and Arabs diminishes the interdependence of territory and security that once existed. New weapons, such as the surface-to-air missile, although designed for defense against attack aircraft, could pose a threat to the airspace of an adversary's territory.

Arabs argue that another war will be different from past ones. An Arab defense expert remarked that "there will be quick strikes with high losses of civilians and aircraft on both sides." He later argued that in the long run, "agreements over security guarantees could be more important than deciding who shall hold hill one, two, or four."

The possibility of basing sophisticated American or Soviet ground, sea, or air forces in the immediate region is disturbing for the Arabs, including many Egyptians. Many oppose the idea and see it as inevitably resulting in direct superpower confrontation in their neighborhood. Many Arabs privately noted that they could understand why the two great powers would prefer to fight on Middle East soil rather than European soil. A Syrian officer inquired, "Why should they risk Poland, Austria, or Norway when the same purpose can be achieved over Syria, Jordan, or Israel?" Although both the Arabs and Israelis realize that their primary arms dependency will continue to cause reliance on the two great powers, there is a fine line drawn between military assistance and military influence that borders on domination. In addition, there is a growing interest in the region to consider, as part of a comprehensive peace agreement, a mutual pact to limit direct U.S.S.R. and U.S. military presence in the area to a certain agreed (fixed) number of advisers.

- *Need for a new kind of* detente

Arabs believe that the concept of *detente* would be applicable to the Arab-Israeli situation in the early stages following a comprehensive settlement. Almost every Arab who participated in the Task Force discussions said that security must be based on an Arab understanding that Israel wants peace more than war, a desire that they claim the Israelis have yet to demonstrate. Neither Israel nor the Arab states, including a Palestinian state if that is established, can be expected to disarm following a settlement of the conflict. A Jordanian official said, "What we are talking about here is an end to sabre-rattling and a start of building some basic confidences by actions, such as notifying a neighboring state of troop maneuvers or exercises which might be misinterpreted . . . things like they are trying to develop in Europe between East and West." A Palestinian professor spoke of the need to establish a "kind of mini-*detente.*" He continued:

> The Israeli military will always be strong for that is their mentality. . . . Their possession of sophisticated weapons, and of course the nuclear weapon itself, is a deterrent in much the same way our Arab numbers and quality of weapons demonstrates to Israel that an unacceptable cost would be inflicted if there was another war. . . .

- *Israel will rely on its own guarantees*

Arabs believe that Israel can guarantee itself compensation for any of the fine points of its *maximum security needs* that cannot be realized in a comprehensive settlement. For example, Arabs cite probable United States military alliance with Israel. In addition, Israeli participation is expected with neighboring Arab governments in the establishment of limited armament zones, demilitarized areas, and the establishment of confidence-building measures.

Most Arabs would still agree that Israeli preoccupation with *secure and defensible borders* is a "cover-up for real Israeli intentions to continue Israeli expansion and annexation of Arab lands in accordance with long-stated Zionist goals." The Lebanese political official continued, "Is not the real issue now facing Israel the need to publicly define what it envisions as its future borders with the West Bank?" A Syrian officer asked how Israel can explain its ideas of a final border on the West Bank when "the whole idea has always been to annex it. . . . All of this autonomy talk has been a clever effort towards realizing Israeli goals. . . . Unfortunately the United States fell for the trap believing that they [Americans] knew something Begin did not. . . ."

Arabs consistently reemphasize that they do not accept the Israeli concept of *secure and defensible borders* or the Israeli tendency to isolate topography as a major determinant for border definition. Arab planners do not understand how factors like population, resources, and the insecurity of Arab neighbors fail to enter more heavily into Israeli security considerations. A summary of the Arab viewpoint was made by an Israeli Arab lawyer from Jaffa. He noted, "The Arabs do not see Israeli confusion over defining secure borders. . . . They see collusion. As I recall, the definition of collusion is some secret set of agreements [between several persons] for a deceitful or possibly fraudulent purpose. . . . Their definition is related to annexation and expansion of Israel."

Arabs believe that the Israeli agreement to withdraw from the Sinai was not an act of good will, but rather an effort to divide the Arab world and buy time to pursue their expansionist efforts in the West Bank and Lebanon. The Arabs demand that the territory seized by Israel during the 1967 war be returned. Barring a willingness to release the territory, Arabs believe that Israeli cries of numerous critical security needs represent a facade designed to keep Western support and delay settlement. The Arabs carefully follow Israeli debates over the question of whether occupied land in the West Bank is essential for national security needs. They view the progress of these debates as an indication of real Israeli long-term intentions.

The basic question for most Arabs is whether the Israelis are willing to negotiate in good faith to secure their basic and realistic security needs. A retired Arab League official asked, "Wouldn't we get a lot further if we were to open negotiations about meeting our security requirements rather than over whether one or another of us has the right to exist? . . ."

The danger perceived within these primary military security considerations exists within secondary military threats as well. These threats, short of full-scale armed confrontation, are seen to menace physical safety of a population, property, and accepted governing institutions.

Israeli Views of Primary Military Security Threats

The notion of secure and defensible borders was added to the Israeli definition of national security after the 1967 war. Prior to 1967, Israeli military doctrine called for an offensive military strategy to compensate for its numerical disadvantage, lack of strategic depth, and absence of acceptable borders with its neighbors. The concept of preemptive war and retaliatory strikes became an essential ingredient of Israeli military policy following Prime Minister David Ben-Gurion's concept of *carrying the war into the enemy's territory*. The Israelis linked this concept of preemptive war with a deterrent theory that advocated an Israel strong in both military manpower and weaponry. This theory held that if the deterrent failed, Israel would use her military power to achieve a quick victory over the numerically superior Arabs.

Out of this doctrine of preemptive warfare and retaliatory strikes and the deterrent theory emerged the concept of secure borders. For the Israelis, a secure border became one which could be defended from attack without necessitating Israeli preemptive actions. Strikes, like those undertaken by the Israelis in Lebanon in 1978 and 1979, are invariably seen by the world community as aggressive and extreme. Consequently, the Israelis would prefer not to resort to them. As a result of the 1973 war, Israelis undertook a number of political and logistic actions to improve their border defense. Among these actions were increasing the number of units (with better intelligence and new structures), the application of a new deployment strategy of armored "fists," the expansion of the fleet of tank haulers, the storage of ammunition and fuel inside tanks rather than in dumps to facilitate rapid deployment, and the redoubling of efforts to improve the reserve mobilization program. The Israelis have long understood that their heavy reliance on the reserve system makes the ratio of Israeli to Arab forces in the first stage of a war a most important determinant of the outcome. "Simply put," noted a senior Israeli defense official, "our nation must be protected not only by its forces, reserves, technology, and will power, but by some minimal geographic security. It's our duty to improve the latter when we are able."

Israeli debate over the need for secure and defensible borders is based today on the concept that such a border should be one that discourages either side from launching hostile activities against its neighbor. Israelis argue that it also means that such a border should be an acceptable distance from areas which are essential to the security of each of the protagonists. Many Israelis agree that from their perspective this should include areas in the West Bank, such as the Jordan Valley, the Jerusalem region, and certain points along the *green line*. In particular, many Israelis believe that the retention of troops in the Jordan Valley is essential to guarantee the effective demilitarization of the West Bank and, in the event of another war, would make Jordan itself the front line. Israeli settlements in the Jordan Valley currently stretch for a considerable distance. (See map on page 116.) An Israeli military officer stated that "these settlements have enabled Israel to seal off its borders from terrorist attacks ... and provide Israel with up-front units which can be quickly integrated into the security plans for the area." Perhaps the simplest formula was expressed by an Israeli defense correspondent: "Most Israelis agree that a secure border is not one secured by treaty or guarantees, but rather one that is secure in itself because of its geographical and topographical location...." Most feel the secure border should *discourage* an offensive movement and serve as an obstacle to save time for mobilization.

Israelis point to a series of universally-accepted geographical features that facilitate any nation's defense and thus help guarantee its security: internal strategic depth to absorb an attack; demographic balance; physical barriers, such as mountains, rivers, or wide expanses of land separating potential adversaries and their major population centers; and self-sufficiency in essential raw materials. Israelis state that they enjoy few such natural defense aids today. A withdrawal to the 1967 borders would take away the few advantages they now hold in these areas. A Foreign Ministry officer argued that "you must understand that Israel is small, has in-

Jewish Settlements in Israeli-occupied West Bank

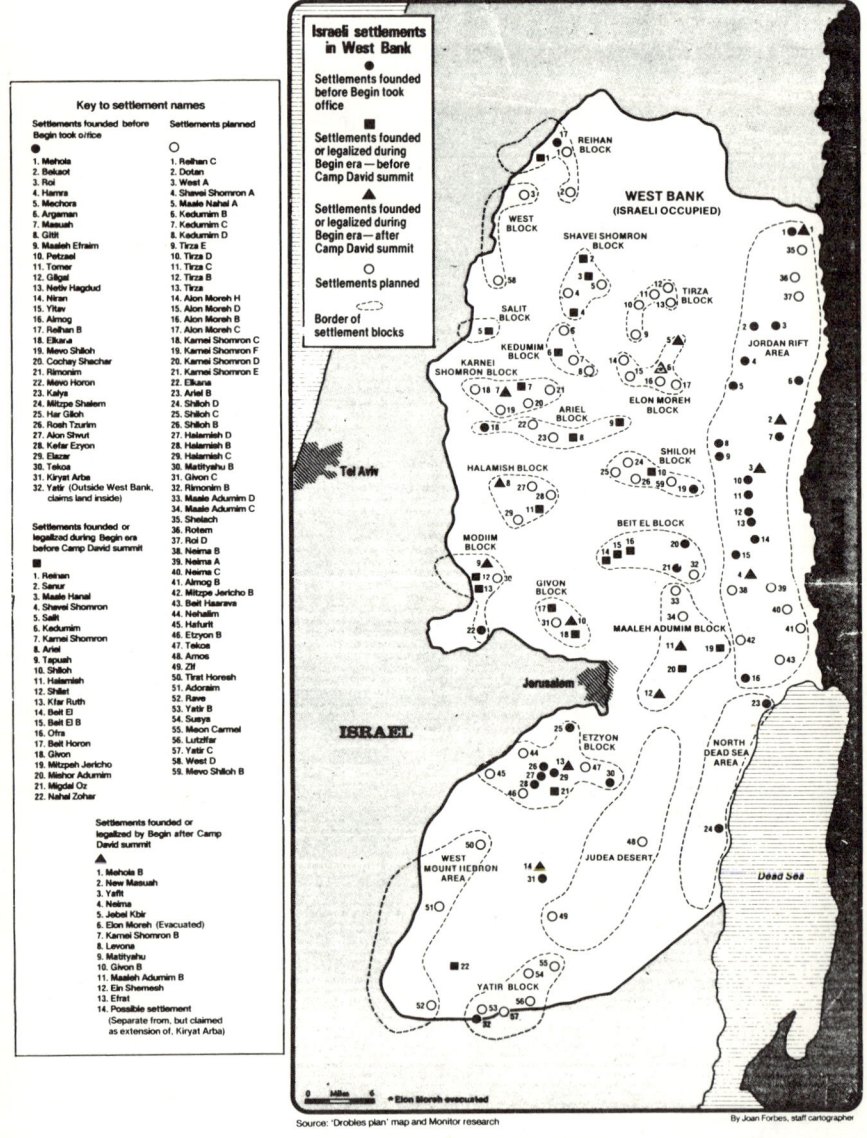

Joan Forbes in the *Christian Science Monitor* © 1980
Reprinted with permission.

adequate natural fortifications, small distances between its neighbors, possesses a potentially restive minority, and is vulnerable to cutoffs of outside supplies of vital resources."

Israelis believe that their concept of defensible borders requires continued superior military strength to deter Arabs from an attack. A senior government official noted, "We are concerned that our qualitative superiority is being eroded. . . . American sale of sophisticated F-15 fighters to Saudi Arabia is a case in point. . . . Our security rests in our superiority." Several Israeli leaders stated that even if peace were achieved, Israelis would worry for some time about irredentionist intentions of the Arabs.

Israeli strategic experts argue that if Israel would withdraw from areas of the West Bank and Gaza, certain basic adjustments would be required in Israel's security doctrine, such as the redefinition of *causus belli* and the increased importance of preemption in overall Israeli strategic policy. In addition, the strategists argue that Israel would have to have improved early warning positions to protect against Arab air forces—as there would be less than two minutes between the time when an enemy plane would enter the airspace over the West Bank and the time it commits serious destruction upon Israel.

Israeli public opinion is badly divided over an agreeable definition of secure and defensible borders. Some Israelis, borrowing from the classic strategic thinking of Liddell Hart, have argued that Israel's small size and geographic situation gives Israel certain wartime advantages. An Israeli scholar noted, "We are able to concentrate our forces at the area of greatest need, achieving local superiority even if we are outnumbered numerically, but then redeploy quickly to another front. . . . This is a great advantage."

Israelis know that their ability to defend their borders also depends upon the size, quality, and coordination of the immediate opposition they must face in battle. A ranking government official said:

> Our talk of the *Eastern Front* threat is based in good degree upon an assessment of equipment and mobility of the Iraqi forces. . . . In October of 1973, some 20,000 Iraqis fought us on the Golan, while Syria received smaller troops from Morocco, Saudi Arabia. . . . We are concerned about these sophisticated weapons reaching our front in a short period of time before full mobilization could be carried out. . . . Remember, the warning times here are almost inconsequential as the distances are so very short.

Arabs quickly retort that because of geographic distance, the Iraqis never coherently or effectively participated in the 1973 war even after three weeks of fighting. Even today there is no effective command and communications coordination. Israeli defense experts note that efforts to improve the latter are carefully watched as an indication of Arab intentions and capabilities. There is an Israeli fear, however, that even a loose grouping of *Eastern Front* countries could torpedo the Egypt-Israel treaty. A strategic planner said, "We just can't know what could happen, but one fear would be if the Arabs invoked the Arab Defence Pact and brought Egypt into the war."

Simplistic talk by outsiders about secure boundaries in the Arab-Israeli conflict is "superficial, if not ignorant, in neglecting the multiple determinants of any country's defense capacity," noted a distinguished Israeli defense expert.[3] He has argued that "any defense formula for Israel must take into consideration such factors as expected balance of forces; future battlefield technologies; probability threat and war scenarios; international contexts and more. A careful signaling of a possible resort to force and the potential consequences of conflict can serve as an inducement to the Arabs to be cautious."

Military considerations aside, the *borders-equal-security* concept has a tremendous psychological appeal for a small nation that has not known peace in three decades. To many Israelis, the establishment of settlements in the occupied territories is helping to create what some Israelis call "facts on the ground" that will help dictate favorable borders for Israel in a peace agreement. Some Israelis express strong disagreement with the simplicity of these equations. A respected Israeli defense analyst stated:

> Much of the standard security concept had been undermined in the 1973 war when it was found that defensive areas are not proof against the strategic consequences of surprise ... There are in Israel serious thinkers, among them past and present army men known for their ability to think in comprehensive military terms, who hold that peace with the Arab states, even in borders effectively those of 1967, is the missing security component.[4]

Other Israelis privately stated that heightened fear of an immediate attack from the *Eastern Front* is not a fair representation of the facts. They noted that almost a third of Syria's army (including substantial numbers of troops for resupply and rotation) is tied down at any given moment in the Lebanese operation. In addition, they note that the Syrian army is not structurally prepared for the logistic requirements of waging a two-front war. The inter-Arab communications network is neither well-established nor tested for use in a coordinated war. However, Israelis point to the Iraqi railroad and the continued development of an infrastructure that could support an offensive operation against Israel. According to some Israeli strategic thinkers, Iraqi preoccupation with Iran and the Gulf further decreases the likelihood of a direct military threat to Israel.

Perhaps the most bitter disagreements in Israel today, however, center on the tendency to intermingle religious, historical, and legal arguments with security considerations as a rationale for continued occupation of the West Bank. A Jewish religious leader argued that "those who mix security needs with moral and historical arguments are diluting the impact of both.... It weakens all the arguments based on right.... One will not be able to revert to them after Israel is offered a solution which the world may consider to be an acceptable firm security guarantee."

Numerous Israelis have pointed out that, prior to the 1967 war during which Israel gained the occupied territories, a force of a few thousand troops was sufficient to guard its borders. In contrast, several divisions of tens of thousands of soldiers are required for the same duties today. Similarly, a retired Israeli general noted, "A budget taking 12 percent of our GNP for military expenditures was adequate before we had the additional territories; today that figure is reportedly near 35 percent." Most Israelis, however, are willing to pay whatever price is required for being totally prepared for an expected renewal of Arab hostilities. Others note that over time Israel has come to face larger and better equipped armies. Whereas in the past Israel faced brigades—today it faces divisions. Hence, according to some Israeli experts, the costs of new technology, which Israel is said to need to deal with the changing power balances in the region, is as much a reason for the higher military expenditures as is the addition of more territory. An Israeli diplomat said:

> Most significant is the psychological security we have gained from having the territories. Giving up the lands again would be unacceptable... 65 percent of our population and 50 percent of our industry would be vulnerable to an armored attack which could be accomplished, theoretically at least, in an hour on some dozen roads. Although I recognize that Israeli missiles near the Jordan River would pose a threat to Amman, Palestinian mortars on the West Bank would threaten Jerusalem.... It is unacceptable perhaps for both of us, but the Arabs must worry about their own security as we worry about ours, for no one else really cares, in the last analysis.

The reader's attention is drawn to the maps on pages 120-123, which show how Israeli and Palestinian publications portray similar facts, in this case the 1947 partition plans. Arab and Israeli military officials agree that the lack of strategic depth necessitates the establishment of security arrangements such as demilitarized or limited armament areas. Most Israelis believe that the West Bank must never be returned to Arab control unless there is a guarantee that it will be demilitarized. Numerous Israelis, however, privately comment that the publicly expressed concerns over the dangers of a small Palestinian entity are politically motivated. A former Israeli intelligence chief and defense analyst wrote publicly about these Israeli fears:

> The current policy of the Israeli government is wrong because it focuses on only one dimension of the conflict — the kind of

120

PLO Views Partition of Palestine

THE PARTITION CONSPIRACIES 1946-1948

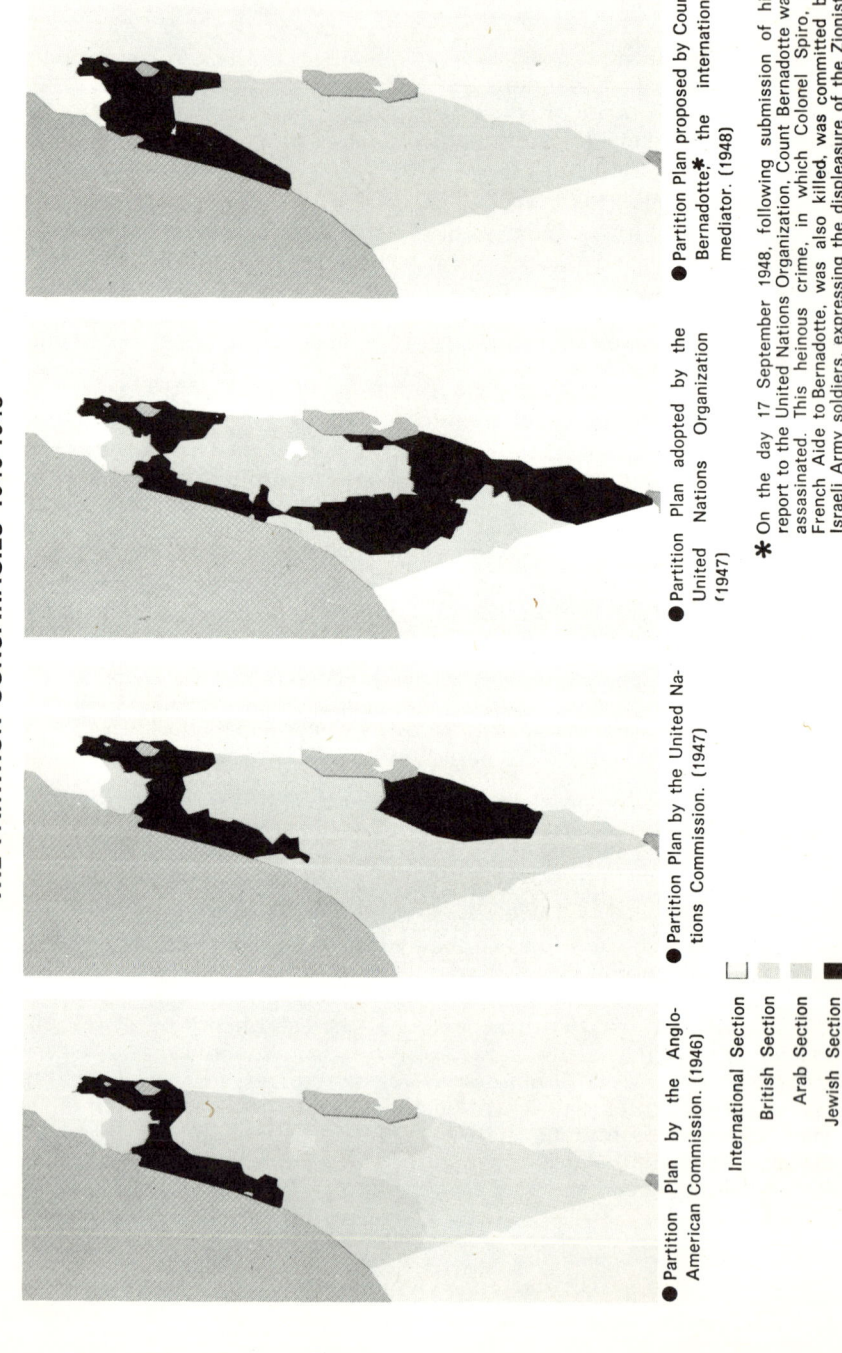

- Partition Plan by the Anglo-American Commission. (1946)
- Partition Plan by the United Nations Commission. (1947)
- Partition Plan adopted by the United Nations Organization (1947)
- Partition Plan proposed by Count Bernadotte,* the international mediator. (1948)

International Section
British Section
Arab Section
Jewish Section

* On the day 17 September 1948, following submission of his report to the United Nations Organization, Count Bernadotte was assasinated. This heinous crime, in which Colonel Spiro, a French Aide to Bernadotte, was also killed, was committed by Israeli Army soldiers, expressing the displeasure of the Zionists over the mediator's « unfavourable » report.

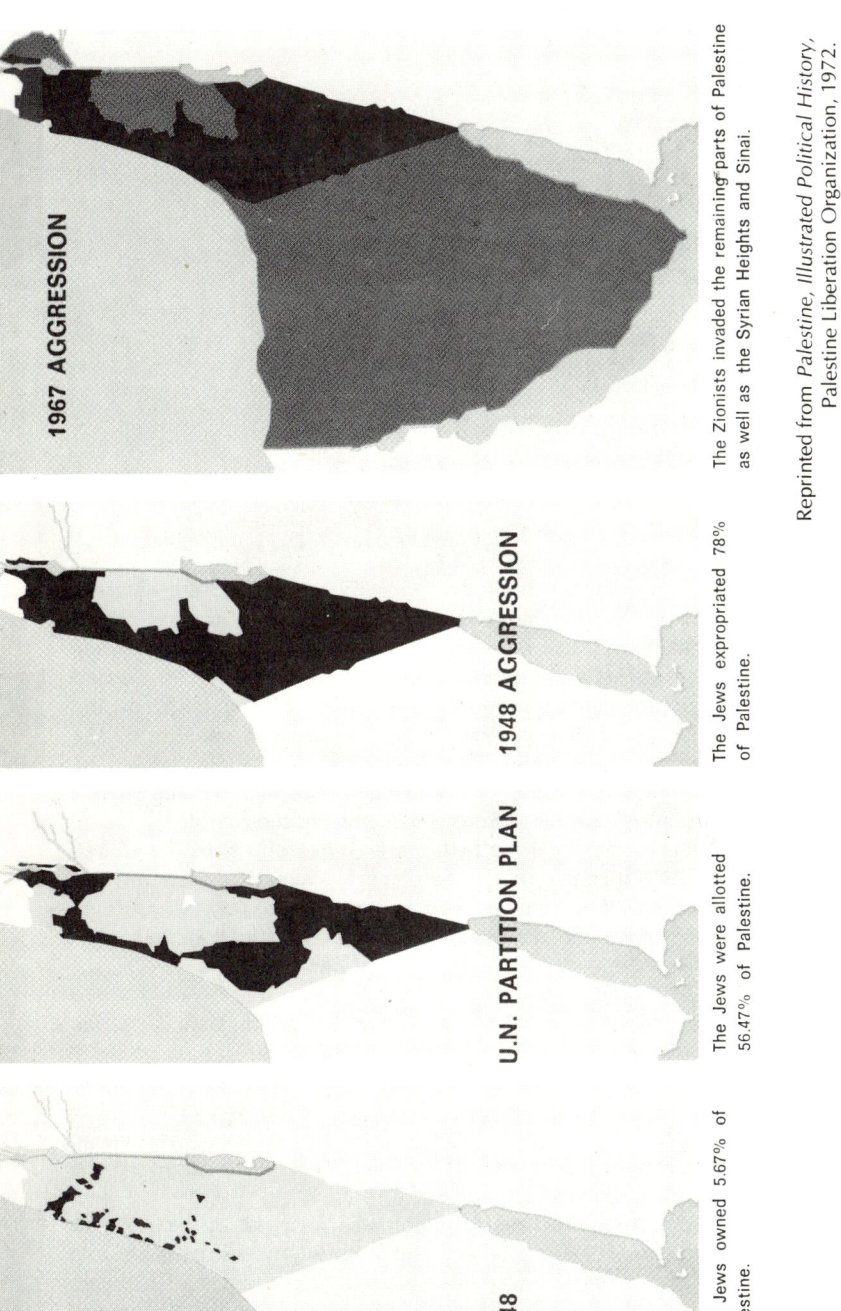

Reprinted from *Palestine, Illustrated Political History*, Palestine Liberation Organization, 1972.

Israel Views Partition of Palestine

SECURE AND RECOGNIZED BOUNDARIES

ISRAEL'S RIGHT TO LIVE IN PEACE WITHIN DEFENSIBLE FRONTIERS

© Carta Jerusalem, 1971

★ Even before outbreak of World War II Britain closed the gates of Palestine against Jewish immigration in appeasement of Arab terrorism and extremism (which had been fanned by Nazi support). Even when faced with the tragedy of European Jewry, Britain refused to rescind the restrictive measures enforced in violation of the spirit of the Mandate from the League of Nations and in spite of censure by the League's Permanent Mandates Commission.

★ After the Nazi holocaust in Europe and the plight of the Jewish refugees, pressure rose for absorption of Jews in their land.

★ Ultimately, Britain decided to transfer the problem to the United Nations. On 29 November, 1947, the General Assembly decided, with substantially more than the required two-thirds majority, to partition the Land once more into three parts, to be connected together in an economic union.

★ As shown in the map on the opposite page, there was to be a Jewish State and an Arab State, with the Jerusalem area a **corpus separatum.**

The plan would have cut the area of sovereign Israel still further to only 14,400 square kilometres. Yet in the interest of peace, and to provide an instant haven for Jewish refugees who could endure no longer in their camps overseas, the Jewish community accepted the proposal.

Instead of peace, the UN Resolution was followed by an outbreak of violence by Arab groups, aided and abetted by the neighbouring Arab countries. The Arabs were determined to prevent the establishment of any Jewish State, whatever its borders. Instead of peace and economic union, there followed war and sieges. Israel lost six thousand of its sons and daughters in its War of Independence.

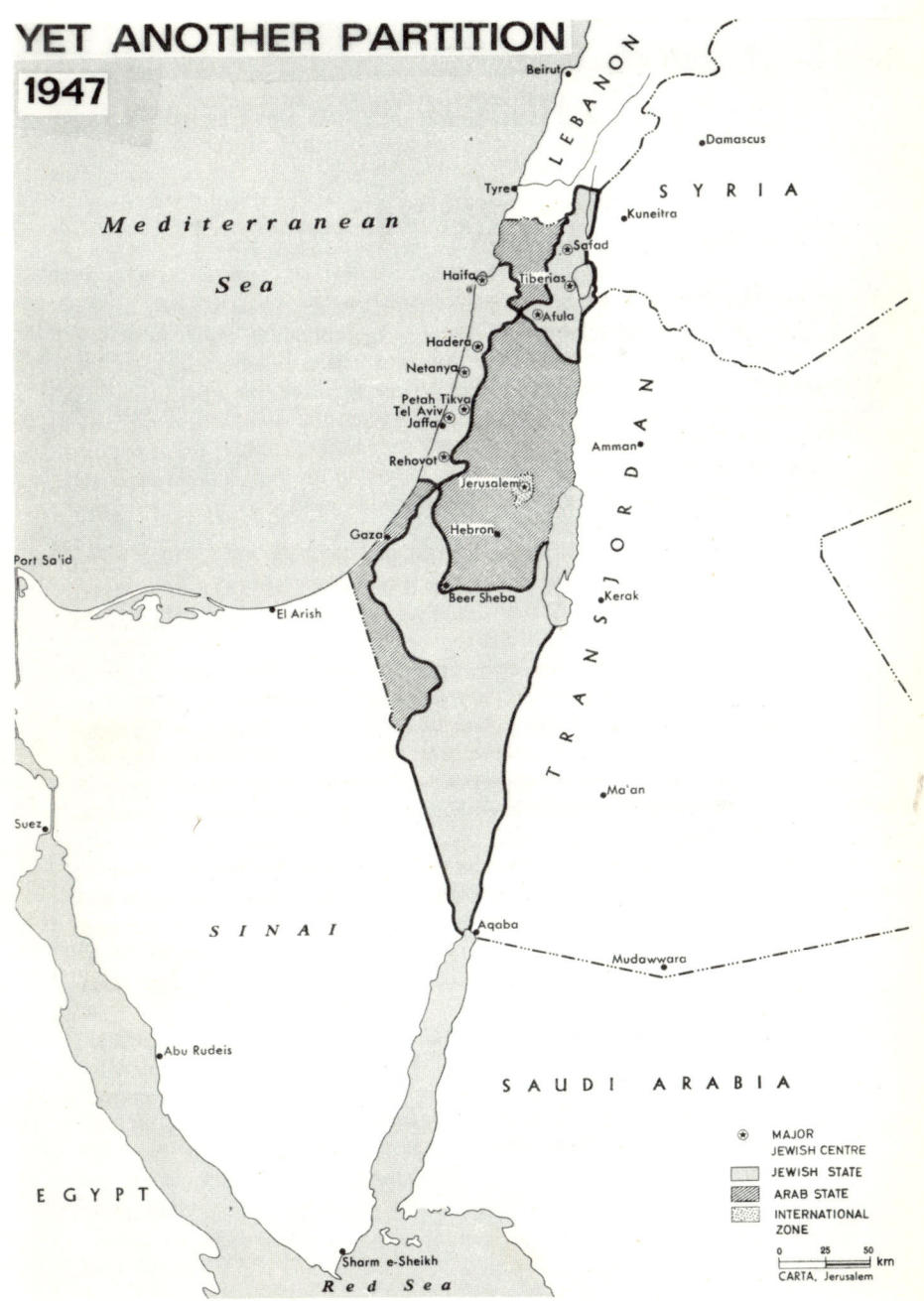

security that comes from holding on to territory. I do not believe we are so weak and helpless that an Arab regime or an Arab mini-State on the West Bank will mean the end of Israel. The Palestine Liberation Organization, which has always feared that it might have to accept a mini-State for lack of an alternative, understands the real balance of power between itself and Israel better than most Israeli politicians.[5]

Israeli strategists argue that there is a positive dimension to retaining the occupied territories — as a buffer which helps keep Arab armies away from Israel's vital population areas. An Arab attack, however, is more likely, many argue, if the occupied territories are retained. Continued occupation gives cause to Arab states to increase their armies and weapons procurement, and assists the PLO in their diplomatic and political offensives.

A fear is that if the territories are returned, terrorism would continue. A more basic fear of the Israelis, however, is that after peace this land would be used as a base to demand more from Israel. The question of the Palestinian's right of return to land in pre-1967 Israel is a particularly sensitive issue, as previously noted.

The debate in Israel over the definition of security continues unabated. A respected journalist said that "so far, we have decided what security is not — but we can't yet agree to what it is...."

Secondary Military Security Threats

Secondary military security threats, in contrast to the primary military security threats considered in the previous section, are those most frequently discussed in the region on a daily basis by both Israelis and Arabs. Whereas the primary threats are potentially damaging, these secondary threats are actualities of daily life. These threats, as presented in the previous chapter, include the following:

- Israeli fear of Arab population growth (p. 51)

- Israeli fear of terrorism (p. 59)

- Jordanian fear of Israeli attempts to force emigration of Palestinians from the occupied territories (p. 63)

- Jordanian fear of the permanent loss of the Arab sector and character of Jerusalem (p. 66)

- Syrian fear of Israeli retention of the Golan Heights (p. 75)

- Lebanese fear of Israeli annexation of Lebanon south of the Litani River (p. 84)

- Lebanese fear of Syrian annexation of Lebanon north of the Litani River (p. 85)

- Palestinian fear of denial of rights to self-determination (p. 91)

- Palestinian fear of Israeli efforts to change the character and economy of the West Bank and Gaza (p. 92)

A senior Jordanian official stressed that "for the Arab people, these fears are as real and dangerous as direct military attacks.... They are perhaps worse because the latter are something that could happen and the former are things that are happening now."

Arab Views of Secondary Military Security Threats

A Syrian foreign affairs official noted that "thirteen years of occupation of our territory makes the heart grow colder and the memory sharper.... Fears by our people that their lands will not be returned for the indefinite future does not contribute to security, and indeed it represents a real psychological burden upon our people, in particular our soldiers."

The fight to regain the occupied territory seized by Israel during the 1967 war remains the single most important objective of the Arab people. What the Israelis call terrorism, the Palestinians and other Arabs consider action in a just struggle. The Palestinian attempt to regain a homeland is widely supported by the Arab people. Arabs argue that political imprisonment in the West Bank and Gaza or retaliatory bombing raids in Lebanon are what a Lebanese banker called "every bit as much acts of terrorism as a commando raid in Nahariya." For every child killed in Israel in terrorist attacks, nearly twenty are killed in Lebanon, according to Arab statistics. Palestinian and Lebanese hospitals are filled with civilians injured or dying from Israeli retaliatory raids which occur on a regular—sometimes daily—basis.

Western reports that most Arabs privately do not wish to see a Palestinian state established are not well supported. It is true that a number of Arabs do not wish to see a heavily-armed Palestinian state, but today it is rare to find Arabs who do not believe that the conflict will be resolved only when the Palestinians have exercised their right to self-determination. Arabs frequently point to Mr. Begin's record as a terrorist during the fight to achieve an Israeli state. A remark by one of the West Bank mayors to the Western press in 1978 is typical: "As head of the Irgun in the 1940s, Begin organized bombings and attacks that killed hundreds, mostly innocent people, and now he is Prime Minister of a Jewish state. How can Palestinians look down on violence when we have such a shining example of what it can accomplish in Mr. Begin?"[6]

Most Arabs privately and publicly agree that acts of violence against Israel will cease once the Palestinians have been given the opportunity to exercise their right to self-determination. The greatest fear, however, shared by most Arabs, is that a protraction of the conflict will cause irreparable harm to the people and land of the occupied territories. Some Arabs questioned whether one day Israel might have some special formal relationship with the United States, thus making any Arab efforts to regain occupied lands impossible without declaring war on the most powerful country in the world. A strategic studies expert in an Arab capital noted, "It may sound preposterous to you now to hear me say that Israel might be the fifty-first state of America, so to speak, but honestly, look at it [the situation] from our viewpoint ... is it impossible?" The fear of an annexation of territory by Israel (or any other state) is a very real fear for many in the Middle East.

The Israeli policy of establishing new settlements in the occupied territories represents a strongly felt threat for the Arabs. A Syrian official noted the visit of Egyptian Defence Minister Hassan Ali to Israel. Gen. Sharon took the Egyptian military delegation, headed by the Egyptian Defence Minister, on a personal tour of the settlements. According to published reports, General Sharon believed that the Minister would see for himself the problems that necessitate Israeli expansion of the settlements in the West Bank. The Egyptian Minister, however, concluded his tour with a statement that as a military man he did not think Jewish settlements in Arab areas added anything to Israel's security. Arabs devote considerable attention to such assessments of the growing Israeli settlement policy, noting that more than 90 percent of the land seized by Israel in the occupied West Bank for the purpose of establishing Jewish settlements since 1967 is privately owned Palestinian land.[7] An Arab official ridiculed the Israeli claim that the settlements would help to show that Israelis and Arabs can live together in peace: "They [Israeli settlers] live behind barbed wire with armed guards.... They are trying to show how to live and work together? Rubbish."

The Arab views on these problems defined as *secondary military security threats* were well summarized by a Jordanian diplomat as follows: "Many Arabs would rather undergo another Israeli war than continue to experience the suffering and despair of what we call low-level violence, which is being extracted from our people every day by the Israelis." Arabs argue that analysts must look back to history to understand long-term Israeli goals and objectives. For instance, in the 1949 documents of the *Foreign Relations of the United States*, one can see Israeli objections to extension of the August 6 Jordanian Defence Treaty with the West Bank. A senior Egyptian official argued that "one must be careful not to forget that the British denied the

Palestinian people their sovereign rights after the war [World War I] and that history books show that this Palestinian issue is a case of an incredible wrong undertaken to make up for another incredible wrong."

Israeli Views of Secondary Military Security Threats

The Task Force noted that the overwhelming majority of the Israeli *1979 Middle East sample* believe that terrorist attacks on Israel are a direct corollary to Palestinian efforts to regain a homeland and were not part of a more general Arab effort to destroy Israel. However, a clear majority of the *sample* believes that terrorism would continue by fringe groups even if a Palestinian entity were established as a result of an exercise in Palestinian self-determination. A senior Israeli defense analyst noted:

> We can see a real possibility of fringe groups who are unsatisfied among the Palestinians even after the establishment of a Palestinian state.... Who will be able to prevent them? ... Now, if we go back to the 1967 borders, any kind of terrorist activity can be done within one night back and forth to a secure place like a Palestinian state in the West Bank.... Now, that is not imagination, but fact based on distances ... because it's ten miles, and in some cases five, to make a raid and come back.... Now, how do we prevent such a thing?

The border that resulted from the land gains of the 1967 war offers relatively little concealment for clandestine movements. Most of the Jordan Valley has miles of desolate wasteland between the population centers, as does the valley south of the Dead Sea. An Israeli defense spokesman noted, "The only area in fact in which we were highly vulnerable was the border with Lebanon, but that has been addressed somewhat since March of 1978." A respected, former government official said, "Terrorist acts will always be seen as a form of limited *causus belli*.... Israel will move in and occupy the area if that is necessary. We have no choice.... We call it retaliation ... you call it what you like."

The Israelis have constructed a sophisticated defense perimeter of mine fields, electronic warning sensors, barbed wire, and other means of surveillance along areas where a border breach is possible. "The fear of the capabilities of the terrorists," says an Israeli Knesset member, "is reflected in the statistics. Did you know that terrorist operations from Gaza alone in 1955 took more Israeli lives than the annual losses on all fronts in the 1970s?"

The settlements are defended in Israel for various reasons. General Sharon said that "without settlements such as Eilon Moreh [in the West Bank] there was no stopping the establishment of a second Palestinian

Road Map of Israel/West Bank/Jordan Area

state."[8] The Israeli Chief of Staff stated that he favored settlements everywhere in the territories for security reasons, noting that "no agreement with the Palestinian Arabs will ever be possible."[9] The ultra-right Gush Emunim makes its intentions clear: "No concessions can be made to surrender Israeli ownership of Eretz Israel of which Judea and Samaria [West Bank] are integral."[10] Yet, former Foreign Minister Dayan stated that "the settlements shouldn't be an obstacle to peace negotiations. . . . Boundaries won't be determined by settlements. Rather, decisions about settlements will be made according to boundaries."[11]

An Israeli businessman and Knesset member decried the bitter division within Israel over settlements and related policies in the occupied territories. He noted that the Arabs can be sure that "we are truly as divided and unsure of ourselves as it appears to be the case from our debates [Knesset]. . . . We can agree on little except perhaps what we disagree about. Security is important to us, but so is justice, democracy, and strength of our belief in ourselves."

The conflicts among security, democracy, and justice also spill over into the Israeli considerations of population imbalances. As explained in the previous chapter, there is widespread concern in Israel over the projections of this imbalance between Jews and Arabs in Israeli-occupied territory. A Hebrew University professor noted, "There is no question but that the demographic imbalances, current and projected, are a major security concern to the government and every Israeli." In brief, the basic security needs and concerns of Israel surpass the number of tanks, F-15s, or nuclear warheads in her arsenal. A senior army figure noted, "Let's face it; only peace will bring us the kind of security we all need and long for. . . ."

Non-Military Security Threats

The third and final component of *security*, as defined in the Arab-Israeli conflict, is the relative freedom from serious shifts by outside parties in their influence or support of a particular government, or from domination by outside parties of the essential elements that constitute national sovereignty. The following specific threats, presented in the previous chapter, fit into this component:

- Israeli fear over an alteration of Israel's special relationship with the United States (p. 56)

- Jordanian fear of Arab vulnerability to radicalism and external influences (p. 65)

- Syrian fear of Israeli cultural and economic penetration of the Arab world (p. 76)

- Palestinian fear of a complacency in world public opinion (p. 95)

- Egyptian fear of Soviet domination of the Middle East (p. 99)

Arab Views of Non-Military Security Threats

Both the Syrian and Iraqi Baath parties traditionally have held a world view imbued with the belief that some global conspiracy exists against the Arabs in general, and against the progressive Arabs in particular. Syria has been the Arab state most adamant in advocating sealed borders with Israel, even after a comprehensive peace agreement is reached. Israelis and Jordanians noted that, whereas the Armistice agreement provided for bilateral contacts between officers under the Military Assistance Commission, few contacts were made by the Syrians.

Task Force members held lengthy discussions with numerous Arabs over the subject of *non-military security threats*. It is important for the reader to understand the depth of Arab suspicions about Israeli intentions. In particular, there are grave concerns over Israeli efforts to achieve a status of developed nation among underdeveloped countries in the region. Regional economic agreement scenarios for the future gravely worry many Arab leaders. For example, discussion of an economic union of Israel with its Arab neighbors appeals to some Arab businessmen, but worries most Arabs. "Until we begin to build some confidence in each other, I doubt such an idea would ever gain support in the Arab capitals," noted a Lebanese official.

Apart from economic fears are a series of other Arab concerns regarding the threat that Israel poses to Arab security. A Syrian professor of international law summarized the situation as follows:

> Syrians, like many other Arabs, both conservative and radical, fear that the Israelis represent a serious challenge to their values and institutions.... This is true, of course, in the military sense, but it is also true in economics, politics, and moral values.... The best thing to do for every Arab is to be aware of the threat and act to dampen the influence which it tries to gain over us.

The possibilities for outside domination have caused the Egyptians to fear a growing Soviet menace and Syrians to fear American meddling in the internal affairs of states in the region. An Egyptian correspondent, who had recently returned from a meeting with Israelis, said that "the Israelis identify with Sadat's fears of Soviet intentions but they cannot seem to understand why Syria and the Palestinians equally fear an American alliance and heightened involvement in the area...." He continued, "They

[Israelis] argued that the Americans would not try to dominate the region in the same way as the Russians. . . . I told them that this was one perspective. . . . They could find opposite perspectives in some of the Arab capitals." Numerous Palestinians pointed out that the Soviet Union since 1948 has supported Israel's existence, including recent pressure upon the PLO to recognize Israel's right to exist. They argue that the very existence of Israel in the midst of the Arab world serves as an irritant to the Arabs and prevents the Arab world from being entirely pro-Western and anti-Communist.

A Palestinian official argued that in the name of security

> Israel has become a colonialist power taking over our economy, and trying to determine our cultural and social preferences. . . . They closed Bir Zeit University on security grounds that would not satisfy the rulers of South Africa. . . . Security for us Palestinians has become protecting our way of life and our values as much as our jobs and homes, and our lives.

Palestinians and other Arabs argue that the Israelis are encouraged to undertake such bold and aggressive moves because of the *carte blanche* support they receive from the United States. The Arabs understand the need to win public support in the West, especially in the United States, as a wedge against the Israelis and as an attempt to have the richest country on earth recognize that there are two sides to the conflict. Since the five Arab protagonists are not oil suppliers to the West, they have little or no influence over the Western system of deliberations as compared to the influence of the Gulf States and Saudi Arabia.

Consequently, the Arab protagonists of this conflict view their status as one of arguing from a position of basic inequality with Israel. "The role of justice is with us, but the just are often not allowed to get what is rightfully ours. . . . Sometimes justice is not enough. . . . We need better guarantees than we have had and we will get them," argued a Palestinian who has recently retired from active politics.

Israeli Views of Non-Military Security Threats

There is little talk in Israel about the economic, cultural, or institutional challenges that the Arab world would pose to Israel should full normal relations be established in the region. However, there are some Israelis who expect the gradual transformation of the Israeli economy from war to peace to be painful. There is also a great deal of concern regarding the relative influence of outside parties.

A leading Israeli defense analyst stated that there are three major factors, apart from geographic borders, that make up the strategic balance from the Israeli perspective: "Israeli military capabilities as compared to Arab military capabilities; the nature and depth of the American commitment; and the application of military capabilities, especially the question of strategic surprise. Unfortunately the second is as important as the first and third."

Prime Minister Begin, however, is aware of the domestic constraints within the United States. In Washington he stated:

> May I say, respectfully, we don't want even one American soldier to fight our battles or lose his life.... We can sustain our independence.... From time to time we need some tools.... We are entitled to receive them because on the other side there are often unlimited stores of Soviet weapons given to our enemies.... If there should be a treaty of common interest between the two countries suggested, we, of course, will greet such a suggestion.[12]

Most of the Israeli arguments against the military implications of a Palestinian state center on the fact that such a state would become a "North Vietnam of the Middle East." A senior Israeli official argued:

> Because a Palestinian state even in union with Jordan cannot be economically viable, it would have to rely on someone and that would have to be a big power; who else but the Soviets?... We would have Moscow under our nose immediately closer than the Americans have Moscow under their nose with Cuba.

The Israelis are interested in, almost obsessed with, the implications of great-power involvement in the region. The Russians are seen to pose a direct threat to Israel. But more importantly, Israel's dependence upon the United States makes any change in that relationship a potentially serious threat to the state of Israel. An Israeli media personality remarked that "a withdrawal of American primary support from Israel would not only damage our economy, morale, stability, and security, but encourage neighboring states and their allies like the Soviets to complete a task begun long ago of destroying the Jewish people and their homeland."

The greatest frustration for Israelis is that they must be so heavily reliant upon another state and another people. The possibility of a change in the degree and strength of American support is seen as a potential threat of the highest order to Israeli security.

Observations

Very little has been said about the role of other parties in the conflict, such as the Christians living in Arab lands and Israel. A strong statement was made by a Christian religious leader in Israel. He deplored the

> blatant and the creeping domination that continues to enter our region from every corner of the earth. . . . I suppose none of us could do much fighting if the outside parties would leave us alone, which would make many people very unhappy. . . . I also suppose that third parties could do as much good to help as to hinder and harm us. . . . One way or the other, they will not go away. . . . Our job is to make their involvement constructive for the improvement of the daily lives of our people.

There is little doubt that the continuation of this conflict has hardened the attitudes and limited the expectations of Moslems, Jews, Christians, and other residents of the region. Central to the personal concerns of nearly every person with whom the Task Force members met in 1978 and 1979 was the need for clarification of the intentions of the other protagonists. The most frequently mentioned impressions about the other protagonists were simply that they were not in a hurry to seek peace. In fact, many doubts were expressed over whether leaders desired peace at all.

Most members of the *1979 Middle East sample* stated that third parties would play a key role in helping to bring about the transition from war to peace. This could be done by refusing to sell certain armaments, providing regional economic assistance for development, participating in transitional arrangements during which time confidence-building measures would be implemented, and generally contributing to the diminution of the violence and tension in the region.

The Task Force members spent a considerable amount of time discussing specific suggestions for meeting what might be described as *mutual security requirements* of the protagonists, based on defined threats as presented in the previous chapter. The interesting result of this effort was that Arabs and Israelis, in their private discussions, frequently suggested similar ideas for meeting specific problems.

The lengthy discussions about security requirements seem to indicate that an important personal reassessment process is now under way among both Arabs and Israelis concerning the nature of possible coexistence as peaceful neighbors. The Egyptian-Israeli Peace Treaty has given sufficient food for thought to both peoples. Most promising, perhaps, for facilitating joint initiatives is the extent of concern over the widening influence of outside powers over regional policies and events. There is a growing belief that more effective efforts must be made to harness these outside forces to serve regional interests before they gain even greater influence or control over regional policies. In addition, Arabs and Israelis expressed the belief that more innovative roles for objective third parties must be developed.

Task Force members discerned a difference in the personal attitudes expressed about the peacemaking process from 1978 to 1980. The willingness to openly discuss specific security apprehensions and suggestions in 1979 did not exist in 1978. An Arab graduate student argued that his younger generation "realizes that the old political vanguard in all these countries is nearing the end of its tenure. . . . Look at Israel. Who are the leaders: Rabin, Begin, Peres, Dayan . . . all names from the 1940s . . . and look at Sadat, Assad, Hussein, and so many others. . . ." He went on to say that his talks in Europe with Israeli and other Arab students seem to "demonstrate that we are going to be willing to take the initiatives to build confidence and end the basic conflict . . . not because we are afraid or tired of fighting so much as because we see the new dynamics of the 1980s and beyond as a tide that will sweep over all of us if we don't."

Younger Arabs and Israelis argued that the next generation of leaders who may assume power in the 1980s must, above all else, demonstrate their intentions — their desire for a just peace and their willingness to make decisions to bring it about. A Palestinian graduate student stated, "The best place to start is to understand what the others really are afraid about . . . and for them to learn our fears. . . . Then we'll see that to survive, we must all live here together, or we shall never know peace."

Perhaps the most interesting sidelight of the Task Force visits was the unceasing requests for information. Officials frequently asked what others were saying about the same problems and events. For example, the Israelis wished to know what Palestinians said about certain problems and about Israeli policies. Palestinians wished to know what Israelis, Syrians, or Egyptians said about certain issues. In fact, much of the impetus for this book came from persons in the Middle East who wished to see a comparison of what the various protagonists privately thought about certain basic security problems as expressed to the Task Force.

When discussing, in general terms, the next phase of the Arab-Israeli conflict, there was considerable, though guarded, optimism that private attitudes were slowly changing from highly confrontational to something more conciliatory. This tendency shows a shift toward the acknowledgement of the *right to existence* for each of the six protagonists. Many Arabs and Israelis continue to fear, however, that the limitations of the political environment, together with the personal biases of the current leadership, impede the process of shifting more conciliatory private views into the realm of public policy.

Younger Arabs and Israelis drew lessons from the analogy of Rhodesia, where both the Smith government and the guerilla leaders were intransigent and unwilling to make concessions. When finally one side offered a concession that the other would have accepted at an earlier moment in the conflict, the other now claimed it was too late. The fighting persisted. As the cycle repeated itself, each time the level of violence intensified. With this in mind, an Arab diplomat at the United Nations recently noted, "The irony of the Rhodesian situation is that now there is a situation which probably should have been accepted by everyone, in particular the Smith regime, back in the late 1960s. . . . Those of us involved in the Arab-Israeli conflict will probably also find ourselves in such a situation before the end of this century. . . . The tragedy is that we are not far away now from an honest settlement."

It becomes evident that current reassessments by Middle East individuals acting in their private capacity could become the basis for meaningful negotiations. This will probably not happen in the foreseeable future, or at least not until each of the protagonists shows a more earnest desire for seeking a just and lasting peace in a way that would be clear and unmistakable to the other protagonists. Basically, there is an immediate need for confidence-building measures. The severity and imminence of most perceived security threats, military and otherwise, are largely a response to the understanding each has of the intentions of its adversary(ies). Until some confidence is built among the protagonists, there seems to be little if any chance that these security concerns will be addressed or a comprehensive peace made possible.

4
Some Options for Resolving Security Threats

It is one matter to examine perceived threats and security requirements; it is quite another to discuss solutions for meeting the threats and fulfilling security needs. Our review of how perceptions of threats influence the determinants of national security in the Arab-Israeli conflict leads us to the exploration of potential scenarios for their resolution.

There is a tendency in the West to forget that security is a basic requirement for each of the protagonists in this conflict. Acceptance of full peace will necessitate significant psychological shifts in the perceptions of each of the protagonists.

Neither the Arabs nor the Israelis believe that the leadership of the other desires a true peace, although both claim that they are ready for a negotiation to achieve such a peace if their adversary made certain concessions. The lack of any confidence or trust in the others' intentions lies at the heart of the problem. As a step toward exploring possible good intentions, the Task Force asked Arabs and Israelis if they favored specific solutions to some of the perceived threats they had listed.

During the private discussions, forty-three specific options were proposed for meeting some of the basic threats that characterize the conflict in the 1980s. Nearly a dozen of the ideas were restatements of official policy positions and seemed to represent established governmental bargaining positions with no room for adjustment. Two dozen other options were mentioned infrequently. A clear majority of co-nationals expressed a sense of disapproval for these latter options as initial solutions.

For example, the idea of establishing a common market of the Middle East to bind Israel and the neighboring Arab states together in some association caused many Arabs to fear Israeli domination, and many Israelis opposed the idea, seeing it as threatening potential Arab domination. Although some Arabs and Israelis recognized that such an economic association was a future possibility, all but a very few members of the *1979 Middle East sample* agreed that it could evolve only over a period of time, if ever.

The options selected for presentation here are those considered by a majority of the *1979 Middle East sample* of Arabs and Israelis as possible components of a comprehensive peace. In regard to the Palestinian issue, it must be noted that a handful of the respondents argued that the Palestinians must never be allowed to have an independent state. Most Israelis, however, acknowledged privately that in their lifetime there is likely to be some form of a Palestinian entity, although most sought to avoid the use of the word "state" and many argued that Israel should do everything possible to delay the establishment of a Palestinian state. Most Israelis supported the concept of a long period of limited autonomy for the West Bank and Gaza. They did not seem to know where and how such limited autonomy would be translated into a final settlement of the Palestinian issue. Most Palestinians demanded immediate self-determination and the right to establish a Palestinian sovereign state on the West Bank and Gaza. There were a number of variations of these themes expressed by Palestinians, other Arabs, and Israelis—two of which will be discussed as sample scenarios of what might be done to resolve the Palestinian issue in a way that could meet the basic requirements of each of the protagonists.

Since there is overwhelming agreement in the region that the Palestinian issue must be resolved and that even limited progress would help open the way to a comprehensive settlement, most attention has been given in this chapter to that issue. The majority of Israelis who met with the Task Force agreed that the status quo would not continue unchanged. All Arabs and much of the rest of the world support the Palestinian right to self-determination. The ability of Israel to keep a million and a half Palestinians under occupation for much longer is privately questioned by more than three-quarters of the Israelis who participated in the 1979 Task Force discussions. The fears for security, however, by all parties cannot be ignored. Accordingly, the Task Force members asked for specific suggestions that might meet the mutual security needs of the parties.

Frequently discussed were the benefits which could be derived from working toward a neutralization of the region, in particular from reducing the direct military influences of the great powers. A region of such limited geographical size cannot continue to support the enormous arsenals which have been built by the Israelis and the Arabs since 1973. Economic development of a region as fragile as this depends also upon the eventual cooperation among the states over water resources, transportation, tourism, agriculture, and related areas. Such cooperation would be facilitated if political tensions were not complicated by great power involvement. Few current leaders in the region would advocate immediate or complete demilitarization of the region. If peace were agreed, however, many Arabs and Israelis believe that there could be a common program for limiting deployment of certain types of weapons, and restricting certain quantities of offensive weapons. In addition, a phased series of policies might be initiated leading to a gradual neutralization of the region.

Palestinians have expressed an interest in serving as a catalyst within the region, for example, in the field of economic development. In addition, they note that their state would require some security assurances. Other states in the region have also expressed concern over the nature of their security needs should a Palestinian state be established. The Israelis, for example, have argued for the complete demilitarization of any Palestinian entity. Some Palestinians have advocated a strong Palestinian state. It is interesting to note, however, that one of the few ideas which was frequently mentioned by Palestinians, other Arabs, and some Israelis was a *neutral* Palestinian state. Such a state might represent a first step in neutralizing the area. Since neutrality is a much misunderstood concept, it is presented in more detrail in the following pages. The purpose of this exercise is not to try to support neutrality as a preferred solution, but rather to review the concept as one model of a type of arrangement which might be adopted in a comprehensive settlement should the parties convince one another that peace is the true goal. It should be noted that many Palestinians would see neutrality as a punishment if it was imposed upon the Palestinian people. The Palestinians who discussed this option did so on the basis that the Palestinians might choose neutrality of their own will during an exercise of their right to self-determination. History reminds us that imposed neutrality against the wishes of the local populace is doomed to failure. Neutrality per se refers to war-time activities and does not preclude participation in political, economic, and other arrangements which the neutral state might decide to undertake. A fuller discussion follows.

A Neutral Palestinian State

Some Arabs and Israelis in the Middle East who voiced support and interest in neutrality admitted that they were unsure of the legal dimensions and the ramifications of the neutrality concept. An Israeli scholar who admitted that he had not carefully investigated the concept said, "Neutrality could be one of those compromise positions that might just meet the basic security fears of every party in this conflict. . . . From that standpoint alone it must be examined further, something which has not yet been done adequately." A Palestinian political figure on the West Bank noted that Palestinians had thought of this idea and that "it certainly could be a way out of the impasse which might otherwise be blown apart into another costly war. ... the question is for me, do we freely accept neutrality as having advantages for our people or do we have it imposed on us? ... The latter we would not accept." The critical question that should be addressed is how the process of establishing neutrality can be tailored to the process of self-determination.

Significantly, those who claimed not to take the neutrality option seriously admitted that they had not explored it themselves, or seen studies that investigated its advantages and disadvantages. A senior Israeli political leader has argued privately that neutrality is not an option because the Palestinians were incapable of renouncing their ultimate goal — the destruction of Israel. Similarly, a Palestinian lawyer said that neutrality is seen as a Western concept—even though Islamic law and mores allowed for it prior to its acceptance in the West as a code of conduct. Therefore, this study presents a preliminary outline of the concept of neutrality that is designed to raise questions for debate and further research.

The idea of applying the concept of neutrality to the West Bank and Gaza received considerable support or interest from both Arabs and Israelis in the region. Many of the negative comments seemed to be based on a lack of information. Following is an explanation of the basic parameters of the neutrality concept.

What is neutrality?

Most people share an understanding of the word *neutrality* that is similar to the ancient Swiss legal definition—neutrality is the act of sitting still while others fight. To some, neutrality implies impartiality, while to others it means nonbelligerency. Neutrality under international law imposes obligations and gives rights. Although international lawyers and politicians continue to argue over variations of the concept and what it means, three basic categories of neutrality have gained wide acceptance and should be understood by the reader. The first, which is often called *temporary or common neutrality*, is invoked when a state refuses to participate in a specific war.

The second is a form of *permanent neutrality based upon unilateral political decisions* that can be changed by the state. The best known example is Sweden. Such states are uncommitted in times of peace with no specific obligations required under international defense or other treaties, which in turn secures their neutrality during times of war. Sweden's neutrality, credited for helping keep Sweden out of World Wars I and II, is not guaranteed under international agreements. In fact, Sweden has rejected such steps on the grounds that they would pose a risk that the great powers, who backed the guarantees, might create "some kind of a dependence on these states by Sweden."[1] Swedes worry that the great powers, then, could raise objections, if in their view Sweden's foreign policy contravened the terms written into an international agreement. Sweden's neutrality also is not written into its constitution or laid down as permanent state doctrine. The concept of neutrality, however, remains an unchallenged mainstay of Swedish policy.

Sweden's adoption of this form of neutrality was in large part due to its geopolitical location and fears for its security. The Swedes decided that their neutrality could be respected only if they possessed an armed capability to defend their neutrality in time of war. The Swedes note two basic limitations that result from their neutrality: no commitments (alliances, for example) can be made in peacetime that would interfere in Sweden's fulfillment of its obligations as a neutral power; and all peacetime policies must sustain the confidence held by the rest of the world in Sweden's determination to remain neutral in wartime.[2]

The Swedes argue that neutrality cannot be equated with passivity or an unwillingness to take a stand. They deny that a neutral state must equally balance all of its contacts with other states. A Swedish official argued that "this would place quite unreasonable demands on the neutral state which must, of course, have the right to develop its contacts with other countries according to its own values and interests."[3] Many Palestinians believe that this type of neutrality could be a compromise if the more extensive Austrian variety was not politically feasible.

The third category of neutrality, and the one that is seen to hold some promise for the Palestinian case, is termed *permanent neutrality*. A permanently neutral state is one that has had its neutrality guaranteed by outside powers, *or* is bound by deed or agreement under international law. Austria and Switzerland are examples. A permanently neutral state under international law is considered sovereign, as are most other states. It is true that a few international lawyers believe that the right to go to war is so fundamentally important that a neutral state should be placed under the category of qualified full members of the community of nations.[4] A critical consideration is whether neutrality is imposed upon a state or freely chosen.

The most famous case of a permanently neutral sovereign state is Switzerland. The Swiss voluntarily adopted their neutrality in the 1600s, and had it guaranteed in 1815. Austria achieved its freedom and expressed its neutrality in the *State Treaty* of May 15, 1955. Both examples have elements which are of particular importance to any discussion of establishing a neutral Palestinian state on the West Bank and Gaza. The Austrian case, in particular, will be used as a reference in discussing a possible Palestinian example later in this chapter.

The Swiss trace their commitment to neutrality to the early sixteenth century. After several serious military defeats, the Swiss chose to avoid, whenever possible, entanglement in the great-power conflicts that engulfed Europe. Most of these conflicts were linked to religious disputes. Swiss participation would undoubtedly have caused increased strife within the Swiss Confederation, since the composition of the Confederation was divided on religious grounds. Swiss leaders feared that such involvement would destroy the independent character of the Confederation.

In 1647, an army of the Confederation was established to protect Swiss territory, setting the important precedent for armed neutrality based on a people's willingness to defend their neutrality. As a political principle, permanent neutrality was adopted in Switzerland in 1674, when the Swiss Confederation decided to regard itself as neutral.

The Congress of Vienna in 1815 recognized the permanent neutralization of Switzerland. The agreement by the great powers concluded that such neutrality was in the best interests of all of Europe and had to be defended. For the first time, it is argued by many international lawyers, the sanction of international law was applied to the doctrine of permanent neutrality. However, there is theoretical precedent in established Islamic law as well — which predates the Swiss usage.

The 1907 Hague Peace Conference dealt in some detail with the right of neutrality.[5] According to the agreed definition, a country having decided in favor of non-participation in a war between two states assumed certain rights, such as inviolability of its territory, and some duties, such as withholding military support from belligerents. Together, the rights and duties composed the law of neutrality. The Treaty of Versailles in 1919 renewed the international community's recognition of neutrality.

The Swiss argue that their neutrality is not an end in itself but a means to an end, namely the "self-preservation of a small country."[6] Those interested in applying the neutrality concept to the Palestinian question might note the developments in the Swiss concept of neutrality since the sixteenth century. In the earlier years, both the norms of international law and Swiss law allowed the Swiss to permit troops of belligerent countries to transit through their territory, to provide ammunition and arms to belligerent parties and even to supply mercenary soldiers to both sides. The restriction was largely one of even-handedness.

After the eighteenth century, these customs changed. The new practice, which became part of the commonly accepted modern definition of permanent neutrality, included, in wartime, the following factors:

- prohibition of transit or stationing of foreign troops on the territory of the neutral state

- prohibition of assistance to belligerents, including financial assistance, munitions, and arms
- prohibition of involvement in conflicts by the neutral state
- prohibition of abandonment of sovereign rights to any belligerent
- willingness to grant asylum to political and religious refugees

The Swiss concept of neutrality is a political and military one. The state, not the individuals within the state, is neutral. Individuals, the press and groups within the neutral state have the right to free speech and freedom to support causes and concerns in their personal capacity, provided that these activities do not impinge directly upon the neutrality of the state. The neutral state need not be neutral in its economic dealings nor carry out balanced trade with belligerents. The neutral state has special opportunities for serving humanitarian causes, such as Swiss involvement with the Red Cross and the Austrian sponsorship of the transit center for Russian Jewish emigrés. It can also provide useful good offices for parties in dispute. Finally, the neutral state must have the right and obligation to possess a sufficient armed capability to defend its neutrality against outside threats.

The Swiss note that their long embrace of neutrality has not always been easy. Challenges have come from outside and from within. During the nineteenth century, for example, religious groups tried to challenge neutrality as a state doctrine so that they could aid their religious brethren abroad. Prominent politicians demanded that Switzerland help neighboring peoples in their struggle for freedom, raising the slogan of "solidarity of the people." The national commitment to neutrality overrode these arguments. Swiss officials today attribute this steadfastness to the Swiss people's understanding of the relative power ratio in the region and their concern for protecting the peaceful conditions of Swiss life. One of Switzerland's foremost authorities on this subject wrote:

> Neutrality is a principle of foreign policy, not of ethics. It presents a program of foreign relations, not a moral ideal.... For the Swiss it is a method of political diplomacy, not the goal of their being a nation. Switzerland is not there for neutrality, but neutrality for Switzerland.[7]

In summary, the Swiss regard their neutrality as, above all, a means to the preservation of their independence, their national character, and their sovereignty. A senior Swiss diplomat noted that "should we renounce our neutrality, we would be exposed to the risks of losing all that we have built.... Therein lies our commitment to permanent neutrality."

Austrian interest in neutrality is often traced to 1919 when the Austrian Empire's last Prime Minister proposed the establishment of a neutral state. Historians note that his memorandum, distributed to the Allied powers in Berne, argued that a neutral Austria together with Switzerland, could create a useful buffer zone in the heart of Europe. The proposal was rejected by the Republic because it ran against the objective of Austrian unification with the Weimar Republic. The question of Austrian neutrality was to be raised again; it would serve as the key to the end of Soviet occupation of Austria following World War II. Austria has become the experiment in neutrality that some in the Middle East believe could serve as a model for the West Bank and Gaza.

The West Bank and Gaza as a Neutral State

The assumption that Israel will not annex the West Bank and Gaza raises a series of questions about interim strategies that could eventually allow the local Palestinian populace to exercise full sovereign rights. The emotions and fears among Israelis and Palestinians are so volatile and deep-rooted that accommodation appears difficult to achieve. Neutrality has been suggested as one of those possible accommodations that might address the security fears of both the Israelis and Palestinians and provide the Palestinians with the national sovereignty for which they have long struggled. Equally important, the neutrality concept addresses a basic Palestinian objection to the autonomy talks and the peacemaking process. Many Palestinians on the West Bank and Gaza refused to consider participation in the autonomy talks because they could not see where the process was going. A West Bank mayor argued, "We have no idea what the final picture might look like from this kind of process, so we cannot embark on this [negotiation]. . . . If there were some general principles of agreement about the future which were acceptable to the PLO and to others directly involved in this conflict, then we could possibly become involved in the process." To a number of Palestinians and others in the region, the neutral state concept represents such a possible general goal which could be agreed upon. The critical issue for Palestinians is that neutrality cannot be imposed, but must be discussed and freely chosen by the Palestinian people.

Despite an expected public outcry, one of Israel's two Chief Rabbis ruled that Jewish law would permit the government to relinquish part of the Biblical Holy Land to Arab rule, if the cession would prevent war.[8] Government officials immediately responded with sharp arguments that for security and religious reasons the occupied lands of *Judea and Samaria* (West Bank) could never be surrendered.

A member of the powerful Knesset Defence and Foreign Affairs Committee argued that "most Israelis honestly believe that the central intention of any Palestinian state would be to destroy the state of Israel." An Israeli scholar painted the following picture of what most Israelis expect will happen if there is a Palestinian state on the West Bank:

> First, the new state would call in needed specialists from the Arab and socialist countries, including military specialists.... Then they would enter into arms negotiations with Western and Eastern nations while they requested temporary security assistance from another Arab state.... The scenario would unfold from there with the end result that a highly armed ally of the Soviets and radical Arabs, to whom the Palestinians owe so much, would be ready to pounce on Israel in another Arab all-front war....

A senior Palestinian political official objected to such a scenario, noting that it would necessitate that several intolerable factors be accepted by a newly independent Palestinian state: the stationing of foreign troops on Palestinian soil, and an alliance or dependency upon the Soviet Union. He envisioned the scenario developing along different lines: "The minute an Iraqi or Syrian division, or advanced Russian weapons and advisers, entered the new Palestinian state, they would be the victim of a massive Israeli preemptive raid.... What would be the result?... I will tell you: a reoccupation of our land by the Israelis...."

Palestinian scholars have argued that a new Palestinian state would need immense outside financial resources to develop its economy. One noted, "It is difficult envisioning such help coming from the Soviet Union.... Even if some were offered, it would be tied to military strings which would necessitate Israeli actions against us." Most PLO officials agree that a Palestinian state would benefit economically from states like Saudi Arabia, the Emirates, Kuwait, France, Germany, the United Kingdom, and perhaps Japan and the U.S. A PLO official argued that "our record shows that we take support from any source who offers help, but that we are beholden to none." He gave several examples to the Task Force which showed the PLO did risk Soviet ire when forced to choose between a Soviet backed position and one which the PLO leadership believed was better for their cause.

A Jordanian official summarized the problem this way: "The creation of a Palestinian entity will force all Arabs to face certain realities including the continued existence of a strong Israel and the need to develop an alternative system to settle our economical, historical, and political grievances...." An Israeli military officer argued that "maybe one day we could live with a Palestinian state, but why should we trust them and risk our security?"

The most critical problems in the Arab-Israeli conflict are the settlement of the future status of the West Bank and Gaza, and the right to Palestinian self-determination. Most Arabs and Israelis privately equate Palestinian self-determination with an eventual independent state. Palestinians see current Israeli and Egyptian discussions of *limited autonomy* for the residents of the West Bank and Gaza as a ploy, similar to the Russian overtures from 1945 to 1954 in Austria. An influential West Bank mayor summarized Palestinian feelings: "The Israelis are committed to the belief that a fully independent Palestinian state must never be allowed to exist.... They will delay and postpone as long as possible any actions that might bring this about."

This first reference to the Austrian case is interesting. The negotiations over Austria's independence had been deadlocked since 1945, preventing the Austrians from gaining their desired independence and putting an end to the four-power Allied occupation. In 1947, two important political parties in Austria called for neutrality as part of their respective platforms.

Soviet Foreign Minister Molotov, in 1954, demanded that Allied troops remain in Austria until a German peace treaty came into force. The Austrians refused, believing that the presence of any foreign troops was incompatible with their independence. Many Austrians believed that this demand was a ploy by the Soviets to guarantee that their troops would remain in small security pockets, thus delaying the final end of occupation. These Austrians felt that the Soviets would then be difficult to evict. Current Israeli proposals for withdrawing military forces into security pockets in critically important strategic areas of the West Bank are rejected by Palestinians in much the same way as the Austrians rejected the Soviet offers thirty years ago. Israeli officials discard the analogy and are quick to point out that their occupation is considerably different from the Soviet occupation of parts of Austria following the last World War. But Palestinians and other Arabs believe there is a strong resemblance between the two cases.

Some Palestinian officials and scholars have inquired about Israeli motivations in spending billions of pounds to develop housing and other settlement projects throughout the territories. They are reminded of the German assets problem which confronted the Austrians after the war.

Agreement for granting independence to Austria was expected as early as 1949. The principal obstacles were the so-called German assets in Austria. These properties in the Soviet zone of Austria alone included oil and shipping properties and some 300 business and industrial enterprises. The governments of the three Western powers offered to turn over their German assets to Austria, but the Soviets refused. The Soviets were unwilling to withdraw their military forces from the occupied territory or to give up the economic benefits they had received since 1945 in this area. Western diplomats complained at one point in the negotiations that the Soviets were preventing agreement by objecting to an article in a draft treaty that was stated in the exact terms they had earlier proposed themselves.

Arab historians admit that the specific cases are different but note that the enormous economic investment made by the Israelis on the West Bank will carry some price tag for the Palestinians during final negotiations.

Arabs frequently cite Israel's efforts to tie the West Bank and Gaza's economies to a dependency status with Israel.

Many Arabs and Israelis responded with guarded caution to the idea of a neutral state on the West Bank and Gaza. The Arabs and Israelis who raised the neutrality option noted that no systematic thinking about a neutral Palestinian state had been discussed or even properly researched in the region. A few greeted the idea with hostility. One Israeli said that a Palestinian state was "to be avoided at all costs, whether it was neutral or part of the Warsaw Pact." A Palestinian professor argued that a neutral state "did not have certain rights, such as the ability to enter a war or an alliance, which belonged to any sovereign, independent state, and thus was unacceptable." A larger number of other Palestinians, however, queried whether they would ever succeed in securing their homeland if some concessions are not made. The Palestinians see their difficulty in negotiating with the Israelis as greater than that which confronted the Austrians in 1950. Palestinians believe that Israeli policy-makers are guided by an immediate self-interest in delaying settlement of the Palestinian issue. They also believe that the Israelis have yet to define what they want as a final scenario. Labor leader Peres and others have begun to discuss more fully their ideas about the future. Some of these Israeli public figures have scorned neutrality in their public talks, yet advocate principles which are byproducts or inherently part of neutrality.

The course of public events, including Stalin's death in 1953, helped to create a breakthrough in the negotiations over the future status of Austria. The Soviets proposed an agreement in 1954 whereby Austria would prohibit the establishment of foreign military bases on its soil and refrain from engagement of foreign military advisers and specialists. This proposal was rejected by the Austrians and the Western powers who saw it as an imposition of neutralization upon Austria. Shortly thereafter, in Berlin, the Austrian Foreign Minister voluntarily expressed Austria's willingness to refrain from joining military alliances or allowing foreign military bases on Austrian territory.

The breakthrough came in the spring of 1955 during the bilateral Soviet-Austrian talks in Moscow, which resulted in the *Moscow Memorandum*. There were several pledges made by the parties in the *Memorandum* that are worth noting:

Declaration by Austria (Part I of the *Memorandum*)

• To declare itself to permanent neutrality of the type practiced by Switzerland including agreement to refrain from joining military alliances and allowing foreign military bases on Austrian territory

• To strive for international recognition of the declaration of neutrality

- To welcome the guarantee by the four major powers of the permanent neutrality and inviolability of the territorial sovereignty of Austria

Declaration by the Soviet Union (Part II of the *Memorandum*)

- To sign the *Treaty* of independence without delay

- To withdraw all Allied troops from Austria by December 13, 1955

- To recognize the declared permanent neutrality of Austria

- To participate in a collective guarantee by the four powers of the inviolability of Austrian territory according to the Swiss model

The *Memorandum* is considered important because it marked the beginning of Austria's neutrality and smoothed the way for an agreement that would result in the 1955 *State Treaty* of independence. From the political and historical point of view, the *Moscow Memorandum* represents the decisive agreement that bartered Austrian independence and departure of Soviet and other troops in return for Austria's commitment to permanent neutrality.

When discussions of the *Treaty* were held among the Austrians, French, British, Americans, and Russians, all but one of the items of the *Moscow Memorandum* received favorable attention. The exception was the call for a collective guarantee by the major powers of Austria's national sovereignty. Such a guarantee raised problems regarding the role of guarantor powers. Would guarantor powers by compelled to intervene when Austria summoned them, or could they freely decide if the case at hand required their immediate involvement to fulfill the guarantee obligation? The representatives of the major powers also questioned whether one of the guarantor states could act unilaterally or if the four had to agree among themselves to act. The Austrians feared the guarantor states' interference in domestic affairs. The Western states were not enamored with the possibility of signing a specific, collective security agreement with the Soviet Union. These same questions are being raised today in the context of security guarantees in the Arab-Israeli conflict, although most discussions now focus on Security Council guarantees.

During the negotiation process leading to the Austrian *Treaty*, the Austrians were able to gain agreement for eliminating certain provisions, such as a strict numerical limitation of the proposed number of Austrian armed forces. They also refuted lingering arguments that Austria would not be economically viable. Such arguments were frequently raised between 1919 and 1939. Palestinians are very much aware of the way that economic viability arguments are used as justification for rejecting proposals for independence. Arabs point out that the era of colonialism has ended since Austria achieved its freedom. Many members of the United Nations, they note, are less economically viable than would be a Palestinian state consisting of the West Bank and Gaza. They point to suggestions and private discussions with Arabs and Europeans that address the possibility of transforming the Palestinian state into a commercial and financial center for the Middle East.

A letter from a leading European banker was quoted by a Palestinian:" 'Many of us can envision high-rise buildings in a Palestinian state — something like the old Beirut — in which Arab countries, and thus the remainder of the world's commercial interests, would concentrate their regional commerce and investment activity.' " A West European diplomat stationed in the Middle East asked the Task Force members:

> Can you imagine a greater reason to prevent acts of violence and unstable relations with Israel than creating a Palestinian state which would become the Switzerland of the Middle East?... Low unemployment, good wages, a favorable climate, an educated people to fill new white-collar jobs, together with a skilled construction industry which has been built up in the occupied territories by the Israelis.... It's the answer to the 'lack of economic viability' arguments raised for so long about a Palestinian state... and it's not an Arab pipe-dream... but rather a probable vision.

It is true that arguments about the inability of a people to be economically viable are not raised as often as they once were in this region. It is also true that the Palestinians stand to collect more "IOUs" than most newly emerging countries, and it must be noted that the Palestinian people have a large proportion of highly skilled and professional workers.

A Palestinian political leader noted that many of the Arab world's most gifted scientists, doctors, engineers, bankers, financiers, and social scientists are Palestinians. He stated:

> And tell me, where are all of them today?... Kuwait, America, Saudi Arabia, Lebanon, Jordan, England, Switzerland. And why are they there?... Because there is no occupation... there is freedom... and good wages... and growth... and an environment for them to use their talents to their fullest.... But let me tell you that if our Arab brothers pay us back what is due for our suffering all of these decades by building our economy and making us a center for economics, medicine, and technology in the Arab world, our people will come back and thrive in their own land.... This is in direct opposition to what the Americans say.[9]

Arguments that a new Palestinian state could not be economically viable do not carry weight with Palestinians. Many economists in Western Europe also believe that the new state would benefit from a highly educated populace, some of whom would return to the area with a tremendous influx of working capital. A Palestinian lawyer noted that "like the Austrian example, there are many arguments about what we are unable to do, and like the Austrians we will demonstrate otherwise." There are serious concerns, however, about population problems. There are an estimated four million Palestinians of which two million are scattered in Arab countries apart from the occupied territories, Jordan, and pre-1967 Israel. If even one-third of those living outside the West Bank and Gaza were to return immediately to a Palestinian state, there could be a serious over-population condition. Most experts believe that a West Bank/Gaza Palestinian state could take in 500,000 new residents on a full-time basis over five years. Many Palestinians, it is believed, would opt to remain working and living where they are now.

On May 15, 1955, the long-awaited *Austrian State Treaty for the Re-Establishment of an Independent and Democratic Austria*[10] was signed. It restricts Austria from certain actions. For example, under Article 13, Austria is prohibited from possessing atomic weapons, self-propelled or guided missiles, submarines, guns with a range in excess of 30 kilometers and specialized types of assault craft. The military and air clauses (Article 17) were to remain in effect until modified by agreement of the four powers, or by agreement of the Security Council of the United Nations, once Austria gained admission to the United Nations. The *Treaty* includes provisions for the withdrawal of Allied troops (Article 20) and lists procedures for the settlement of disputes (Article 30).

Austrian acceptance of the *State Treaty* and the *Moscow Memorandum* was voluntary. The signatory four powers did not condition the *State Treaty* or its implementation on a guarantee of Austria's territorial integrity and neutrality. Austrian legal experts cite a series of factors that together provide a basis for acceptance of Austrian neutrality, including the *Moscow Memorandum*, the letters exchanged between Austria and the major powers at the time of the signing of the *State Treaty*, the notification to all nations of Austrian neutrality,[11] its acceptance by the international community (as reflected in Austria's acceptance into the United Nations), and adoption of Article One of the *Federal Constitutional Law of October 26, 1955*.

When the last Allied soldier departed from Austria on October 24, 1955, the Austrian National Council decided to adopt neutrality in the *Federal Constitutional Law of October 26, 1955*. Article One contains a declaration of Austria's permanent neutrality; its willingness to use all available means to defend and maintain its neutrality; and an agreement to refrain from joining military alliances or permitting foreign military bases on its territory.

An Arab who has pursued the possibility of establishing a neutral Palestinian state on the West Bank and the Gaza noted with particular interest the wording and "parallelism to the Palestinian case" of Secretary of State Dulles' *Report to the President on the Austrian State Treaty*.[12] Part five of that *Report* included the following passages:

> Those who have observed the conduct and demeanor of the Austrian people during recent years [of occupation] can, I think, have little doubt that this present intention of the Austrian Government [permanent neutrality] will become the permanent will of the Austrian people.
>
> They have shown a courage and steadfastness which is remarkable in the face of repeated disappointments of their hopes. Despite, or perhaps because of, the occupation of much of their land by the Soviet Union and despite intensive efforts by the Soviet Communists in developing a Communist Party in Austria, that party has never been able to rally more than 5 percent of the vote. Despite the drain year after year of their economy by the Soviet exploiters, the Austrian people have courageously and skillfully rebuilt the economy which was left to them.
>
> They have never succumbed to the temptation to accept a treaty which gave them less than genuine freedom and independence.[13]

Lengthy discussions about neutrality with both Arabs and Israelis resulted in the collection of several ideas regarding the obligations and rights, advantages, and disadvantages of a neutral Palestinian state. The following list indicates specific areas where greater research attention must be focused. The most frequently cited advantages and disadvantages of a Palestinian neutral state were the following:

ADVANTAGES TO THE PALESTINIANS

• Neutrality could be a breakthrough concept for the deadlock over the Palestinian issue. Neutrality would address both the question of Palestinian sovereignty and the concerns over security for the Palestinian state's neighbors, including Israel.

• Under international law, a neutral state is allowed to have a defensive capacity to protect its sovereignty and neutrality. A neutral state is not prohibited from participating in a self-defense treaty.

• Transitional arrangements for a Palestinian state could include an international presence on its borders, which would provide an opportunity for developing an indigenous defense capacity.

• A neutral state would make the Palestinian state more appealing for large-scale Arab and Western financial investments because the risk of a pending war with Israel would be greatly reduced.

• Neutrality does not prohibit involvement in the United Nations and regional organizations, providing that that involvement does not include participation in certain military security agreements.

• A neutral Palestinian state could be a logical center for Arab affairs since it would be removed from the military and political in-fighting that characterizes the Arab world at this time.

• A neutral state could avoid entanglements which might drag the Palestinians into an undesired conflict caused by the political ambitions of another state in the region.

ADVANTAGES TO THE ISRAELIS AND NON-PALESTINIAN ARABS

• A declaration of neutrality would signal a commitment by Palestinians to live in peace with their neighbors.

• Offensive arms could be restricted.

• Foreign troops could not be stationed on or transit the territory of the neutral state.

• A neutral state is prohibited from giving assistance to belligerents.

• A clear understanding of Israeli perceived security needs could be established by defining a violation of neutrality as a *causus belli* for Israel.

• The Palestinian state could not become involved in another violent conflict without sacrificing its neutrality and possibly its independence. (The exception would be if its neutrality were violated through an act of aggression.)

• An economically viable Palestinian state could benefit the entire region economically and politically.

• Minor border rectifications might be agreeable as part of a comprehensive settlement.

DISADVANTAGES TO THE PALESTINIANS

• Neutrality is seen as a limitation on the sovereignty of a state.

• Outside guarantees securing neutrality could result in outside interference by the guarantor powers.

• The Palestinian people would be prevented from aiding another Arab state. A Palestinian educator argued, "Would we be expected to sit by while another Arab people was under attack by Israel, Iran, or other outside powers?"

• The neutral state would be unable to form certain military alliances with other Arab states, although they are not excluded from regional security pacts that are defensive in nature.

• Neutrality would prevent the Palestinian state from allowing transit of foreign troops from friendly countries.

• The military imbalance between a heavily armed Israel and a lightly armed, neutral Palestinian state would put the Palestinian state at the mercy of Israel.

• The Palestinians cannot be forced to accept neutrality against their wishes but must be allowed to exercise their right to national self-determination.

• Transitional arrangements toward such a goal would not be well-received, particularly those that called for a staged withdrawal of the Israeli defense forces over time.

DISADVANTAGES TO THE ISRAELIS

• Any Palestinian state would pose a threat to the security of Israel.

• The neutral state would be armed. Even such a defensive capability could pose a threat to Israeli population centers.

• The neutral state would be unable to prevent terrorist attacks on Israel by fringe groups and individuals.

• The movement from today's situation to a neutral state would necessitate a period of transitional arrangements that Palestinians would not accept.

• The neutral state could discard its neutrality and join an attack on Israel.

• The other Arab states would not recognize its neutrality.

• The Palestinians could never peacefully select and maintain a leadership; the PLO, for example, would form a clique that Western-educated Palestinians returning to the area would challenge, generating instability.

• The state would not be economically viable.

• The Palestinians could not maintain neutrality in affairs that dealt with their co-religionists.

These Israeli comments seem to stem from a belief that, even after a comprehensive settlement, the Palestinian goal would be the destruction or damage of the state of Israel. These remarks demonstrate the Israelis' lack of confidence in the Palestinians. An Israeli retired public servant noted that "the sad thing for me is that few people here are willing to try to build confidence and bridges with them [the Palestinians]. . . . Unless we do so, how can we ever agree to anything?" In a similar vein, Palestinians noted that Israelis would not believe that Palestinian intentions were anything but evil. Likewise, the Palestinians lacked confidence in Israeli words and intentions.

It should be noted that the Palestinians and Israelis modified many of these listed objections during subsequent private discussions. Both groups noted that each side would have to accept some compromises if there were to be a comprehensive agreement. A few Israelis speculated that PLO acceptance of neutrality would be a Palestinian ploy to secure their independence. No Palestinians made such allusions in the public or private discussions. In every case, those who discussed the option of neutrality became more obviously enthusiastic about its possibilities as discussion turned to its specific components. One Palestinian businessman, who said earlier that he was a PLO sympathizer and opposed anything short of a full sovereign state, remarked:

> This neutrality could be the answer to many of our own problems. . . . The modern history of permanently neutral states is a good one and it does not mean that we would be rejecting the Arab world, quite the contrary, we might become the arbiter of their disputes—and perhaps the logical place to center the Arab League as well—it doesn't really belong in Cairo or Tunis, nor in Baghdad or other places where power concentration is a major goal.

It is important that acceptance of neutrality by the Palestinians not place them at a disadvantage vis-à-vis their neighbors. A series of steps can be taken to guarantee evenhandedness. For example, it is proposed that Israel, Syria, Jordan, Lebanon, and Egypt agree to prohibit foreign military bases on their soil as part of the security package of a comprehensive settlement. It is also suggested that a symbolic reciprocal repatriation system be established, whereby an agreed number of Jewish and Arab people enter the Palestinian state and Israel, respectively. It should be remembered that this concept of neutrality is part of a larger system which would be established — part of a comprehensive settlement based on a commitment of mutual recognition and peace. A Palestinian lawyer with PLO sympathies argued, "Some dismiss neutrality without thinking of what it could mean to our people: it could help ensure us freedom from more wars and violence—and it will set an example for this war-ravaged area to put improvement of standards of living above improvement of warmachines."

Special Considerations

Other important considerations must be taken into account when reviewing such a scenario. One is that the scenario assumes that such actions will take place only when the Israelis and Arabs have provided convincing evidence to one another of their genuine desire for peace. This must include their demonstrated good faith to participate in comprehensive peace negotiations. The concept of good faith implies the existence of a political will to make mutual adjustments on the most difficult issues.

Both the Arabs and Israelis traditionally have pitted various factions of their adversaries against one another. The very nature of comprehensive peace negotiations requires agreements on a wide range of subjects. Each of the protagonists must make efforts to understand the perceived threats of the others and to determine its priorities in making adjustments in the best interests of a total peace. Several other issues arose during the discussions in the region concerning the neutrality concept, and some of the most important are presented here.

Transitional arrangements. Most Israelis argued that Israel would insist on a specific transitional period prior to the establishment of a neutral, sovereign Palestinian state. This transition could include a period of full demilitarization of the West Bank and Gaza. United Nations troops might be stationed along border areas during the transitional period; local police would be armed for maintaining internal order. Some Israelis argue that Israeli demands for retaining security pockets of Israeli Defence Force (IDF) military units in strategic locations along the border areas might be reduced if certain measures were taken. Included in these measures would be internationally recognized guarantees by Syria and Jordan not to deploy their forces and certain types of offensive weapons within specified geographic areas near the neutral Palestinian state. In addition, the neutral Palestinian state would agree not to allow foreign military personnel to be stationed on its territory and would refrain from obtaining certain types of weapons during the transitional period. Violation of these agreements serve as a *causus belli* for Israel, argue Israeli strategic thinkers. The Palestinian state would, in turn, be given assurances by members of the Security Council to protect its neutrality and assist, if requested, in protecting the state from acts of external aggression.

Palestinians offer counter proposals that entail Israeli agreement to limit its deployment of specific arms within a certain distance of the demilitarized area. Limited armament zones might be established on all border areas of the new state, perhaps manned by United Nations peacekeeping observers. The difference, noted an Israeli journalist, is that "this time they [United Nations peacekeeping forces] would be keeping a *real peace.* . . ."

These ideas are not universally accepted, however. Israeli estimates of a fair transitional period range from one to ten years. Some Israeli officials have argued that a division-sized force (10,000 to 12,000 troops) must be kept in West Bank security pockets after a main Israeli military withdrawal from the West Bank. Israeli Defence Force officials have argued that prior to a large Israeli withdrawal, it would be essential for the IDF to secure better operational units, increased anti-aircraft, early warning and command and control capabilities, prepositioning of supplies, and guarantee of freedom of movement. Egyptian officials concerned with the recent autonomy talks spoke of a possible 5,000 to 10,000 Israeli troops, with light arms being deployed in small security areas during a transitional period. Their role during the transition would be "like the British in the canal zone," noted an Egyptian official. The Israeli argument for this military presence is that during the transitional period, sufficient mobilization time is needed to repel any Jordanian or Syrian attacks. Palestinians argue that an Israeli military presence is unthinkable and that third parties, many suggest Jordan, could be stationed in the area during the transitional phase(s).

From the point of view of topographical defense, the Jordan Valley is Israel's preferred border. The vulnerable parts of the 230-mile border between Jordan and Israel today are less than 20 miles of relatively weak defenses, "specifically the region of the Bet Shean Valley on the eastern side and the relative lowlands of the upper Jordan Valley and Irbid region on the western side."[14] In any transition on the West Bank, "we would want to hold onto some of these Jordan Rift military positions until the very end," said an IDF spokesman. Most Israelis believe that some security arrangements deemed as essential to Palestinians and Israelis could be agreed upon for the transitional phase without great difficulty — once a decision was made to negotiate and make peace.

The clear majority of the combined *1979 Middle East sample* of Israelis and Arabs believed that if basic confidence-building measures were mutually undertaken, some combination of elements might create an acceptable formula that would not require a physical Israeli military presence during the transitional stage. Such elements would include demilitarization, assurances of neighboring states and outside powers, a third-party peacekeeping presence that would include sophisticated anti-tank fields or other devices which would give the peacekeeping forces some strength in the face of any aggression, and limited armament zones. Nearly half of the Israelis of the *1979 Middle East sample* believed that the deciding factor could be Israel's continued threat of a preemptive attack, should agreements be broken or a hostile act be committed by the neutral state or its Arab neighbors. It is likely that the Palestinians would not accept the presence of Israeli military forces on the soil of a Palestinian state, even in the transitional stages. Other arrangements involving Jordanian or other outside parties would need to be developed.

The importance of limiting certain armaments during a transitional period is seen as essential, since even regular field artillery can pose a threat to strategic targets in the area. For example, the Soviet ML-20 (152mm) gun has a maximum range of some 10.5 miles. This means that a shell fired from the West Bank could hit Ben Gurion Airport or locations in Tel Aviv. An IDF spokesman noted that the Israeli military is also capable of inflicting substantial damage "on any inch of West Bank soil."

In addition, some Jordanian, Palestinian, Egyptian, and Israeli officials have suggested that the guarantor powers should restrict the supply of specific new offensive weapons to the neutral state *and* its neighbors. Similar to the provisions of Article 13 of the Austrian *State Treaty*, the agreement could also prohibit certain other weapons in the defense force arsenal of the neutral state.

Israeli settlements. The continued expansion of Israeli settlements in the occupied territories poses a serious problem. According to Israeli polls in 1978[15] and 1979,[16] some 69.8 percent of Israelis believed that peace within secure and recognized borders was more important than the right to settle on the West Bank and Gaza; and some 64 percent opposed the new settlements on the West Bank as an obstacle to peace. Yet, Israeli government officials have argued that even after a resolution of the West Bank problem, the settlements should remain. Israelis base this argument on the idea that Jews have the right to live on the West Bank for religious and historical reasons and as a segment of what a retired Israeli general called an "early warning defense system in case of another war."

The problem of Palestinian repatriation or compensation is "the other side of this coin," noted a Jordanian businessman. He added, "I think that when the will to achieve peace is present, we will both [Arabs and Israelis] find this issue a mutually uncomfortable and painful one, which should result in a fair and swift solution." Palestinians are understandably adamant that forced Israeli settlements built on seized Arab land are illegal and must be removed. Most Palestinians argued that they had no difficulty welcoming anyone back to the West Bank who legitimately owns land or who wishes to become a citizen in all its aspects. "This applies to Jews as well as anyone else," stated a West Bank mayor known to be involved with the PLO.

Current security. Austria experienced a bitter terrorist problem over its disputed border area with Italy in the South Tyrol. The Austrian army was deployed to prevent Austrians from conducting raids across the border in a fashion similar to the deployment of the Jordanian army in the 1970s against the PLO. During the transitional stage, the United Nations or other peacekeeping force(s) stationed in the demilitarized zone, together with Palestinian militia and police, could be made responsible for preventing low-level commando attacks on Israel, Jordan, or Syria, as well as for preventing such attacks launched from neighboring states upon the new Palestinian state.

A Palestinian defense capability would be designed during the transitional period and implemented gradually prior to the date of the establishment of the independent and neutral Palestinian state. Austrian and Swiss civilian advisers on military affairs could be retained as consultants during the transitional phases.

Despite such arguments, many Israelis doubt that Palestinians could seal off their border from attacks on Israel, once the transitional stage ended. An Israeli journalist argued that "it will take our people a while to mentally accept this scenario. . . . When push comes to shove, we are afraid that terrorism or worse things would result."

A West Bank businessman suggested that a careful reexamination be made by the Israelis of the Jordanian success, since 1970, in sealing off its borders from violent attacks into Israel. He continued:

> There is no doubt that most governments can restrain the extremist elements when there is a desire and reason to do so. . . . We Palestinians are so tired of fighting and death that I can assure you of the unbelievable determination we would have in our own state to prevent extremist attacks on Israel which would result in retaliatory or preemptive attacks on us as a response.

Those familiar with the internal workings of the PLO argue that Chairman Arafat's Fateh faction holds some 80 percent of the Palestinian fighting capability and public support. A Gaza leader argued that "there is no doubt in our minds that if Fateh accepts a state with certain international safeguards, then we all [Palestinians] will be prepared to accept it." A West Bank mayor wrote that "I am not saying that we won't have differences of opinion — we will — but we will solve them democratically. How do the Israelis satisfy their Communist Party, Gush Emunim right-wingers, and all the others?" A careful review of the composition and election process of the Palestine National Congress (governing body of the PLO) demonstrates that it is perhaps the most democratic of Arab regimes.

Similarly, Palestinians argue for the need of an agreement by the Israelis not to launch preemptive attacks upon the demilitarized area as retaliation for isolated commando raids which might elude the United Nations peacekeeping and local forces. Establishment of a transitional committee composed of representatives of Israel, the new Palestinian leadership, and Jordan (and perhaps Syria and Lebanon) was proposed. It could be chaired by the U.N. Secretary-General's Special Representative. Its tasks would include facilitating discussion of potential or low-level problems that otherwise might escalate into large-scale hostilities.

Limitations on sovereignty. Several Palestinians expressed specific reservations about the neutrality concept. For example, a group of Palestinian educators expressed the fear that permanent neutrality would prevent a Palestinian state from fully participating as a member of the Arab League. They cited Austria's refusal to join the European Economic Community (Common Market). Austria's refusal was based on the EEC *Treaty*, Articles 224 and 225, both of which could affect its status. No such article exists in the twenty-article *Pact of the League of Arab States*.

Austria, however, did join the Council of Europe in 1956, noting that Austria saw no contradiction between the obligations arising out of permanent neutrality and international or interparliamentary collaboration in the non-military field. A prominent Austrian official summarized the attitude: "A neutral state's competence to conduct independent economic or other non-military policies with other countries remains completely intact." A respected Palestinian scholar noted:

> ...When a comprehensive peace is agreed, the Arabs will find the need to completely revamp the Arab League...its purposes, structure and capabilities.... It should not be difficult at that time for some consideration to be given to accommodate special cases like a neutral state as a member of the League at least for a specified period.... But everyone must remember that in the long-time [sic], we, as all of the Arabs, are commited to the vision of an Arab nation.

An Arab official who stated that he had never in the past "listened to any talk about neutrality" added:

> Many of us rejected that idea [neutrality] because it seemed a capitulation to the Israelis.... But in fact it could give us some advantages that we might otherwise not get, for example, our own state in my lifetime ... or the right to have a defense capability ... and influx of great sums of money to build a service economy....

> My only reservation is that one day, many, many decades from now, it is our dream, like all our Arab brothers, that there will be a single *Arab nation*.... When that day comes, international law and all nations will have to realize that our choice will be to become part of that single *Arab nation* ... for that is our destiny as Arabs.... But do not put this in current terms, for no Arab I know maintains that this can happen in the next twenty-five, maybe fifty or one hundred years ... and then the world will be so different in its economics, military weapons, politics and everything, that speculation is not sensible.

Several Palestinians questioned neutrality because it would "restrict our ability to fulfill the obligations of collective security under the United Nations Charter." Two primary arguments support neutrality as being compatible with United Nations membership. First, Article 51 of the Charter,[17] while allowing all Member states to come to the aid of a Member [state] suffering aggression, does not impose such assistance as an obligation. Neutrality can be preserved except if the Security Council has determined, in accordance with Article 39 of the Charter,[18] the existence of an act of aggression and ordered sanctions. The Security Council, however, is not obligated to compel all members to participate in the sanctions. Article 48 states that the action required to carry out decisions of the Security Council for the maintenance of international peace and security "shall be taken by all Members of the United Nations or by some of them as the Security Council may determine." Second, Austria was admitted to the United Nations with full recognition by all member states of its permanent neutrality and without prejudice due to its neutrality. It is conceivable that Switzerland will reverse its past unwillingness to become a member of the United Nations and will apply for membership in the early 1980s.

Several Palestinians who support the PLO argued that the world should note that the Palestinian people have already given up so much — a large part of their original homeland. Their willingness to recognize and accept Israel's permanent right to exist in part of Palestine is also agreeable if the Palestinians are to exercise the right to self-determination. However, these Palestinians said that acceptance of the neutrality idea, which they favored, was yet another limitation of Palestinian full sovereignty. One Palestinian professor argued, "Let the world see that my people want peace enough to consider sacrificing even more the little that we might have. . . . It is true that we could benefit from neutrality, but it is also true that we would have to accept another limitation on our full sovereignty — just remember our possible willingness to accept these things is yet another indication of our willingness to end this unending war."

Other Palestinians raised the argument that those who have lived with great injustices for many years should not adopt "something like neutrality which prevents our moral conscience to assist those suffering injustices elsewhere." An Austrian diplomat addressed this argument: "A neutral state can often do things to help the oppressed which other states cannot do, for example, look at the scores of activities called *good offices* or humanitarian projects which we [Austrians] and the Swiss are doing at this very moment . . . and do not forget that in the single instance where economic sanctions were ordered by the Security Council against Rhodesia, we [Austria] decided to comply with the sanctions request." A Swiss legal expert added, "Being neutral does not . . . and cannot mean that one is without morals or indifferent in the face of the world's injustices."

A distinguished Austrian military officer added, "We know what occupation and suffering means . . . that is why we often offer our troops for U.N. peacekeeping missions when these troops can do good in troubled areas, and why we serve as a bridge between East and West at the highest level. . . . Being neutral in this world is not a curse. . . . In many ways it is a blessing and an opportunity to do good things others cannot do. . . ."

States Admitted Under Conditions

Some Israeli and Western lawyers have argued that the Palestinians should be admitted to the community of nations only under rigid conditions, such as their agreement to abide by certain restrictions on armaments, regulations, and mode of conduct. They argue that the international legal category, *states admitted under conditions*, like permanently neutralized states, assume special obligations through free acceptance of the treaty that creates their independence. It is this element of free choice that guarantees their recognition as sovereign under international law.

An Arab official asked to respond to these points argued, "Are these conditions imposed as a penalty for losing a war or being a bad boy?... They are unacceptable." A Palestinian colleague added, "If *we* suggest some modest restrictions as a way to resolve an impasse ... things we are willing to freely accept, then that is another story, but we will not be treated as a defeated prisoner of war or such a thing...." A senior Israeli diplomat had earlier noted:

> Let us face the fact that assurances will be needed and demanded by both sides.... We can look at this as pressure and penalization or as acting like statesmen in making mutual concessions which will actualize peace.... It is off the record, but each party is known to either have fall-back positions or is willing to consider alternatives to current demands.... None of us will get what we want and concessions will have to be made on both sides....

Security Assurances

One of the most misused and misunderstood concepts in the Arab-Israeli peacemaking process is *security guarantees*. In its basic sense, a guarantee is a pledge or assurance. It is relatively simple to understand a government guarantee to depositors that the money they place in certain savings accounts will be available to them in the future. There are other aspects of guarantee that also must be understood. For example, there is often a tendency to view guarantees as absolute. Any person who has filed a claim with his insurance company, for example, to receive reimbursement for incurred damages, knows that oftentimes the claims are rejected or adjusted to something less than one expected. There is often the uncertainty that a loophole or oversight will be discovered by the guarantor party that permits it to refuse to honor all or part of the guarantee.

The same basic analysis applies to the international context of security guarantees. In the Middle East, the term *guarantee* has been defined as a commitment to "protect — by force unless otherwise specified — another and weaker state's independence, territorial integrity, or other specified attributes."[19]

A security guarantee is rarely absolute; it is, rather, a limited safeguard and provides additional feelings of security to the state receiving the guarantee. It is also a warning to other parties that threatening harm to the guaranteed state could bring responsive measures from the guarantor state. The term is often misunderstood or loosely used in international relations. For example, many outsiders were perplexed by the unwillingness of the Soviet Union to come to the military assistance of Vietnam when the latter was subjected to a Chinese attack in 1979. The Chinese actions were said to be retaliation for Vietnamese aggression in Cambodia. The Soviet Union and Vietnam had previously concluded a detailed Mutual Assistance Pact. It did not, however, *require* the Soviet Union to send military forces to the defense of Vietnam if attacked. The Soviets did send enormous amounts of military matériel but did not enter the conflict directly.

This is, perhaps, the most important first lesson to learn about the nature of security guarantees. They are not absolute. Like the insurance company that wants to avoid paying a particular claim, the guarantor power can often find loopholes for not intervening. Japanese and West European officials question whether the United States would risk a direct nuclear confrontation with the Soviet Union if its allies were attacked by Soviet forces. In this sense guarantees are better called assurances, as the word "guarantee" connotes an absolute sense that cannot be justified in international politics.

The second important lesson that can be culled from the history books is that outside security guarantees cannot adequately replace the establishment of normal relations between neighboring states. *Security guarantees are most effective when they supplement, not replace, peaceful relations between states.* Basing one's security in a hostile environment upon outside guarantees is a risky business.

Over the past twenty years, there has been considerable discussion about the possibility of American security guarantees in the form of mutual pacts with Israel and, perhaps, Egypt, as well as other states. [20] The history of mutual defense pacts is a varied one. The United States, for example, currently engages in three types of security pacts with its allies. The most notable is the North Atlantic Treaty Organization (NATO), which commits all NATO members to consult when a member's national security is threatened. The NATO-type agreement is based on the principle that an act of aggression upon any member is an attack on all members and must be given a response, including the full use of force.

American treaties with Korea and Thailand are examples of another type of defense pact in that they require each party to confront a security threat in accordance with its established constitutional processes. The third type is the American treaty with Japan that guarantees that the United States will defend Japan, but does not require Japan to come to the assistance of the United States.

The differences among these three currently practiced forms of security guarantees are important. The NATO-type has been the most desirable from the Israeli view because it would obligate the United States to come to Israel's aid if attacked. The more standard type of security guarantee pact requires Congressional approval before it is invoked and is seen by many in Israel and Egypt as a potentially unreliable guarantee. Changes in the membership of Congress and pressures from certain constituencies could cause Congress to refuse implementation of the guarantee. The possibility of joint American-Soviet assurances, including the token presence of U.S. and U.S.S.R. observers as part of an international supervisory force, is currently being discussed in the region.

United Nations Security Council guarantees raise other problems that must be noted. In 1974, Cypriots discovered one of the problems inherent within its 1959 *Treaty of Guarantee* by the United Kingdom, Turkey, and Greece. These three guarantor powers had assumed the right to take joint or separate action to maintain the independence and constitutional integrity of Cyprus. In 1974, the Turkish government invoked the terms of the guarantee agreement and sent a military force into Cyprus for the purpose of protecting the Turkish Cypriot minority. Turkish troops remain on the island today enforcing a *de facto* partition of the island. A related problem for the Middle East protagonists is that securing any agreement by the five permanent members of the Security Council—China, France, United Kingdom, United States, and U.S.S.R. — would be extremely difficult. Each Middle East state would understandably want to allow its particular, trusted ally [guarantor] to intervene alone in time of aggression should that be necessary. This problem is often debated in the Middle East. No suitable alternative has yet been found.

The weaknesses of security guarantees, as witnessed by the above examples, underscore the importance of using such measures as *supplemental actions* to a comprehensive agreement. In the case of a neutral Palestinian state, there must be agreement and basic confidence that the normalization of relations will create a condition where outside guarantees are not likely to be needed. A Jordanian official spoke of the problem of security guarantees and noted:

> I hear the Israelis say that they don't particularly want the U.N. involved in their transition with Egypt, but rather favor joint Egyptian-Israeli patrols ... and the Palestinians claim that a peace agreement would bring normal border relations between Israel and their Palestinian state.... The trend, I think, is obvious.... We want to create a stable peace here ... then security guarantees are an extra bonus that makes us feel a little more secure as we build confidence about each other ... remember that the guarantees are needed for all of us, not just the Israelis or a Palestinian state.

An Israeli defense analyst and former senior defense official agreed with this assessment. He added, "I don't object to certain kinds of security guarantees after the fact [of peace being established], perhaps as a way to express the endorsement by the world community of the peace, and as a little reminder to each of us to remain honest and committed to our course of peace."

Other defense experts in the West have argued that there are other benefits of certain security guarantees, such as their possible utility as a provider of early warning against surprise attack, and more important as a deterrent to a potentially hostile party not to launch an attack. Few would argue, however, that security guarantees can actually prevent aggression or stop it once it begins. As a Palestinian scholar noted, "We must have the belief that we will all honor our commitments.... We have all suffered enough death in our families.... We now must turn to the economic matters at hand and build a region where fighting is no longer our most discussed and practiced skill." There is a recognized need in the region to devise new forms of security assurances and to remember that such assurances are not guarantees in the absolute sense of that word.

A Confederation of a Palestinian (West Bank/Gaza) State with Jordan

Palestinians note that Israelis and Jordanians frequently use the terms *federation* and *confederation* interchangeably. More Arabs and Israelis preferred to speak freely with the Task Force members about the possibility of some form of federation between a Palestinian entity and Jordan than about neutrality. Recent Arab history has included various forms of federation, making the concept more understandable than neutrality to some. It has been discussed as an option for many years in the region, although relatively little has been written about the nature of the proposed federation. King Hussein of Jordan presented a plan for federation of a West Bank with Jordan in 1972, and recently there have been efforts in the region to study the concept in greater detail as it might apply to the Middle East.

Arab and Israeli motivations for supporting a form of confederation differ greatly. Many Israelis, for example, spoke of the need for King Hussein to remain in complete control of defense matters and foreign affairs. One Israeli Finance Ministry official said that he could support this idea only if it were "evident that Hussein could keep a lid on the Palestinians." Jordanians are completely unwilling to consider confederation with a Palestinian state if it meant a new form of domination. Senior Jordanian officials argue that the Palestinians must exercise their right to self-determination without outside interference.

The Task Force members noted that one of the reasons why so many Arabs and Israelis feel comfortable discussing the federation concepts between Jordan and a Palestinian state is that it has become an ambiguous concept that means many different things to many people. It is also clear that many people who claim to support the principles are unaware of the legal and historical traditions and definitions. For example, numerous Israelis asked why Palestinians insisted that they be given their independence and national sovereignty *prior* to agreeing to enter some sort of a confederation with Jordan.

More than half of the Israelis who discussed confederation ideas raised this question; most speculated that it was another demonstration of underhanded Palestinian ploys to gain public support and achieve independence. "We know that they would gain independence and then renege on their promise to join a federation with Jordan," argued a Tel Aviv lawyer who had served as a periodic advisor on Arab affairs to the Israeli government.

More than two-thirds of the Arab members of the *1979 Middle East sample* believed that a confederation type of relationship would benefit the Palestinians, Jordanians, and the Arab world as a whole. Their arguments included historical, socio-economic, and political overtones. Most frequently mentioned was the fact that some 60 percent of the Jordanian population is Palestinian. Some reservations were expressed in reference to the Gaza Strip, which had previously been under Egyptian administration. Palestinians, however, showed no flexibility when discussing the basic requirements of their state—it must include the West Bank and Gaza, both of which are inhabited by Palestinians. Gaza Palestinians were not opposed to a confederation with Jordan after independence, although they were clearly not as receptive as their colleagues on the West Bank.

Overall, it must be noted that many Palestinians saw attempts to force the creation of an immediate confederation of the Palestinian entity with Jordan as an Israeli goal to deny the Palestinians their national sovereignty and to subjugate the new Palestinian state to Jordanian interests. A senior Palestinian official argued that "just as independence and national sovereignty are prerequisites to joining a confederation, so a confederation is a step toward a federation. . . . Isn't that the historical experience?" Many West Bank residents who favored confederation argued privately that it was not politically feasible if the PLO was excluded. A moderate Palestinian businessman noted, "You must remember that the PLO are not a bunch of radical misfits. They are our leadership and cannot be excluded . . . . Whether I vote for Arafat or Mayor X as my duly elected head of state is my business later—but for now my loyalty and that of all my people is to the PLO and Mr. Arafat—and achieving our right to self-determination." Such views appear to be widely held by Palestinians in the occupied territories as well as by those in Lebanon, Jordan, and the other Arab states.

What is a confederation?

Although both federations and confederations were discussed by the Arabs and Israelis with Task Force members in 1979, the option presented here is confederation. Few Palestinians were willing to look beyond a possible confederal relationship with Jordan and numerous Israelis familiar with the legal distinctions favored confederation as more practical than federation. International lawyers define a confederation as a number of independent states linked by a treaty in a union with a central government. The central government has specific powers over the confederation's member states but not over its citizens. This confederation brings states together for a specific purpose but leaves each member state sovereign and independent in other respects.

International law theorists argue that doctrines of international law on the matter of federations and confederations declare that both are unions of *sovereign states*. As in all matters of law, practice does not always conform to doctrine. The example of the Canadian confederation is a case in point. Although Canada is officially called a confederation, it is argued by many Canadian constitutional experts that it is in fact a federation. In either case, however, it must be noted that the establishment of the Dominion of Canada in 1867 by an enactment of the British Parliament proclaimed, in fact, a union of upper and lower Canada. Although they were separate entities, both were subject to the colonial administration of Great Britain and not sovereign states as understood in international law.

Under the accepted norms of international law, confederation normally is not considered an *international person* and each of its component states remains sovereign and subject to international law. In the 1700s both the United Provinces of the Netherlands and the Swiss confederations were considered not to impair the sovereignty of their individual component states. The United States experienced a confederate form of government from 1781 to 1789. The governmental agency of the American confederation was accepted as speaking for its component members, although the component states retained their sovereignty and independence. It was understood that the independence resided in each state's right to reassert control over its foreign affairs through dissolution of the Union.

Under international law, a component unit of the confederation may maintain its own diplomatic representation abroad, conclude treaties, and enter alliances with other states as long as the treaties do not prejudice the confederation's interests. The most frequently cited example is the German Confederation of 1815 to 1866.

Confederations have had a tumultuous history. In every modern case, a structural form different from confederation has replaced the original union, usually the federal form or *federation*. A federal state is a *permanent union* of several previously independent states with governmental organs of its own *and* power over its component states as well as over their citizens. The federal state alone has the right to declare war, make peace, and conclude international political or military agreements. Domestic constitutional provisions may permit limited international activity by its members. The component states, however, cannot be considered members of the community of nations.

It should also be noted that there is a special form of confederation called a *real union* that exists when several sovereign states are linked by treaty under the same head of state and act as one state for international purposes. The union is not a single state but a real union of two separate states acting together as a single international person. Despite popular opinion, the union of Syria and Egypt in 1958 into the United Arab Republic is *not* legally considered a *real union* but rather a merger of two sovereign states into a single unitary state. Examples of *real unions* include Sweden and Norway (1814 to 1905), Austria and Hungary (1867 to 1918), and Denmark and Iceland (1918 to 1944).

A perfunctory glance seems to indicate that the differences among federation, confederation, and a *real union* are not substantial. The differences, however, are quite important for the Palestinian people, who believe they have lived long enough without having control over their own affairs. A distinguished Arab journalist familiar with discussions on these matters argued, "No Arab can honestly envision that the Palestinians would welcome a federation plan now.... But a confederation which would give certain specified powers to the central government while preserving powers for each state and freedom for each state to govern its own individuals in domestic matters, is a possibility, especially with Jordan."

Several Israelis who had spoken in favor of a federation or confederation altered their views when they learned that by definition a confederation is entered into by two sovereign states. A Palestinian West Bank official remarked that "on first glance, it appears that a confederation is keeping more sovereignty for ourselves than neutrality, but in the balance it is not that simple.... We want to gain our sovereignty and independence, not trade it off right away."

A Jordanian-Palestinian Confederation

Some Middle East observers, including Arabs and Israelis, believe that the East and West Banks of the Jordan River represent essentially one people, history, and culture. Palestinians make up a clear majority of the population on both sides of the river. Israelis often ask privately, what would eventually happen to the Hashemite Kingdom of Jordan and the ruling family if there were a real federation? Over a period of several years, it is expected that Palestinian leaders could assume control, through some evolving democratic means or a *coup d'etat*. This possibility is seen as a clear threat by many Israelis and by some Arabs as well. West Bank residents often mention that they do not wish to return to Hashemite rule. A mayor on the West Bank said, "Look, it is very simple, we have been denied the right to govern ourselves for too long.... Now that is about to change.... Why should we again trade it away ... for what?" Most Palestinian leaders, however, agree that after achieving independence, they would favor some form of union with Jordan as a practical matter.

Jordan proposed a federation of the East and West Banks in 1972. The suggestion was rejected by the Palestinians through their spokesmen, the Palestine Liberation Organization. The PLO argue that consideration of plans like confederation, while not being ruled out, must be decided only *after* the achievement of independence by a Palestinian state. Jordanian officials have also added that the determination to confederate will be open to scrutiny by the Palestinians and Jordanians alike. One added, "Too often people forget that perhaps the Jordanians won't wish to be part of a confederation."

King Hussein's proposed federation plan in March of 1972 called for the establishment of a United Arab Kingdom with two autonomous regions, a Jordanian one on the East Bank and a Palestinian one on the West Bank. There would be separate authorities in each district under a single army. The King would be the head of the army and the state. A leading Palestinian figure on the West Bank said:

> This idea was slightly possible some ten years ago, as the Palestinian people were still relatively weak and did not enjoy world public support for their cause.... But why should we accept this today? ... I think even the King would agree that the events and circumstances have changed.... Total federation is just not practical until we have our state and then decide what to do....

This entire issue revolves around the fact that Jordan has been accepted as a member of the community of nations. Jordan is also a valuable member of the Arab community of nations. Jordan has earned wide respect for its U.N. and global conference participation. The world community agrees that it must be protected. A Lebanese scholar noted that "the world agrees that Jordan, like Israel, must not be destroyed.... But the Palestinians must also be given their rightful seat in the community of nations, although the state that will be created now will be quite different from what might have been established forty years ago." Arabs acknowledge that they must make do with the artificial borders and political units that were determined by the colonialist powers. A Kuwaiti diplomatic official remarked that "we will suffer as our African friends suffer over the shameless way the old imperialist powers artificially divided peoples and uprooted some from their age-old homelands... Palestinians should be in Palestine, not Jordan and Lebanon... but what can we do but adapt?"

Similar to the prevailing belief in Africa, Arabs believe that any attempted redrawing of their borders, based on topographical or historical grounds, could set loose an endless stream of violent conflicts that would persist for decades. The essential importance of respecting the principle of internationally recognized borders was supported by an overwhelming majority of the *1979 Middle East sample*. A Syrian official argued that "if this does not become accepted by everyone [Arabs], then there can never be peace in our region, never...."

Palestinians note that most Western and Israeli support for the concept of confederation is tied to the belief that an independent Palestine will become uncontrollable and will represent a threat to its neighbors. Fears that the Palestinian state would become another Cuba are deeply held by many Israelis and Westerners. Most Israeli support for the confederation option includes the provision that the Palestinian component of the confederation be permanently demilitarized. Demilitarization is completely unacceptable to the Palestinians. Their arguments are based not only upon the desire for some independence, but also on security concerns.

It is important to determine what advantages a confederation would hold for the protagonists. For the Israelis, there are perceptions that a more moderate policy would be followed by a new confederated Palestinian entity. For some Palestinians, confederation represents a very important opportunity to end Israeli domination of the West Bank and Gaza, and to achieve more independence than the Palestinians have had in their entire history. For the other Arab states, the confederation could serve as a model for additional Arab efforts to establish unity. Some Arabs also believe that confederation would help keep the Palestinians restrained in their international activities.

There are differences of opinion as to whether or not this type of union would truly benefit the economic viability of either the Palestinians or the Jordanians. Both would have to carefully consider the options. Jordan certainly is more advanced in terms of both its industry and its prosperous service economy. The West Bank and Gaza, on the other hand, are largely agricultural areas, with Gaza also having the potential to be an important port. As previously discussed, the West Bank could become a major finance and commercial center for the region.

Some Palestinians argue against the economic benefits that many outside observers say will accrue from a combined Jordanian-West Bank/Gaza economy. Neither Jordan nor the West Bank and Gaza have an abundance of raw materials, sufficient water, or a strong industrial base. Both will continue to be dependent upon service industries and the assistance of outside states, they argue. Others point to Jordan's booming economy, efficient management, and the possibility of discovering oil in Jordan.

Israelis point to the resolutions of the Eighth Session of the Palestine National Council, which met in Cairo in the winter of 1971. It was affirmed that Jordan and Palestine are bound together by a national bond. It was agreed that they represented a single geographical unit united by history, culture, and language. It was noted that the establishment of political entities east and west of the Jordan River was void of legal basis and represented the outcome of divisions caused by the colonialist powers after 1919. An Arab League official responded:

> Just as we have come to accept the idea that Israel is here to stay in what should be Palestinian lands, they [Israelis] must come to accept that a Palestinian state is coming to stay.... The question is not whether it is our preference or theirs, but it reflects the reality of our age.... The 1971 statements reflected that time.... You will remember that the situation in 1971 was quite different than today.... But remember, you cannot sweep the whole issue under the rug any longer.

A PLO representative noted that the Israelis refuse to talk publicly about a Palestinian state because "they know that we will compete with them in everything, including economic and technological superiority." He added, "Did you know that there is a reason why the West continues to focus on a Palestinian *entity*? ... It is their dream that we will fall (out of desperation) for any solution."

Emotions run high when discussing the future of the West Bank and Gaza. Most Israelis publicly talk about a possible Palestinian *entity*. Even in private discussions, the words *Palestinian state* are rarely used by policymakers and others in the mainstream of Israeli public opinion. The word *entity* has a connotation that implies a denial of the right to full national sovereignty.

A Palestinian asked, "Have you ever looked up the definition of this term *entity*? ... I will tell you what Webster's [dictionary] says it means—*existence* or *being*.... So let us think of this Western talk about a Palestinian *entity*.... It means we will be given our existence? ... No, thank you .... We already exist." A colleague argued, "How can you take an occupied territory and make it confederate with a sovereign state and say that the problem is over? ... What problem is that supposed to solve?" A Jordanian businessman who is a Palestinian added, "The joke of all of this is that Israel is mentioned as *giving* the Palestinians the right to some demilitarized land providing we accept a confederal arrangement with Jordan.... Tell me what confederations in history have been so established ... and what ever happened to your Western doctrine that *sovereign states* make up a confederation?"

Jordanian officials agree that a confederation is composed of sovereign states and that discussion of confederation must be determined by the Palestinians and Jordanians following the achievement of national self-determination of the Palestinian people.

Special Considerations

Arabs believe that the ability of the Palestinians to achieve freedom for the West Bank/Gaza depends upon whether Jordan and the PLO are able to achieve a limited amount of agreement, prior to their negotiation with the Israelis, on a joint bargaining position and plan of action for the transitional phases as well as on the details of the election and an overall framework of agreement. An Israeli political official in Jerusalem admitted that the "inability of the Arabs, in particular Jordan and the Palestinians, to plan and undertake common positions strengthens our [Israeli] hand. . . . The best chance they probably have is agreement on confederation."

Several Israelis who favored confederation noted that most Western officials who support this idea tend to do so because "they feel that a conservative Jordan will temper a radical Palestinian state." They note that the opposite possibility could result as well. Most Arabs and many Israelis believe that the Palestinian state will act as a responsible member of the community of nations upon gaining its independence. A PLO representative remarked, "Begin became respectable, didn't he . . . and let us consider the enormous amount of work that must be done for our people — we must regain generations of lost economic and social opportunities. . . ." Arabs and Israelis are closely watching the Zimbabwe elections in Africa. A Jordanian official argued that "you should wait and see if Mugabe wins in Zimbabwe. . . . He has been called a Marxist by the Western press. . . . He is not a Marxist but a nationalist and you people in the West better begin to realize that there is a difference."

A Syrian diplomat asked, "Why is the talk of confederation restricted to Palestine and Jordan?. . . There is a possibility that other states in the region would be interested as well. . . ." An Israeli who strongly favors confederation of the West Bank with Jordan noted, "I would not be so happy if the confederation extended to include Syria or, almost unimaginable, Iraq." He had earlier noted, "Yet the idea of confederation is usually used in history for a short period . . . ten to fifty years, and in that way we must be open-minded. . . . One cannot plan for fifty years away, but we must find a way to resolve this impasse of having an intelligent and now popular people [Palestinians] without a state of their own. . . . It just cannot work like this much longer."

A Palestinian political leader on the West Bank was asked to comment on confederation. He said:

> A confederation someday, why not?.... But it cannot be forced on us and it must be thought through carefully which has not yet been done.... It is interesting to us why Israel and its friends believe that only this idea of confederation can solve the Palestinian problem.... Why do American presidents continue to deny our right to statehood, yet recognize that we should be part of a confederation with Jordan? Perhaps their advisers should go study international law and history.

The confusion continues over how a confederation would be established. There is no doubt that a transition from Israeli occupation to confederation would be a difficult and time-consuming process. An Egyptian scholar summarized the problem this way:

> The irony of the confederation approach is that whereas it represents a possibly good solution for everyone in the future, it is quite difficult to implement in the short term.... However, this matter must really be decided by two and only two groups headed by King Hussein and Mr. Arafat.... If they believe it's workable, then who are the rest of us to say it's too difficult?

An Israeli government official added his personal comments, after explaining some of his government's ideas on confederation: "Quite honestly, I'm confused about it.... Many people think it's the solution, but we just don't know all that it involves.... In fact, we doubt if anybody from Washington to Amman understands how the idea might possibly be implemented ... but it's worth a try, I suppose." A PLO official noted that "I am certainly not opposed to the eventuality of some union with Hussein's Jordan, and it's good to dwell on the possibilities, but first let us take the prerequisite — national statehood — and go from there...."

The reader must understand that, for the first time in the last forty years, the Palestinian people see that world opinion favors their right to self-determination and establishment of their own state. The gradual shifts in European attitudes on this matter have particularly reinforced these beliefs. Similar to the Rhodesian struggle for independence, ideas (such as immediate confederation of Jordan and the West Bank) that might have been acceptable five years ago are unacceptable to most Palestinians today. An Israeli Knesset member recently stated, "I am afraid that our delaying tactics have caught up with us. Now we will pay a price that few Israelis like to pay—seeing the Palestinians established in their own state. I'm afraid it's only a matter of time now."

United Nations involvement. The transition of the occupied territories from Israeli occupation to confederation could require a substantial involvement by objective third parties. It is commonly assumed that a confederation agreement between Jordan and a Palestinian entity would take place in transitional phases. A key question is whether such phases can take place prior to the granting of self-determination to the Palestinians. Most experts agree that a confederation must take place between two or more sovereign entities. It is expected that one or more official plebiscites would require new types of third-party roles. Most Arabs and Israelis believed that the United Nations would be best suited to carry out such activities. The United Nations' role in the Middle East has included a long-time peacekeeping presence. The record includes observation duties as fulfilled by UNTSO (United Nations Truce Supervisory Organization, 1948 to present), together with peacekeeping missions in the Gaza, UNEF I. (United Nations Emergency Force I., 1956 to 1967); the Sinai, UNEF II. (United Nations Emergency Force II., 1973 to 1979); the Golan Heights, UNDOF (United Nations Disengagement Observer Force, 1973 to present); and Lebanon, UNIFIL (United Nations Interim Force in Lebanon, 1978 to present). These international missions have overall earned the respect of the protagonists. Confidence in their ability is undermined only by the realities of international politics. For example, a peacekeeping force deployed between two or more protagonists is most effective when it has the support of the active protagonists in the conflict. The UNIFIL force in Lebanon is in a precarious position because some of the parties clearly do not want it to succeed. An Israeli journalist pondered the difficulties this way, "I believe that UNIFIL will not succeed because many of us lack the will to let it succeed. . . . Either give UNIFIL teeth [heavy armaments and the like] or resign yourselves to the fact that it cannot succeed." When asked about the performance of other U.N. peacekeeping efforts, the journalist replied, "Oh yes, they have been quite good on the whole in carrying out their duties — but that is because each of the parties had vested interests in assuring their success. Take the Golan force [UNDOF], for example — Syria and Israel clearly want the Golan quiet."

The United Nations' record for supervising plebiscites is extensive and well-respected. It includes successful cases in the Togoland (1956) and the Cameroons (1959 to 1960). There is little doubt that the United Nations could agree to accept supervision of elections and transitional peacekeeping responsibilities in the Middle East. The European Community, the Commonwealth, or other international organizations could also be asked to play a role.

Limited Armament Zones. One of the most important ideas that could help to assure the success of this option is the willingness of Israel, Egypt, Syria, and Jordan to agree, during the transitional period, to restrict certain armaments from a designated area bordering on the West Bank and Gaza. It has been suggested that tanks, field artillery, surface-to-surface missiles, surface-to-air missiles, and mortars be prohibited from these areas as a confidence-building measure for both the Palestinians and Israelis.

The Israelis fear that Arab weapons could quickly be transported into a Palestinian state, thus posing an immediate threat to Israeli security. Similarly, Palestinians fear sophisticated Israeli weapons massed on its borders. It is hoped that the three states—Israel, Jordan, and Syria—might agree to some mutual limitations of offensive weapons during the transitional period. One Arab military officer suggested that the restriction be considered a permanent one to help build confidence and reduce tensions in the area.

Supervision of the special limited armament zones and demilitarization of the Palestinian state itself during transition could be made by United Nations observers, together with a combined supervisory force made up of unarmed military representatives of the Palestinian state and its neighbors. Surveillance technology would include satellite reconnaissance (with information relayed to the United Nations staff); air reconnaissance (similar to that employed in the Sinai peacekeeping experience); night viewing optical equipment; electronic and electromagnetic observation stations; and mobile supervisory units.

The technology and the experience of international peacekeeping does exist. The steps envisioned now for the transitional stages are meant to provide and build confidence. In addition, they serve as an early warning capability should any one of the protagonists decide to violate the spirit or letter of agreements. Greater attention will be given to these problems in the author's next study, to be completed in 1981.

Other Ideas for Consideration

Most of the many options suggested by members of the *1979 Middle East sample* dealt with the West Bank and Gaza. There was a shared belief that progress over the Golan, Jerusalem, or Lebanon depends upon progress being made over the Palestinian issue. An Israeli military official remarked that "most of us realize very well that Golan and Lebanon are as good as resolved once the Palestinians are happy." In order to demonstrate to the reader, however, the kinds of private thinking that were expressed to the Task Force members during the 1979 visit, several brief examples are presented on these other components of the conflict.

A Demilitarized Golan Heights

Egyptian military officials remarked that the most confusing policy discrepancies they had seen in Israeli official statements concerned the Golan. One officer noted:

> I understand that the Western plateau of the Golan is a steep precipitous cliff rising to heights from 425 to nearly 1700 feet

above the floor of the valley. [Hula Valley is some of the richest agricultural land in Israel.]... And yet an Israeli cabinet member told a press meeting that Israel would practically offer the Syrians the return of the Golan Heights in exchange for a peace treaty.[21]

Prime Minister Begin and Mr. Rabin have stated that they could consider only a partial withdrawal from the Golan in a peace settlement, with an adjustment being required in the international boundary. Yet, Mr. Begin later told an interviewer:

> We shall never withdraw from the Golan Heights.... There is no such thing as sacrificing security in return for peace. There is no peace without security. Without the Golan Heights, there is no security. We shall therefore make peace while we are still on the Golan Heights....[22]

The Golan Heights represents the largest concentration of Israeli settlements in the occupied territories. (See map on page 77.) One Israeli businessman noted that there were at least three plausible reasons for Israeli settlements: "Either they are meant to show that Israel intends to keep the territory indefinitely; or because they are needed for current security; or that they represent a pressure and bargaining card during a protracted negotiation." An Israeli defense analyst added that "one can make a good case that security is not the major purpose of these settlements ... although they could play a marginal role in that the reservists in the Golan civilian settlements would be on the spot if an attack took place." Other Israeli defense experts argue that Israel cannot forsake its Golan settlements, due to security considerations, as they are said to provide an on-site infrastructure necessary in wartime.

Syrian President Assad has frequently stated that Israel has never claimed the Golan for religious, historical, or legal reasons. Syria is completely opposed to any territorial adjustments. A Syrian military official argued, "Why should we make concessions on what has always been our land and what has never been claimed by them [Israel] as their land? ... Even today they do not claim this except as security requirements." A military officer in Damascus referred to an article on the military significance of the Golan that was published in an American book edited by two Israelis.[23] He said:

> Let me tell you what it said — If a friendly neighbor controlled the Golan, it was not of importance to Israel ... and yet in the hands of a foe, it is a great threat as it is only 50 miles to Haifa....
>
> Now I ask you, do you think that it also mentioned that the distance from the same plateau to Damascus is something like 35 miles? No, it did not. So the American reader sees a poor

threatened Israel and a mighty, protected Syria.... You [the author] have stood on Mount Hermon with the United Nations and looked down to Damascus.... Now you tell me, is this a one-sided affair?

An Israeli defense analyst noted that the 1967 cease-fire line and its modification of 1974 is not a defensible border for either the Israelis or Syrians. He explained that "for the Syrians, it exposes the entire Bashan plateau and the plains to Damascus while for us the line provides depth but not a good positional defense." (See map on page 176.) Syrian leadership has accepted, in principle, the establishment of a narrow demilitarized strip with the conditions that Israel withdraw totally from the lands occupied in 1967 and establish an identical zone of demilitarized territory on its side of the border. Privately there are signs of greater flexibility regarding the role of third parties in a Golan settlement including discussion of early warning problems and defense of the two areas where a tank crossing could be made across the Golan. Israel's three major security concerns on the Golan are two tank-crossing areas, the need for early warning capability, and assurances of restriction of SAM (surface-to-air missiles) which could neutralize the Israeli air force if heavily deployed.

An Arab journalist suggested that any consideration for adjustment by the Syrians or Israelis must relate to *people*. He continued, "Some 100,000 Syrians are refugees from the Golan even today ... and don't forget that Syrian artillery on the Heights again would jeopardize the Israeli population in north Galilee." A distinguished Arab diplomat said that "the solution seems a fairly straightforward one to me.... The Israeli top defense and strategic thinkers all say we [Israel] can afford to give back all of the Golan except the 15 to 20 kilometers closest to Israel.... Well, then that could be a formula.... Israel withdraws from all of the Golan and the area of the 15 to 20 kilometers becomes demilitarized Syrian land with an international presence... perhaps one with teeth...."

This argument suggests a scenario which is similar to one frequently alluded to by Arabs and Israelis during the Task Force discussions in 1978 and 1979. According to such a scenario, it would be possible to demilitarize, under international supervision, the belt of land of the Golan, some 20 kilometers wide which borders on Israel. The United Nations force currently serving with success in the Golan, UNDOF, could be reduced in size and given a new mandate to permanently observe the adherence to the demilitarized nature of this zone. In addition, the remainder of the Golan evacuated by the Israelis and a proportional area on the Israeli side of the Golan could be designated limited armament zones. These zones would be restricted to offensive weapons such as tanks, field artillery, surface-to-surface and surface-to-air missiles, armored infantry, and commando units. The construction of fortifications would not be permitted. A team of

Syrian Map of the Region

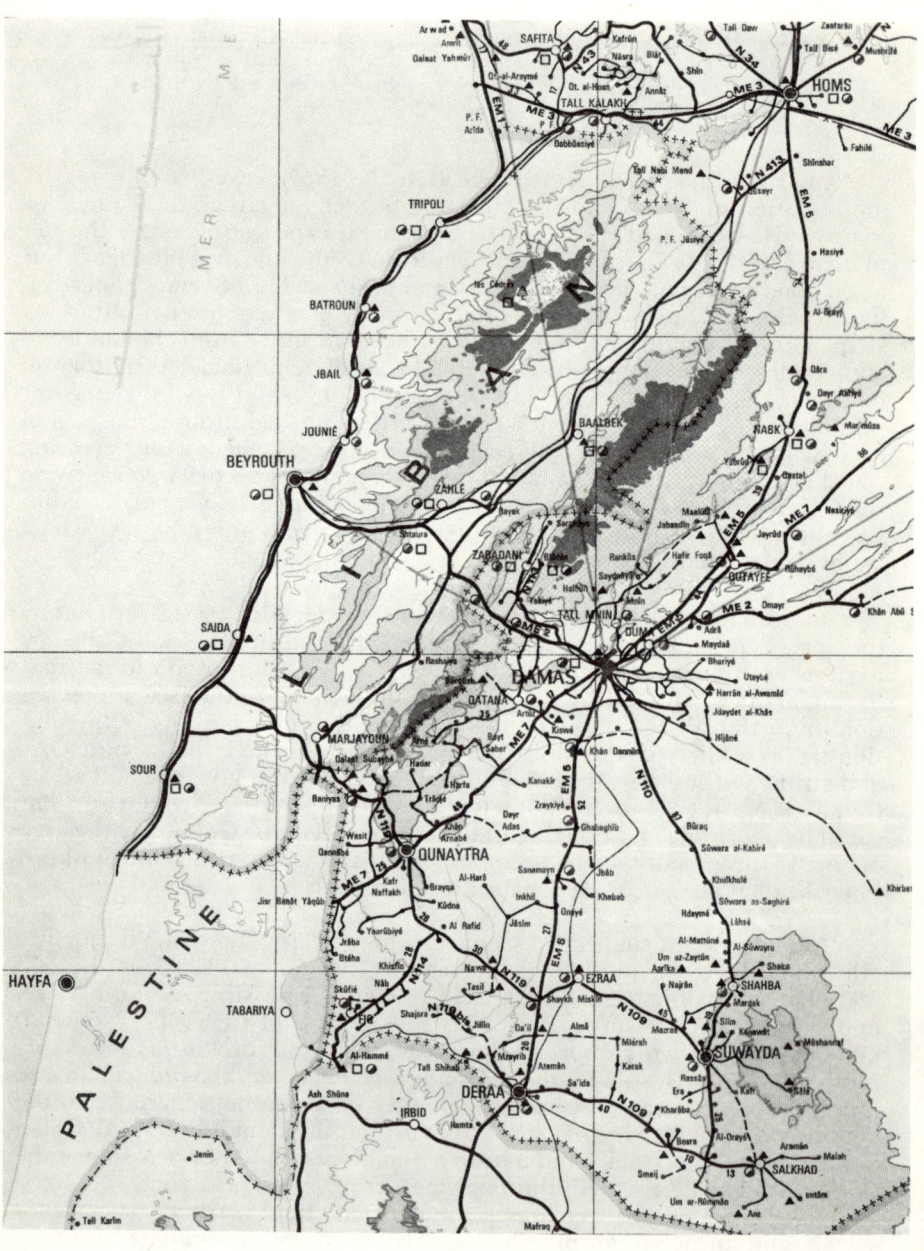

Syrie Carte routière et touristique, Damascus.

UNDOF observers could be assigned to verify compliance with the terms of the Israeli-Syrian limited armament agreement. The 20 kilometers could be reduced to one-third that amount if certain specific defensive measures were provided by the third party in the demilitarized area.

In this scenario, UNDOF could be given electronic observation posts to be stationed in the eastern and central sectors of the Golan Heights. Some experts suggested that the United States and the Soviet Union be asked to supply teams of civilian experts to be based in the demilitarized zone. All of the occupied territory would be vacated by the Israelis, including the settlements. An agreement would be made between Syria and Israel regarding compensation for damages and the determination of the future use of Israeli settlement property.

Joint Israeli-Syrian supervisory teams could be established to work in cooperation with the UNDOF forces. Confidence-building measures would be instituted by the two protagonists to relieve further the tensions of mistrust and hostility that exist between Israel and Syria.

Other ideas suggested to meet particular concerns raised by Israelis and Arabs include the establishment of wider, limited armament zones on either side of the demilitarized area; and the possibility of employing a satellite channel by the United Nations that would provide information to each state on major troop movements. The satellite information would be interpreted with a team of civilian experts drawn from states that are permanent members of the Security Council. An Arab educator asked if an office could "be established in Vienna or Geneva with both states having a small representative delegation to review the satellite photographs and meet with the teams of civilian experts to analyze the materials." An Israeli defense analyst responded, "I am not sure how we [IDF] would react to such an idea. . . . Since we already have better information than they [Arabs] do. I suppose they would benefit from it more than we would, but I don't know yet."

Numerous Israelis stated that they would be comfortable living with a demilitarized Golan Heights, provided that the United States made a security guarantee that if Syria should break the agreement, American supplies of essential weapons and other support would be forthcoming. An Israeli politician stated, "Yes, we want that extra insurance policy. . . . Of course, if it is real peace, we shall never need to cash it in, so to speak, but we cannot trust the Syrians, of all of them [the Arabs], we cannot trust the Syrians most of all."

Other Israelis believe that an alliance or merger of Iraq with Syria would cause most Israelis to reject acceptance of a demilitarized Golan Heights. As we have seen, there is a great deal of Israeli concern over the combined fighting capability of the *Eastern Front*. Short of such an alliance, a vast majority of Arabs and Israelis noted that this demilitarization scenario is possible and perhaps probable. The Syrians, however, make it clear that Syria will not consider resolution of the Golan problem while the Palestinians continue to be denied their basic right to self-determination.

The composition of the third-party presence in the Golan is of particular concern to the Israelis. One Israeli official was quoted in the press as saying, "Who's going to guarantee [demilitarization]? ... the United Nations? The U.N. only knows how to write reports."[24] A senior Israeli diplomatic official disagreed:

> I must tell you privately that despite our periodic pronouncements about the ineptness of the U.N., we are of course pleased with its performance on the Golan and in Sinai, prior to the Treaty.... We detest its [U.N.] politicization in the General Assembly, but we do recognize that it has a role to play, particularly in the peacekeeping area.... We all must remember that in peacetime there is goodwill of all parties ... that makes a large difference for U.N. effectiveness.

One Israeli retired military officer stated, "I think the wider the demilitarized area and adjoining limited armament zones, the harder it will be for either side to launch a strategic surprise attack." A Syrian tradesman remarked, "Do not forget that we have more to fear about their [Israeli] violations than vice versa, so we would prefer some arrangements whereby their [Israeli] preemptive attack would necessitate killing American, French, Russian, British peacekeeping troops.... Isn't that a deterrent of some sort?"

A distinguished Egyptian military officer noted that "the agreements on limiting weapons in certain areas have worked very well.... Those kind of agreements are easy to implement if there is the political will.... In peace there is the political will and what you are talking about is in peace, isn't it?"

Most Israeli members of the *1979 Middle East sample* agreed that the occupied strip of territory Israel holds on the Golan is too narrow to serve as a useful land warning zone that would give adequate time for the mobilization of reserves in case of a Syrian attack. A surprise attack in the brief scenario presented here would require breaking a peace agreement; introducing troops into the limited armament zone and crossing a demilitarized zone, both manned by international forces (including possibly personnel of the governments of the great powers); and meeting other obstacles that might be set by the international guarantor force. It is this latter area that offers most promise to strategic thinkers of both sides. For example, it has been suggested that automatic explosive devices be planted under critical roadways and paths where tanks and personnel carriers of either side might try to pass in an attack. The UNDOF commander would have detonator controls to destroy the roadways by activating the automatic explosive devices. Additional measures of varying degrees of sophistication could be undertaken as well, including sophisticated minefields and antitank trenches to inhibit a tank assault by Israel or Syria on the other through the Golan.

A Syrian official noted, "As part of a comprehensive settlement, we Syrians are willing to resolve the conflict, but Israel must withdraw from occupied territory that even it does not claim as its own land. . . . Security in the long term can only come when neighbors are not occupied . . . and when there is peace." Most Israelis agree that the Golan issue will be resolved when there is the political will for peace although many express a deeply-held reluctance to trust the other.

The Future Status of Jerusalem

The Jerusalem issue, more than any other, arouses emotion among both Israelis and Arabs. All of the protagonists agree that access to religious places must be allowed for people of all faiths to exercise freedom of worship, and to transit and visit the holy places without discrimination or harassment. An overwhelming percentage, of the *1979 Middle East sample* agreed that the holy sites should be administered by representatives of the respective faiths.

Jerusalem has been conquered more than three dozen times in its 4,000 year history. There have been more than three dozen detailed plans submitted for resolving the Jerusalem problem since 1967. The Israelis and Arabs claim that Jerusalem will never again be divided. The Arabs demand that all of East Jerusalem be returned to Arab rule. Many of the plans submitted for resolving the impasse call for the internationalization of the city, although such proposals have been completely rejected by the Israeli government.

The reader must realize that Jerusalem has an equally strong religious, historical, and emotional attraction for Jews and Moslems alike. The Task Force found no Israelis or Arabs who were willing to cede Jerusalem to the other. The Task Force members believe that the Jerusalem issue will be the most difficult to resolve. An Israeli politician noted, "Americans would enjoy being arbiter of this one [issue] since it is a clear case of two parties with legitimate reasons and arguments of equal strength. It's perfect for an American concessionary compromise attempt — which I doubt will succeed."

Jerusalem Mayor Teddy Kollek has argued that Jerusalem's problems will not be resolved by stating immutable positions, "such as Jerusalem being the eternal capital of Israel." Mayor Kollek has suggested a borough plan for Jerusalem, but he has noted that "the city has 100,000 residents who hold Jordanian passports and regard themselves as alien in Israel."[25] He and other Israelis are in no hurry to see changes in the current status. Kollek has argued that a divided city would bring back the barbed wire and minefields of the past and was clearly unacceptable. He argues that current conditions are satisfactory in Jerusalem. Few Arabs would agree. Most of the *1979 sample* believed that Jerusalem would be the last problem resolved during comprehensive negotiations. All members of the *sample* who addressed the Jerusalem question believed that a compromise solution could be found if there was a mutual desire for full peace.

Most Arab and some Israeli *sample* respondents told Task Force members that a possible compromise formula might call for an undivided Jerusalem municipality with two districts, one under *Israeli* administration and sovereignty and one under *Arab* administration and sovereignty. A phased transitional plan would have to be designed by the Israelis together with officials from an emerging Palestinian government in the West Bank. This might be a Palestinian state, or a Palestinian entity in confederation (or federation) with Jordan or other arrangement. This idea presupposes a real peace, not a temporary truce.

Some of the specific ideas which are mentioned include the following:

- A joint municipal board or council representing both Arab and Israeli residents could be established and made responsible for the supervision of basic municipal services and functions in the two districts of the city.

- Freedom of communication and movement between the two districts would be guaranteed and supervised by police patrols consisting of residents of both sectors of the city.

- The entire municipality would be demilitarized during the transitional period. A small United Nations observer mission could be attached to the local police, in particular, to patrol areas near the religious shrines and areas where tensions are high.

The Jerusalem issue, despite its great complexity and the high emotional attachment that all of the protagonists hold for it, is privately considered by most Arabs and Israelis to be a solvable problem once there is the commitment to achieve peace. Confidence-building is perhaps most crucial in this case of Jerusalem. Jerusalem could become the example of how Jews and Moslems can live and work together in peaceful relations. Jerusalem could become a major communication center for the region. Tourism, one of the largest revenue-producing activities in the region, would be expected to increase when violence terminates in peace. Many believe that tourism to the religious sites in the West Bank (such as Bethlehem and Jericho) as well as in Galilee, would increase as joint Moslem-Israeli-Christian tourist ventures were established in Jerusalem. Coordination would increase tourism at the religious sites, which are spread out among Israel, Egypt, and the West Bank, and would clearly benefit each of the parties.

There is, understandably, much bad feeling in Jerusalem over the consequences that have accompanied the Arab-Israeli conflict. But most of the Jerusalem residents to whom the Task Force members spoke were willing to put bitterness aside. There is no reason to believe that Israel would relocate its capital elsewhere. It is possible that the Palestinian state, if it is created, would also choose to locate its capital in Jerusalem. An Arab lawyer asked, "Is that such a bad idea? . . . We all say it cannot happen, but that is what we said about Israel being permanently accepted, and the odds of the Palestinians ever regaining a homeland. . . . Let's stop saying it cannot be done. If God wills, it will be done." His Tel Aviv counterpart argued that "our war mentality makes it a dream—or for some a nightmare—to think of Arab sovereignty over one foot of Jerusalem. But if there were real peace, I could dream it and accept it." Most Israelis were not that willing to consider compromise on Jerusalem in Task Force discussions.

A Federated State of Lebanon

Most Lebanese agree that until the Palestinian question is resolved, there can be no peace for the Lebanese people. There has been some progress in rebuilding the Lebanese army during the past year, but the divisions in Lebanese politics and society remain deep-seated. Yet, a senior Christian leader remarked that Moslems will be treated much better in the *new Lebanon* than they were in the old. Young people are learning that religious intolerance can lead only to terrible violence. Most Lebanese families have been affected directly — many losing sons and daughters — since the 1975 civil war erupted. The civilian casualty list in Beirut alone is staggering.

Lebanese officials estimate that probably less than one-third of the 350,000 Palestinians living in Lebanon would leave to begin a new life in a newly independent Palestinian state. Many Lebanese are willing to accept some Palestinians as Lebanese residents or at least as semi-permanent workers. Most Lebanese believe that hard work, large doses of third-party relief, and rehabilitation assistance, coupled with the establishment of a home for the Palestinians, would enable Lebanon to regain its old stature as a major center of finance, tourism, and trade. It must be noted that most Lebanese do not believe that a *solution* to the Palestinian issue can be successful which excludes the well-entrenched PLO and the 350,000 Palestinian refugees who are in Lebanon from pre-1967 Israel. A senior Lebanese military official presented his concern: "The Jordanian option which is the dream of the Camp David people would address only one aspect of the Palestinian issue — the occupation of 1¼ million Palestinians. It would not answer the larger questions of the PLO and the countless refugees who still would be homeless . . . . You must face that issue."

Many Lebanese argue that a possible solution for Lebanon, once the Palestinian issue is resolved, would be the establishment of a federal form of government, made up of several autonomous units dominated demographically by particular religious sects. A respected Christian leader argued:

> One can easily see that there would be a Christian sector, possibly several, a Druze, and some Shiite and Sunni [Moslem] as well. . . . The areas are quite sharply defined actually . . . and many Lebanese of all faiths are discussing this already at the village level. . . . I myself have attended several religious meetings where people of other faiths and Christians have discussed this idea in some detail. . . .

Most Lebanese believe that the Civil War, which has disrupted Lebanese society, will leave an indelible imprint upon the hearts and minds of the Lebanese people. Although deep power struggles are anticipated among religious groups as well as within them, it is expected that a greater commitment and loyalty to the nation will develop. In addition, Lebanese believe that a system for resolving domestic disputes will be instituted as part of the new system of government that will be ushered in when peace is achieved.

Most Lebanese believe that the government should try to devote more energy to rebuilding its armed forces. In addition, they believe Lebanon should support a process which would facilitate the withdrawal of Palestinian fedayeen and the Syrian peacekeeping force. Some Lebanese believe that the Syrians and Israelis have other plans for Lebanon, including annexing some Lebanese territory. The majority, however, believe that the political situation will change and that the pre-1975 Lebanon will re-emerge with one distinct difference—a more workable and fair federal governing system will be devised.

Most Lebanese are resigned to the continued presence of Syrian and Palestinian armed forces in Lebanese territory. A Lebanese businessman noted, "We live for tomorrow and the past, we tolerate the present because there is absolutely nothing we can do." Suggestions that the Lebanese army should fight Syrian or Palestinian troops have little public support for ideological and pragmatic reasons. The planned withdrawal of Syrian troops from Beirut and their replacement by units of the Lebanese army is an important first step in the process of rebuilding Lebanon.

The Lebanese component of the Arab-Israeli conflict perhaps reflects best the complexities, fears, and misunderstandings of the entire conflict. A Lebanese Christian businessman gave his summary this way:

Lebanon is still in a state of war with Israel, as are Jordan and Syria, and they [Israel] with us. This is not peace, but a time of continued violence in a state of war.... The Israelis are here to stay ... and so are the Palestinians.... If the latter were a refugee problem only, they would have gone away by now — melted out of their camps into other societies.... Violence is two-sided ... Yes, Israeli civilians die in terrorist attacks, but many more Lebanese and Palestinian civilians die in Israeli attacks, even today.... Yes, I want the Palestinians to leave Lebanon, but they have no place to go; so they will stay here.... They cannot stay here forever.... Look, let us face it that unless this whole conflict ends, we are building to the day when a whole people—or peoples—will be destroyed. Its only a matter of conjecture whether this means Israelis, Lebanese, Palestinians, or others. Yes, here in the land of the Bible and the Koran we spend decades working towards killing others. Maybe one day we will understand that this can stop.... I'm afraid it will come too late.

Conclusion

It is understandable that most Arabs and Israelis have grown tired of three decades of stalemate, fear, and violence—characteristics of the Arab-Israeli conflict. It is equally understandable that most Arab and Israeli leaders lack confidence in the basic intentions of their adversaries.

In scores of private discussions, Arab and Israeli leaders attempted to convince the Task Force that they were desirous of ending the conflict. Most argued that the overwhelming majority of their people now accepted the right of the Israeli and Palestinian peoples to live within secure and recognized borders. It was explained that an acceptance of *realpolitik* and frustration over the impasse of *no war/no peace* in the region had led to the softening of the previously immutable positions that denied the right of other peoples — Palestinians and/or Israelis — to exist as independent nations.

These efforts to convince the Task Force members of a basic change of attitude were, however, combined with attempts to persuade us that the private statements of the other protagonists, particularly those which differed from publicly expressed views, were not valid or representative of real intentions. For example, a senior Israeli analyst argued, "You will see that Israelis, in our private opinions, are willing to make concessions. . . .You must study Arab [public] statements, not their privately expressed views or unannounced actions to know that they are unwilling to make concessions on the basic issues."

Similarly, numerous Arab leaders, while expressing a belief that today a majority of the Israeli people desired peace, argued that the privately expressed views of the Israeli leadership were misleading. They were said to be ploys designed to trick Arabs and others into believing that the expansionist aims long held by Israeli leaders had changed. "The Labor Party," argued an influential Arab political leader, "is no different in its goals than Begin — they are smoother in their tactics that is the only difference."

Both Arab and Israeli officials made reference to specific uncompromising public statements made by the leadership of their adversary. These were offered as evidence that the ultimate strategy of that adversary remained unchanged—that is, the adversary is still fundamentally opposed to a comprehensive settlement. The Task Force members often mentioned to these officials that such claims had also been raised by the other protagonists against them.

A Syrian military official emphasized that "the critical problem, then, appears to be how do you build my confidence that they [Israelis] really desire what they say they desire?" An Israeli Knesset member asked, "Why should they [Arabs] believe what I say privately? . . . I don't blame them [Arabs] for thinking [that] I am feeding you a line of bait. . . and so how can I trust what they [Arabs] are saying?" Psychological barriers of mistrust can be broken down, however. Israelis give as evidence the results of President Sadat's initiatives to Israel.

Egyptians and Israelis argue that the Egyptian-Israeli Peace Treaty and the process of its implementation will help build confidence among both peoples that peace can be a permanent condition in the region. Other Arabs contend that such a partial settlement is insufficient. They argue that if Israelis wanted real peace, they would stop their government from establishing new settlements in the occupied territories. "Actions speak louder than words," commented a senior Jordanian official, pointing to a map of new Israeli settlements established since the Camp David agreements in the occupied territories. This issue (of the settlements) demonstrates the need for the reader to objectively analyze motivations underlying words and actions. A significant degree of analysis and subjective judgment is needed in order to reconcile actions with words, or public statements with privately-expressed views.

Thought-provoking questions arise when one considers various points of view of the adversaries. For example, if the PLO's ultimate intention is to be a heavily armed Soviet ally in the region, why does it favor a comprehensive settlement which stipulates exclusion of great power military presence and an agreement to limit arms in the area? If the aim of the *Eastern Front* is to attack and defeat Israel militarily, why do Jordan, Iraq, and Syria fail to coordinate their military systems, communications, logistics, and maneuvers? If Israel's intention is permanent retention of the West Bank and Gaza against the wishes of the United States and the world community, why doesn't it annex these areas? If the PLO is not representative of the Palestinian people, why do Palestinians working outside the occupied territories voluntarily pay 5 percent of their income to the PLO?

There are several types of answers to such questions. "The easiest answers," argued a retired Jordanian official, "are those based on our stereotyped images from the past . . . [based upon] intentions." An Israeli diplomat argued, "If we reflect carefully on such questions, we can argue that there are two or more contradictory explanations depending on the bias one uses to analyze. . . . We have always answered such questions from what I call the *worst case* scenario. . .this is quite fair, I think, but it doesn't give anybody any benefits of doubt about actual intentions. . . ." A Jordanian official gave another example: "Why didn't we destroy Israel's potash project on the Dead Sea?"

For more than a decade, the Israelis have produced potash from the waters of the Dead Sea. Israelis are quick to point out that a simple act of sabotage could easily have been carried out by the Arabs to destroy the mechanical devices required to produce chemicals from the Dead Sea water. Yet, such sabotage attempts were not made.

Today, Jordan is nearing completion of a $450 million Arab Potassium Project on the Dead Sea to reclaim potash, a major source of fertilizer. This project is under the direction of the Hashemite Kingdom of Jordan, with 51 percent ownership. The remaining 49 percent of investment was made by various Arab individuals and states. A senior official involved in this project noted that the Jordanian dock is some 500 meters from the Israeli potash dock. "In addition," he added, "while we are going to be some 200 meters east of the truce line, Israel is 200 meters west of the truce line." Israeli and Jordanian officials agree that relatively small weapons could destroy both projects.

The Jordanians note that the Dead Sea is estimated to contain 22 billion tons of magnesium, 2 billion tons of potash, 12 billion tons of table salt, and 1 billion tons of bromide. Overall, some 145 billion tons of chemicals are said to be contained in the Dead Sea, enough to supply all possible Israeli and Jordanian envisioned needs for such materials for 800 years. A Jordanian official added that "at that time we will sit down with our [Semitic] cousins and decide what to do."

This simple project, located at the southern end of the Dead Sea, 1300 feet below sea level, is less than 200 kilometers from Amman, Jerusalem, and Tel Aviv. Several experts argued that the enormous mineral wealth of the Dead Sea could be a major source of fertilizer (potash), raw materials, export revenue, and an example of cooperation between Jordan, Israel, and a Palestinian entity on the West Bank. There was even discussion of the relative merits of constructing a joint railway to the ports of Aqaba (Jordan) and Elat (Israel). Currently, Israeli trucks carry the potash some 150 kilometers to Elat. And Jordan will have to haul potash to Aqaba. The railway could later be connected to Syria, Turkey, and Europe with a naval link via ferries to the Red Sea and elsewhere. "This scenario," noted a Palestinian business leader, "is the type of project many of us envision for the future of this region. . . .It may seem a distant dream today, but it is a possibility tomorrow."

An Israeli businessman and politician said, "You must understand that all of us in the region see the glass as being half-empty, not half-full. . . .When something happens that could be viewed as positive or negative, we assume the negative is the proper interpretation. . . .We need some confidence built here to overcome this routine mode of thinking." Some characterize private discussions as surges of wishful thinking. An Arab diplomat added, "At least today there is wishful thinking—five years ago we did not even have that."

The art of building an adversary's confidence in one's intentions is a difficult process. Such attempts are often seen as indicators of weakness, deception, or a willingness to achieve a settlement regardless of costs. Like all other fundamental relationships, confidence-building between peoples must be a mutual activity in order to succeed. A Lebanese lawyer argued that "first I must see that others truly desire peace, and then I will work to reduce the tensions caused by high insecurity and assessments of bad intent." That view is widely held throughout the Middle East.

A traditional method for eliminating feelings of high insecurity is to adopt measures that strengthen one's own military and psychological forces against an enemy. This approach could include procurement of more sophisticated weapons, entering into an alliance, launching a propaganda campaign among one's population or one's allies against the enemy, or launching a preemptive military strike. An Israeli defense expert argued that "it is clear that we have entered an era when these methods are inadequate." The alternative, however, is not particularly appealing to policy-makers. The Israeli defense expert emphasized that "each of us [protagonists] is reluctant to appear weak. . . .If we make any gesture toward moderation of our views, they [Arabs] harden their positions even further, thinking we are weak." The very talk of compromise can jeopardize the political standing and domestic or international support of a leader. The fact, however, that Arabs and Israelis are willing to discuss demilitarization arrangements, limited armament zones, neutrality scenarios, limitation of great power military presence, and the like indicates more of a willingness to negotiate in good faith. A Palestinian political official said that "every time a debate rages in Israel or within our PLO about the need for concessions, it makes compromise a little closer. . . .We both used to stand with uncompromising principles and you see what it achieved for us. . . we Palestinians used to say we wanted all of Palestine back. . . .The Israelis not long ago argued that they could never give up the Sinai settlements, airfields and oilfields. . . yet, look at the situation today." There were noticeable shifts in flexibility by Arabs and Israeli leaders' private statements between March 1978 and the winter of 1980.

A West Bank political leader discussed the process this way, "No one will be completely happy with every aspect of a comprehensive settlement." He continued, "We must, however, find a solution that is just and permanent—that means that I cannot go back to my family house in Jaffa or my people go back to 80 percent of their land of 1947. . . but then why can I not expect a homeland on the remaining 20 percent of my land?" An Israeli diplomat urged, "Privately we [Israelis] agree that the old days of fighting over our acceptance in the region must now change to accommodating ourselves to the realities of a permanent existence with Arab neighbors.... .If we cannot learn to live with such a situation, then Israel cannot likely continue to exist in this region." Another Israeli, a defense official, remarked that "in my heart, I can tell you I long for all of Eretz Israel... but I will certainly accept now a secure and permanent home in the region of our ancestors if our neighbors accept our permanent right to exist." Throughout the region soldiers, statesmen, businessmen, educators, and politicians agreed that the wars and acts of aggression must end and arrangements for guaranteed security be invented. Basic security has to be mutual and grounded in normal relations between neighboring states.

Beyond the search for security lies the search for a trust which is based on the confidence that the ultimate intention of each disputant is not a desire to defeat others or affect their religion, ideology, or territory. Without such a basic confidence, all the specific solutions, ideas, and good intentions are wasted. With such confidence, a comprehensive settlement and lasting peace is possible, and, indeed, many Arabs and Israelis would argue today, probable before the end of this decade.

The most frequent expressions made by Arabs and Israelis under the age of 45 with whom the Task Force members spoke are exemplified by a statement of a Syrian junior military officer: "If we must fight to defend our lives and land, or [fight] over our fellow Palestinians' right to self-determination, we will fight, but it appears to us that people throughout the region now want peace.... .I only can pray that this happens before the dreams, limbs and lives of my son and his generation in this area are sacrificed...two generations of this are enough."

Such quotations as presented throughout this publication, although carefully analyzed and selected to represent mainstream private opinions (as presented to Task Force members), remain but words until there is the political will to transform the words into policy.

Whether the political will for accommodation will match the emerging private feelings for peace that pervade the region remains to be seen. The review of perceived threats and security requirements of the Israelis, Palestinians, Jordanians, Egyptians, Syrians, and Lebanese presented in this volume is undertaken to serve several purposes:

- It demonstrates that the legitimate fears in this conflict are mutually held. Understanding the depth of such fears helps to explain the reservations and reluctance of the protagonists to accept proposed peacemaking initiatives.

- It indicates that security considerations in the Arab-Israeli conflict are political and psychological problems, as much as they are military problems.

- It demonstrates that when security problems are viewed from the perspectives of the various protagonists, compromise solutions can be developed to meet the basic security requirements of each party.

- It indicates that third parties might be asked to play a critical role in the resolution of the conflict, especially in the transitional phases of implementing a comprehensive agreement.

- It shows that efforts to dismiss security considerations as unimportant or secondary serve little useful purpose. Similarly, efforts to label too many aspects of relations as security requirements dilute the meaning of the term *security* itself and de-emphasize the importance of certain essential needs.

Security cannot be isolated as the independent variable in the search for a solution to the Arab-Israeli conflict. Security considerations must be taken together with the historical, legal, economic, political, and religious dimensions of the conflict. Yet, security for people and territory remains the cornerstone which must support any settlement.

Understanding the legitimate fears and security concerns of each of the protagonists facilitates discussion of various options for implementing a comprehensive settlement. The design of such ideas must contribute to a confidence-building process within and between the parties to the conflict. Beyond concerns for security lies a mutual lack of confidence in the basic intentions of the other parties to the conflict. Whether the desire by the people in the region for an end to violence and the achievement of a final peace can be translated into political realities in the 1980s depends in great measure upon the future actions of the region's leadership. These actions can either build confidence that mutual security can be achieved or continue to fuel particular security fears of one or more parties. Their choice will determine whether the decade of the 1980s will witness another war or the achievement of peace and an end to a costly and protracted conflict.

Footnotes

Preface

[1]The International Peace Academy is a non-governmental, educational institute devoted to teaching the skills of peacekeeping, mediation, and negotiation. It provides training seminars for government officials, issues publications for the practitioner, and engages in action-research projects which result in curriculum materials, private papers and publications. Several of its previous publications deal with problems related to this study. They include: *The Middle East and the New Realism* (New York: IPA, 1975); *The Thin Blue Line: International Peackeeping and Its Future* (New Haven: Yale University Press, 1974, 1978); *The Peacekeeper's Handbook* (London: IPA, 1978); and *The Elusive Peace in the Middle East* (Albany: SUNY Press, 1975). Additional information on the International Peace Academy may be obtained from the Executive Offices, International Peace Academy, 777 United Nations Plaza, New York, New York 10017. Cable: IPACADEMY. Telephone: (212) 986-3540.

[2]The governing Board of Directors which authorized this project in 1977 included diplomats, businessmen, scholars and other professionals from Austria, Canada, Egypt, France, Guatemala, Indonesia, Iran, Japan, Norway, Sierra Leone, and the U.S.A. A listing of current Board members is available from the Academy.

[3]The *1979 Middle East sample* refers to the group of 108 primary discussants who participated in private conversations with the Task Force during 1979. The breakdown of the sample group is as follows:

Egypt	23 persons including 14 from government
Jordan	17 persons including 11 from government
Israel	27 persons including 6 from government
Lebanon	5 persons including 2 from government
Syria	11 persons including 9 from government
Palestinians	25 persons from the West Bank, Gaza and the PLO

Efforts were made to include in each sample group some persons who disagreed with mainstream opinions. The sample is not scientifically designed. The personal comments quoted in this study were gathered during discussions with Arabs and Israelis during 1978 and 1979, both within the region and in meetings held at the United Nations in New York. They are presented without attribution in accordance with prior agreements.

Chapter One

[1]Mr. Begin's Eretz Israel doctrine espouses a state of Israel encompassing Israel and the West Bank of the Jordan River. This doctrine is based upon Biblical claims.

It denies the possibility of the Palestinian people being given any homeland on this territory.

[2]The original Palestinian National Covenant was adopted in May, 1964, by the First Palestinian Congress in Jerusalem. It was amended in Cairo at the fourth session of the Palestinian National Council in July, 1968. It now states that: the liberation of Palestine is a national duty for Arabs (Article 15); the partitioning of Palestine in 1947 and the establishment of Israel is fundamentally null and void (Article 19); every solution that is a substitute for *complete liberation* of Palestine must be rejected (Article 21); and all zionist [sic] existence and activity must be prohibited (Article 23).

The Covenant has not been officially changed although there have been numerous unconfirmed reports that the PLO would agree to eliminate the articles which advocate the destruction of Israel in return for Israeli agreement to negotiate with the PLO and recognize the right of the Palestinian people to self-determination.

[3]*Jordan Times*, 6/17/79, p. 1

[4]*New York Times*, 6/2/78, p. A-6. **Author's note:** These figures do not correspond to published data.

[5]*New York Times*, 11/29/77, p. 1.

[6]Arabs are quick to point out that the Egyptians have never shared this Arabic approach to negotiations due to the outside cultural influence which has always distinguished Egyptians from other Arabs.

[7]*Christian Science Monitor*, Boston, 10/17/79, p. 1.

Chapter Two

[1]Yigal Allon, "Israel: The Case for Defensible Borders," *Foreign Affairs*, Vol. 55, No. 1, October 1976, p. 38.

[2]"Begin's Tactic Under Fire," *Time*, Vol. 111, No. 10., 3/6/78, p. 35.

[3]"Israel, Interested — But Wary," *U.S. News & World Report*, Vol. 85, No. 9, 9/4/78, p. 15.

[4]*New York Times*, 5/13/79, p. 3.

[5]*New York Times*, 3/4/79, p. 9.

[6]*New York Times*, 9/13/79, p. 3.

[7]*Jerusalem Post*, International Edition, 7/8/79, p. 22.

[8]*Jerusalem Post*, 4/10/79, p. 1.

[9]*New York Times*, 1/14/79, p. E-3.

[10]*New York Times Magazine*, 4/8/79, p. 90.

[11]Abraham S. Becker, *Israel and the Palestinian Occupied Territories: Military-Political Issues in the Debate*, a report prepared for the Office of the Assistant Secretary of Defense for International Security Affairs (Santa Monica, California: Rand Corporation, 1971), Rand report R-882 ISA, p. 51.

[12]*Jordan Times*, 7/26/79, p. 1.

[13]*New York Times*, 11/23/77, p. 3.

[14]*Jerusalem Post*, International Edition, 7/1/79, p. 17.

[15]*Jordan Times*, 6/9/79, p. 1.

[16]*Jerusalem Post*, International Edition, 6/10/79, p. 7.

[17]*Ibid.*, p. 7.

[18]*New York Times*, 1/29/79, p. 3.

[19]*Jerusalem Post*, International Edition, 8/12/79, p. 10.

[20]*Christian Science Monitor*, Boston, 3/8/77, p. 3.
[21]*New York Times*, 8/9/79, p. 10.
[22]*New York Post*, 7/7/79, p. 1.
[23]*New York Times*, International Economic Survey, Section 12, 2/4/79, p. 65.
[24]*Jerusalem Post*, International Edition, 8/12/79, p. 8.
[25]*Diplomatic World Bulletin*, New York, 1/22/79, p. 3.
[26]*New York Times*, 7/25/79, p. 8.
[27]Steven J. Rosen, *Military Geography and the Military Balance in the Arab-Israeli Conflict*, Hebrew University of Jerusalem, Leonard Davis Institute for International Relations, Jerusalem, 1977, pp. 33.
[28]*New York Times*, 5/15/78, p. 19.
[29]After the 1967 war, the Palestine Liberation Organization used Jordanian soil as its base for launching violent attacks against Israeli civilian and military targets. The Palestinian fedayeen (resistance elements) constituted a growing threat to the sovereignty and security of the Hashemite Kingdom of Jordan. Open conflict erupted between the two in June, 1970. In September, 1970, the fedayeen commandeered and destroyed three international airliners in the desert outside of Amman. The Government of Jordan responded with military force and large-scale fighting erupted. On September 22, Arab Foreign Ministers arranged a cease-fire to begin the next day. Sporadic fighting continued, however, until July, 1971, when Jordanian forces won a decisive victory over the Palestinians and forced their withdrawal from Jordan. Most of the fedayeen moved to neighboring Lebanon.
[30]*Jordan Times*, 7/20/79, p. 2.
[31]Meron Benvenisti, *Jerusalem, The Torn City*, Jerusalem, Isratypeset, Ltd., 1976, p. 249.
[32]*New York Times*, 3/2/79, p. 7.
[33]*Jordan Times*, 7/3/79, p. 2.
[34]Angus Deming, Milan J. Kubik, "Israel: Day of the Hawks," *Newsweek*, Vol. LXXXIX, 5/30/77, p. 32.
[35]*Christian Science Monitor*, Boston, 10/16/78, p. 3.
[36]*Jordan Times*, 5/3/79, p. 1; or *New York Times*, 5/3/79, p. 5.
[37]*New York Times*, 12/1/77, p. 3.
[38]*Ibid.* p. 3.
[39]*Christian Science Monitor*, Boston, 9/25/78, p. 4.
[40]*Christian Science Monitor*, Boston, 9/19/79, p. 9.
[41]*Christian Science Monitor*, Boston, 8/30/79, p. 9.
[42]The United Nations Interim Force in Lebanon was initially composed of Iranian troops who were borrowed temporarily from the UNDOF forces in the Golan Heights. The UNIFIL operation was placed under the direction of Major General Emmanuel Erskine (Ghana). The UNIFIL force has included contingents from the Netherlands, Senegal, France, Ireland, Fiji, Iran, Norway, Nepal, Canada, and Nigeria. The reader is directed to Henry Wiseman, "Lebanon, the latest example of UN peacekeeping," in *International Perspectives*, January/February, 1979.
[43]On March 11, 1978, Palestinian commando units staged an attack outside of Haifa during which time a bus was seized. Thirty-four Israelis died in what was one of the worst terrorist attacks suffered by Israel in a decade. On March 14, a large Israeli military force invaded southern Lebanon, the site used by Palestinians as staging area for commando raids upon Israel. The Israelis used all components of their armed forces and succeeded in quickly occupying southern Lebanon up to the Litani River. (See map on page 82.)
[44]*New York Times*, 10/4/76, p. 2.

[45]International Labour Office, Geneva, "Action taken by the International Labour Office at its 59th to 64th Sessions," 1979, p. 43.
[46]*New York Times*, 6/4/79, p. 17.
[47]*Jerusalem Post*, International Edition, 6/3/79, p. 12.
[48]*Jerusalem Post*, International Edition, 5/20/79, p. 6.
[49]*New York Times*, 2/23/78, p. 6.
[50]*Jordan Times*, 7/31/79, p. 1.
[51]*Jerusalem Post*, International Edition, 9/23/79, p. 16.
[52]*New York Times*, 5/24/78, p. 12.
[53]International Labour Office, Geneva, "Action taken by the International Labour Office at its 59th to 64th Sessions," 1979, p. 43.
[54]*Jordan Times*, 7/10/79. p. 2.
[55]*Jordan Times*, 7/15/79, p. 1.
[56]*Christian Science Monitor*, Boston, 4/4/79, p. 27.
[57]*Christian Science Monitor*, Boston, 6/8/78, p. 20.
[58]*New York Times*, 6/9/79, p. 3.

Chapter Three

[1]Hedley Bull, "The objectives of arms control," in *Politics and the International System*, edited by Robert L. Pfaltzgraff, Jr., Philadelphia, Lippincott Company, 1972, p. 504.
[2]Israelis argue that the element of surprise attack was critically important and must be considered when reviewing the outcome of the 1967 and 1973 wars.
[3]*Jerusalem Post*, International Edition, 7/1/79, p. 9.
[4]*New York Times*, 2/26/78, p. E-3.
[5]Yehoshuput Harkabi, "Israel debates Peace," in *Atlas World Press Review*, Vol. 25, No. 8, August 1978, p. 18.
[6]*New York Times*, 3/30/78, p. 12.
[7]*Jordan Times*, 5/23/79, p. 4.
[8]*Jerusalem Post*, International Edition, 6/17/79, p. 6.
[9]*Jerusalem Post*, International Edition, 6/24/79, p. 23.
[10]*Jerusalem Post*, International Edition, 8/5/79, p. 14.
[11]*New York Times*, 1/13/78, p. 3.
[12]*New York Times*, 3/24/78, p. 10.

Chapter Four

[1]Karen Söder, *Sweden's Neutrality Policy*, Ministry for Foreign Affairs, Press and Information Department, Stockholm, 1977, p. 2.
[2]Sverker Åström, *Sweden's Policy of Neutrality*, The Swedish Institute, Stockholm, March 1977, p. 9.
[3]Karen Söder, *Sweden's Neutrality Policy*, Ministry for Foreign Affairs, Press and Information Department, Stockholm, 1977, p. 7.
[4]Gerhard Von Glahn, *Law Among Nations*, Macmillan Company, London, 1969, pp. 619-665.

⁵The Fifth Convention dealt with the rights and obligations of neutral powers and persons in the event of land warfare; and the Thirteenth Convention with the rights and obligations of neutral powers in the event of warfare at sea. Some amendments were proposed under the Geneva Convention of 1949 (application of the right of neutrality to the right of humanitarianism in war).

⁶Daniel Frei, *Swiss Foreign Policy*, Pro Helvetia Press Service, Zurich 1977, p. 11, translation by F.M. Blackwell.

⁷Edgar Bonjour, *Swiss Neutrality*, George Allen and Unwin, Ltd., London, 1946, p. 136.

⁸*New York Times*, 8/22/79, p. 10.

⁹This is a reference to President Carter's statement that a relatively limited number of Palestinians scattered throughout the Arab world want to return to the poverty of that area (meaning the West Bank). See *Jordan Times*, 8/3/79, p. 1.

¹⁰Department of State, *The Austrian State Treaty*, April 1957, Department of State publication 6437, p. 80.

¹¹*Ibid.*

¹²*Ibid.*, pp. 42-97.

¹³*Ibid.*, p. 97.

¹⁴Steven J. Rosen, *Military Geography and the Military Balance in the Arab-Israeli Conflict*, Hebrew University of Jerusalem, Leonard Davis Institute for International Relations, Jerusalem, 1977, p. 18.

¹⁵*New York Times*, 3/25/78, p. 4.

¹⁶"A Growing Struggle on the West Bank." *U.S. News and World Report*, Vol. LXXXVII, No. 6, 8/6/79, p. 30.

¹⁷Article 51 of the Charter of the United Nations: "Nothing in the present Charter shall impair the inherent right of individual or collective self-defence if an armed attack occurs against a Member of the United Nations, until the Security Council has taken measures necessary to maintain international peace and security. Measures taken by Members in the exercise of this right of self-defence shall be immediately reported to the Security Council and shall not in any way affect the authority and responsibility of the Security Council under the present Charter to take at any time such action as it deems necessary in order to maintain or restore international peace and security."

¹⁸Article 39 of the Charter of the United Nations: "The Security Council shall determine the existence of any threat to the peace, breach of the peace, or act of aggression and shall make recommendations, or decide what measures shall be taken in accordance with Articles 41 and 42, to maintain or restore international peace and security."

¹⁹Alan Dowty, *The Role of Great Power Guarantees in International Peace Agreements*, The Hebrew University Press, Jerusalem, 1974, p. 7.

²⁰For a review of some of the Western-suggested proposals, see the following: Richard H. Ullman, "Alliance with Israel?" in *Foreign Policy*, Summer 1975, No. 19, pp. 18-33; George W. Ball, "The Looming War in the Middle East and How to Avert It," *Atlantic Monthly*, January 1975, Vol. 235, No. 1, pp. 6-8; Nadav Safran, "The War and the Future of the Arab-Israeli Conflict," *Foreign Affairs*, January 1974, Vol. 52, pp. 215-236; and Stanley Hoffman, "A New Policy for Israel," in *Foreign Affairs*, April 1975, Vol. 53, pp. 405-431.

²¹*Christian Science Monitor*, Boston, 4/19/79, p. 5.

²²*Jordan Times*, 5/3/79, p. 1.

²³Reference was to *The Syrian Arab Republic*, Anne Sinai and Allen Pollack (Editors), American Academic Association for Peace in the Middle East, New York,

1976, pp. 130-131. **Authors Note:** A review of this article by Irving Neymont entitled, "Military Significance of the Golan Plateau," showed that it was accurately quoted by the Syrian official.
[24]*New York Times*, 2/26/78, p. E-3.
[25]*Jerusalem Post*, 5/27/79, p. 3.

Bibliography

Author's Note: Extensive research and background reading was undertaken prior to and following each of the Task Force trips to the Middle East. The following sources were among those we considered to be particularly interesting.

1. BOOKS

Abu-Lughod, Ibrahim. *The Transformation of Palestine.* Evanston, Illinois: Northwestern University Press, 1971.
Alroy, Gil Carl. *Behind the Middle East Conflict.* New York: C.P. Putnam's Sons, 1975.
American Friends Service Committee. *Search for Peace in the Middle East,* rev. New York: Hill and Wang, 1970.
Amos, John W., II. *Arab-Israeil Military/Political Relations: Arab Perceptions and the Politics of Escalation.* New York: Pergamon Press, 1979.
Antonius, George. *The Arab Awakening.* New York: C.P. Putnam's Sons, 1946.
Aronson, Shlomo. *Conflict & Bargaining in the Middle East.* Baltimore: The Johns Hopkins University Press, 1978.
Art, Robert J. and Waltz, Kenneth N., eds. *The Use of Force: International Politics and Foreign Policy.* Boston: Little, Brown and Co., 1971.
el-Asmar, Fouze, Davis, Uri, Khadr, Naim. *Towards a Socialist Republic of Palestine.* London: Ithaca Press, 1978.
Astor, David and Yorke, Valerie. *Peace in the Middle East: Superpowers and Security Guarantees.* London: Corgi, 1978.
Atiyah, Edward. *The Arabs.* Beirut: Librairie du Liban, 1968.
Bar-Siman-Tov, Yaacov. *The Israel-Egyptian War of Attrition, 1969-70: A Case Study of Limited Local War.* New York: Columbia University Press, 1980.
Benvenisti, Meron. *Jerusalem: The Torn City.* Minneapolis: University of Minnesota Press, 1976.
Blechman, Barry M. and Kaplan, S.S. *The Use of Armed Forces as a Political Instrument.* Washington: The Brookings Institution, 1977.
Blum, Yehuda. *Secure Boundaries and Middle Eastern Peace.* Jerusalem: The Hebrew University, Faculty of Law, 1971.
Bonjour, Edgar. *Swiss Neutrality.* London: George Allen and Unwin, Ltd., 1946.
Brecher, Michael. *Decisions in Israel's Foreign Policy.* New Haven: Yale University Press, 1975.
_____. *The Foreign Policy System of Israel: Setting, Images, Process.* New Haven: Yale University Press, 1972.
_____. *Studies in Crisis Behavior.* New Brunswick, New Jersey: Transaction Books, 1978.
Buehrig, Edward H. *The UN and the Palestinian Refugees.* Bloomington: Indiana University Press, 1971.

Bull, Vivian. *The West Bank — Is It Viable?* Lexington, Massachusetts: D.C. Heath and Company, 1975.
Chami, Joseph G. *Days of Tragedy: Lebanon '75/76.* Nicosia: Printco, 1978.
Cohen, Saul B. *Jerusalem: Bridging the Four Walls.* New York: Herzl Press, 1977.
Collard, Elizabeth and Wilson, R. *The Economic Potential of an Independent Palestine.* London: Middle East Economic Digest, 1975.
Committee on International Relations of the Group for the Advancement of Psychiatry. *Self-Involvement in the Middle East Conflict.* New York: GFAOP, 1978.
Curtis, M., Neyer, J., Waxman, C., Pollack, A. *The Palestinians.* New York: American Academic Association for Peace in the Middle East, 1975.
Dimbleby, Jonathan. *The Palestinians.* London: Quartet Books, 1979.
Dodd, Peter and Barakat, Halim. *River Without Bridges: A Study of the Exodus of the 1967 Palestinian Arab Refugees.* Beirut: The Institute for Palestine Studies, 1969.
Dror, Yehezkel. *Crazy States: A Counterconventional Strategic Problem.* Millwood, New York: Kraus Reprint, 1980.
Dunn, Lewis A. and Kahn, Herman. *Trends in Nuclear Proliferation, 1975-1995.* Croton-on-Hudson, New York: Hudson Institute, 1975.
Dupuy, Trevor N. *Elusive Victory: The Arab-Israeli Wars, 1947-1974.* New York: Harper and Row, 1978.
Eban, Abba. *An Autobiography.* New York: Random House, 1977.
Elzer, Daniel J. *Camp David Framework for Peace: A Shift Toward Shared Rule.* Washington: American Enterprise Institute for Public Policy Research, 1979.
Europa Publications. *The Middle East and North Africa, 1978-79.* London: Europa Publications, Ltd., 1978.
Evron, Yair. *The Middle East.* New York: Praeger Publishers, 1973.
Fabian, Larry and Schiff, Ze'ev. *Israelis Speak.* New York: Carnegie Endowment for International Peace, 1977.
Farrell, John C. and Smith, Asa P., eds. *Image and Reality in World Politics.* New York: Columbia University Press, 1967.
Freedman, Robert O., *Soviet Policy Toward the Middle East Since 1970,* rev. New York: Praeger Publishers, 1978.
_____. *World Politics and the Arab-Israeli Conflict.* New York: Pergamon, 1980.
Frei, Daniel. *Swiss Foreign Policy.* Zurich: Pro Helvetia Press Service, 1977.
Gerson, Allan. *Israel, The West Bank and International Law.* London: Frank Cass & Co., Ltd., 1978.
Glassman, Joh D. *Arms for the Arabs: The Soviet Union and War in the Middle East.* Baltimore: The Johns Hopkins University Press, 1975.
Golan, Galia. *Yom Kippur and After: The Soviet Union and the Middle East Crisis.* Cambridge University Press, 1977.
Gorbatov, O.M. and Cherkasski, I. *Sotrudnichestvo SSSR so stranami arabskogo vostoka i Afriki.* Moskva: Nauka, 1973.
Gray, Colin S. *The Geopolitics of the Nuclear Era: Heartland, Rimlands, and the Technological Revolution.* New York: Crane, Russak & Company, Inc., 1977.
Guillaume, Alfred. *Islam.* Harmondsworth, Middlesex: Penguin Books, 1954.
Hadawi, Sami. *Bitter Harvest — Palestine 1914-67.* New York: The New World Press, 1967.
Haddad, Hassan S., and Nijim, Basheer K., eds. *The Arab World: A Handbook.* Wilmette, Illinois: Medina Press, 1978.
Hanreider, Wolfram F., and Buel, Larry V. *Words and Arms: A Dictionary of Security and Defense Terms.* Boulder, Colorado: Westview Press, 1979.
Harkabi, Yehoshafat. *Arab Strategies and Israel's Response.* New York: The Free Press, 1977.

Harkavy, Robert E. *Spectre of a Middle Eastern Holocaust: The Strategic and Diplomatic Implications of the Israeli Nuclear Weapons Program.* University of Denver Monograph Series in World Affairs, Vol. 14, Book 4, Denver, 1977.
Hassan, His Royal Highness Crown Prince. *A Study of Jerusalem.* London: Longman, 1979.
Heikal, Mohamed. *The Sphinx and the Commissar: The Rise and Fall of Soviet Influence in the Middle East.* New York: Harper & Row, Inc., 1978.
Heiss, Klaus P., Knorr, Klaus, Morgenstern, Oskar. *Long Term Projections of Power.* Cambridge, Massachusetts: Ballinger Publishing Co., 1973.
Heradstveit, Daniel. *The Arab-Israeli Conflict: Psychological Obstacles to Peace.* Oslo: Universitetsforlaget, 1979.
Higgins, Rosalyn. *United Nations Peacekeeping, 1946-67,* Vol. 1, *The Middle East.* London: Oxford University Press, 1969.
Hilal, Jamil. *The West Bank: Its Social and Economic Structure, 1948-1974.* Beirut: Palestine Liberation Organization Research Center, 1975. Original in Arabic.
Hirst, David. *The Gun and the Olive Branch.* London: Futura Publications, Ltd., 1978.
Hourani, A.H. *Syria and Lebanon.* New York: Oxford University Press. 1946.
Huntington, Ellsworth. *Palestine and Its Transformation.* Boston: Houghton Mifflin Company, 1911.
Hurewitz, J.C., ed. *Soviet-American Rivalry in the Middle EAst.* New York: Frederick Praeger, 1971.
_____, ed. *The Middle East and North Africa in World Politics: A Documentary Record,* Two Volumes. New Haven: Yale University Press, 1979.
Hussaini, Hatem I. *Toward Peace in Palestine.* Washington: Palestine Information Office, 1975.
Institute for Palestine Studies. *The Egyptian-Israeli Treaty.* Beirut: The Institute for Palestine Studies, 1979.
International Peace Academy. *The Peacekeepers Handbook.* New York: IPA, 1978.
Israel Academy of Sciences and Humanities, The Israel Exploration Society, The Hebrew University Department of Geography. *Atlas of Jerusalem.* Jerusalem: Massada Press, 1973.
James, Alan. *The Politics of Peace-Keeping.* New York: Frederick A. Praeger, 1969.
Jervis, Robert. *The Logic of Images in International Relations.* Princeton: Princeton University Press, 1970.
Kadi, Leila S. *Arab Summit Conferences and the Palestine Problem.* Beirut: Research Centre-Palestine Liberation Organization, 1966.
Kerr, Malcolm H., ed. *The Elusive Peace in the Middle East.* Albany: State University of New York Press in cooperation with the International Peace Academy, 1975.
Khalidi, Walid, ed. *From Haven to Conquest: Readings in Zionism and the Palestine Problems until 1948.* Beirut: The Institute for Palestine Studies, 1971.
_____. *Jerusalem: The Arab Case.* Amman: The Hashemite Kingdom of Jordan, 1967.
Koury, Enver M. *The Balance of Military Power: The Arab-Israeli Conflict.* Hyattsville, Maryland: Institute of Middle Eastern and North African Affairs, 1976.
Laffin, John. *Rhetoric and Reality: The Arab Mind Considered.* New York: Taplinger Publishing Company, 1975.
_____. *The Arab Mind: A Need for Understanding.* London: Cassell and Company, Ltd., 1975.
Lapidoth, Ruth. *Freedom of Navigation with Special Reference to International Waterways in the Middle East.* Jerusalem: Hebrew University, 1975. Jerusalem Papers on Peace Problems.
Laqueur, Walter. *Confrontation: The Middle East and World Politics.* New York: Quadrangle/The New York Times Book Company, 1974.

Legum, Colin, ed. *Middle East Contemporary Survey.* New York: Holmes and Meier Publishers, Inc. 1978. See especially Part I: "The Middle East and World Affairs and The Arab-Israeli Conflict."
Leitenberg, Milton and Sheffer, Gabriel, eds. *Great Power Intervention in the Middle East.* New York: Pergamon Press, 1979.
Lenczowski, George ed. *Political Elites in the Middle East.* Washington: American Enterprise Institute for Public Policy Research.
Lesch, Ann Mosely. *Political Perceptions of the Palestinians on the West Bank and the Gaza Strip.* Washington: The Middle East Institute, 1980.
Longrigg, Stephen. *Syria and Lebanon Under French Mandate.* London: Oxford University Press, 1958.
Lustick, Ian. *Arabs in the Jewish State: Israel's Control of a National Minority.* Austin, Texas: University of Texas Press, 1980.
Lutskia, N.S., ed. *Arabskie strany: Istoriia, ekonomika.* Moskva: Nauka, 1974.
Mandel, Robert. *Perception, Decision Making and Conflict.* Washington: University Press of America, 1979.
Mangold, Peter. *Superpower Intervention in the Middle East.* London: Croom Helm, 1978.
Mansfield, Peter. *The Arabs.* London: Alan Lane, 1976.
Ma'oz, Moshe, ed. *Palestinian Arab Politics.* Jerusalem: Jerusalem Academic Press, 1975.
McGowan, Pat and Kegley, Charles W., Jr. *Threats, Weapons, and Foreign Policy.* Beverly Hills: Sage Publications, 1980.
Mishal, Shaul. *West Bank/East Bank: The Palestinians in Jordan, 1949-67.* New Haven: Yale University Press, 1978.
Moore, John Norton, ed. *The Arab-Israeli Conflict,* Vol. 3, *Documents.* Princeton: Princeton University Press, 1974.
Nakhleh, Emile A., ed. *A Palestinian Agenda for the West Bank and Gaza.* Washington: American Enterprise Institute for Public Policy Research, 1980.
_____. *The West Bank and Gaza: Toward the Making of a Palestinian State.* Washington: American Enterprise Institute for Public Policy Research, 1979.
National Lawyers Guild 1977 Middle East Delegation. *Treatment of Palestinians in Israeli-Occupied West Bank and Gaza.* New York: National Lawyers Guild, 1978.
Nisan, Mordechai. *Israel and the Territories: A Study in Control.* Ramat Gan, Israel: Turtledove Publishing, 1978.
Nyrop, Richard F., ed. *Israel: A Country Study.* Washington: The American University, 1979.
_____., ed. *Syria: A Country Study.* Washington: The American University, 1979.
Oesterreicher, John and Sinai, Anne. *Jerusalem.* New York: John Day Company, 1974.
O'Neill, Bard E. *Armed Struggle in Palestine: A Political-Military Analysis.* Boulder, Colorado: Westview Press, 1978.
Pajak, Roger F. *Soviet Arms Aid in the Middle East.* Washington: Center for Strategic & International Studies, 1976.
Patai, Raphael. *The Arab Mind.* New York: Charles Scribner's Sons, 1976.
Peres, Shimon. *David's Sling.* London: Weidenfeld and Nicolson, 1970.
Peretz, Don. *The Government and Politics of Israel.* Boulder, Colorado: Westview Press, 1979.
Polk, William R. *The Elusive Peace: The Middle East in the Twentieth Century.* New York: St. Martin's Press, 1979.
Porath, Yehoshua. *The Emergence of the Palestinian-Arab National Movement 1918-29.* London: Frank Cass and Company, Ltd., 1974.
Pranger, Robert J. and Tahtinen, Dale R. *Nuclear Threat in the Middle East,* Foreign Affairs Study No. 23. Washington: American Enterprise Institute, 1975.

Quandt, William B. *Decade of Decisions: American Policy Toward the Arab-Israeli Conflict, 1967-76.* Berkeley: University of California Press, 1977.
⎯⎯⎯⎯⎯⎯, Jabbar, Fuad and Lesch, Ann. *The Politics of Palestinian Nationalism.* Berkeley: University of California Press, 1973.
Ra'anan, Uri. *The USSR Arms the Third World.* Cambridge, Massachusetts: MIT Press, 1969.
Ramazani, R.K. *Beyond the Arab-Israeli Settlement: New Directions For U.S. Policy in the Middle East.* Cambridge, Massachusetts: Institute for Foreign Policy Analysis, 1977.
Reich, Bernard. *Quest for Peace: United States-Israel Relations & the Arab-Israeli Conflict.* New Brunswick, New Jersey: Transaction Books, 1977.
Rikhye, Indar Jit and Volkmar, John. *The Middle East and the New Realism.* New York: International Peace Academy, 1975.
⎯⎯⎯⎯⎯⎯, Harbottle, Michael and Egge, Bjorn. *The Thin Blue Line: International Peacekeeping and Its Future.* New Haven: Yale University Press, 1974.
⎯⎯⎯⎯⎯⎯, *The Sinai Blunder.* London: Frank Cass and Company, 1980.
Roberts, Adam. *Nations in Arms: The Theory and Practice of Territorial Defense.* New York: Praeger Publishers, 1976.
Ro'i, Yaacov, ed. *The Limits to Power: Soviet Policy in the Middle East.* New York: St. Martin's Press, 1979.
⎯⎯⎯⎯⎯⎯, *From Encroachment to Involvement: A Documentary Study of Soviet Policy in the Middle East, 1945-1973.* New York: Halsted Press, 1975.
Rosen, Steven. *Military Geography and the Military Balance in the Arab-Israeli Conflict.* Jerusalem: Hebrew University of Jerusalem. Davis Institute for International Relations, 1977.
Royal United Services Institute. *International Weapon Developments.* London: Brassey's Publishers Ltd., 1979.
Rubinstein, Alvin Z. *Red Star on the Nile: The Soviet-Egyptian Influence Relationship Since the June War.* Princeton: Princeton University Press, 1977.
Safran, Nadav. *Israel: The Embattled Ally.* Cambridge: The Bellknap Press of Harvard University Press, 1978.
Said, Edward W. *The Question of Palestine.* New York: Times Books, 1979.
Salibi, Kamal. *Crossroads to Civil War: Lebanon 1958-1976.* Boulder, Colorado: Westview Press, 1979.
Sampson, Anthony. *The Arms Bazaar: From Lebanon to Lockheed.* New York: The Viking Press, 1977.
Schiff, Ze'ev. *A History of the Israeli Army (1870-1974).* New York: Simon and Schuster, 1974.
Shalev, Brigadier General Aryeh, (res.). *The Autonomy — Possible Problems and Possible Solutions.* Tel Aviv: Center for Strategic Studies, 1980.
Sharabi, Hisham. *Palestine and Israel.* New York: Pegasus, 1969.
Sheehan, Edward R.F. *The Arabs, Israelis and Kissinger: A Secret History of American Diplomacy in the Middle East.* New York: Reader's Digest Press, 1976.
Sinai, Anne and Pollack, Allen, eds. *The Syrian Arab Republic.* New York: American Academic Association for Peace in the Middle East, 1976.
Snider, Lewis W. *Arabesque: Untangling the Patterns of Supply of Conventional Arms to Israel and the Arab States and the Implications for United States Policy on Supply of "Lethal" Weapons to Egypt.* University of Denver Monograph Series in World Affairs, Vol. 15, No. 1. Denver, 1977.
Sobel, Lester A., ed. *Palestinian Impasse: Arab Guerrillas & International Terror.* New York: Facts on File, 1977
Sykes, Christopher. *Crossroads to Israel, 1917-1948.* Bloomington: Indiana University Press, 1973.

Tritton, A.S. *Islam.* London: Hutchinson University Library, 1954.
Tuma, Elias H. and Darin-Drabkin, Haim. *The Economic Case for Palestine.* New York: St. Martin's Press, 1978.
Ushakova, N.A. *Arabskaia respublica Egipet.* Moskva: Nauka, 1974.
Van Arkadie, Brian. *Benefits and Burdens: West Bank and Gaza Strip Economies Since 1967,* New York: Carnegie Center for International Peace, 1977.
Von Glahn, Gerhard. *Law Among Nations.* London: Macmillan Company, 1969.
Wainhouse, David W. *International Peacekeeping at the Crossroads: National Support, Experience and Prospects.* Baltimore: The Johns Hopkins University Press, 1973.
_____. *International Peace Observation: A History and Forecast.* Baltimore: The Johns Hopkins Press, 1966.
Wilson, Evan M. *Decision on Palestine: How the U.S. Came to Recognize Israel.* Stanford, California: Hoover Institution Press, Stanford University, 1979.
Yodfat, Aryeh. *Arab Politics in the Soviet Mirror.* Jerusalem: Israel Universities Press, 1973.
Ziadeh, Nicola. *Syria and Lebanon.* New York: Praeger, 1957.

II. ARTICLES, PAPERS AND SHORT STUDIES

Adomeit, Hannes. "Soviet Risk-Taking and Crisis Behavior: From Confrontation to Coexistence?" *Adelphi Paper,* No. 101. London: International Institute for Strategic Studies, 1973.
Ajami, Fouad. "Stress in the Arab Triangle." *Foreign Policy,* Winter 1977/78, No. 29, pp. 90-108.
Allon, Yigal. "Israel: The Case for Defensible Borders." *Foreign Affairs,* Vol. 55, No. 1, October, 1976, pp. 38-53.
_____. "The West Bank and Gaza Within the Framework of a Middle East Peace Settlement." *Middle East Review,* Vol. XII, No. 2, Winter 1979/80, pp. 15-18.
Amir, Yehuda. "Interpersonal Contact Between Arabs and Israelis." *The Jerusalem Quarterly,* No. 13, Fall, 1979, pp. 3-17.
Astrom, Sverker. *Sweden's Policy of Neutrality.* The Swedish Institute. Stockholm, March, 1977.
Atlantic Council's Working Group on Security. *Security in the Eastern Mediterranean.* Washington: The Atlantic Council, 1978.
Avineri, Shlomo. "Peacemaking." *Foreign Affairs,* Vol. 57, No. 1, Fall, 1978, pp. 51-69.
Avruch, Kevin A. "Gush Emunim: Politics, Religion, and Ideology in Israel." *Middle East Review,* Vol. XI, No. 2, Winter, 1978-79, pp. 26-31.
Azar, E., McClaurin, R.D. et al. "A System for Forecasting Strategic Crises: Findings and Speculations About Conflict in the Middle East." *International Interactions,* Vol. 3, No. 3, 1977, pp. 193-222.
Bailey, Clinton. "Changing Attitudes Toward Jordan in the West Bank." *Middle East Journal,* Vol. 32, No. 2, Spring 1978, pp. 155-166.
Ball, George W. "The Looming War in the Middle East and How to Avert It." *Atlantic Monthly,* Vol. 235, No. 1, January 1975, pp. 6-8.
Becker, Abraham S. *Israel and the Palestinian Occupied Territories: Military-Political Issues in the Debate.* A Report prepared for the Office of the Assistant Secretary of Defense for International Security Affairs. RAND Report #R-882 ISA. Santa Monica, California: Rand Corporation, 1971.
Becker, Abraham S. *Moscow and the Middle East Settlement: A Role for Soviet Guarantees?* A Rand Paper Series Publication. Santa Monica: Rand Corporation, October, 1975.

Bonham, G.M., Shapiro, M.J., Trumble, T.L., "The October War: Changes in Cognitive Orientation Toward the Middle East Conflict." *International Studies Quarterly*, Vol. 23, No. 1, March, 1979.
Brecker, Michael, "Jerusalem: Israel's Political Decisions, 1947-77." *Middle East Journal*, Vol. 32, No. 1, Winter 1978, pp. 13-34.
The Brookings Institution. *Toward Peace in the Middle East*. Washington: The Brookings Institution, 1975.
Bull, Hedley. "The Objectives of Arms Control." *Politics and the International System*. ed. Robert L. Pfaltzgraff, Jr. Philadelphia: Lippincott Company, 1972. pp. 500-509.
Bulletin of Peace Proposals Special Issue. "The Arab-Israeli Conflict." *Bulletin of Peace Proposals*. Oslo International Peace Research Institute, 1976. pp. 291-378.
Campbell, John C. "Soviet Union in Middle East." *The Middle East Journal*, Vol. 32, No. 1, Winter 1978, pp. 1-12.
Churba, Joseph. "The Middle East Power Balance in Transition." *Comparative Strategy*, Vol. 2, No. 1, 1980, pp. 87-96.
Cohen, Raymond. "Threat Perception in International Crisis." *Political Science Quarterly*, Vol. 93, No. 1, Spring 1978, pp. 93-107.
Crittenden, Ann. "Israel's Economic Plight." *Foreign Affairs*, Vol. 57, No. 5, Summer 1979, pp. 1005-1016.
Daly, J.A. and Andriole, S.J. "Problems of Applied Monitoring and Warning: Illustrations from the Middle East." *Jerusalem Journal of International Relations*, Vol. 4, No. 2, 1979, pp. 31-74.
Danilov, Satvro. "The Arab Muslim Image of World Order." *Middle East Review*, Vol. XI, No. 4, Summer 1979, pp. 50-57.
Dawisha, A.I. "Syria and the Sadat Initiative." *The World Today*. Vol. 34, No. 5, May 1978, pp. 192-198.
Dawisha, Karen. "Soviet Policy in the Arab World: Permanent Interests and Changing Influence." *Arab Studies Quarterly*, Vol. 2, No. 1, Winter 1980, pp. 19-37.
Dayan, Moshe. "Israel's Border and Security Problem." *Foreign Affairs*, Vol. 33, No. 3, January 1955, pp. 110-118.
Dellaflar, William A. and Pack, Howard. "Economic Benefits of Peace in the Middle East: Some Cautionary Notes — Some Potential Benefits." *Middle East Review*, Vol. XI, No. 3, Spring 1979, pp. 10-18.
Department of State. *The Austrian State Treaty*. Washington: Department of State publications, April 1957.
Dowty, Alan. *The Role of Great Power Guarantees in International Peace Agreements*. Jerusalem: The Hebrew University Press, 1974.
Eban, Abba. "Camp David: The Unfinished Business." *New Outlook*, Vol. 22, No. 2, March 1979, pp. 9-16.
Evron, Yair. "The Role of Arms Control in the Middle East." *Adelphi Paper*, No. 138. London: International Institute for Strategic Studies, 1977.
Fabian, Larry L. "Toward a Peacekeeping Renaissance." *International Organization*, Vol. 30, No. 1, Winter 1976, pp. 153-161.
Fisher, Thomas L., II, et al. *UN Peacekeeping: An Analysis of the Elements of Past Operations*. Conference on the Prospects for International Peacekeeping. Saranac Lake, New York: Browne & Shaw Research, 1968.
Forsythe, David P. "The UN and the Arab-Israeli Conflict: What Has Been Learned in 25 Years?" *International Organization*, Vol. 26, No. 4, Autumn 1972, pp. 705-717.
Gemayel, Beshir. "An Interview with Beeshir Gemayel." *Middle East Review*, Vol. XII, No. 1, Fall 1979, pp. 58-60.
Ghorbal, Ashraf. "The Way to Perceive Peace." *International Security*, Vol. 2, No. 3, Winter 1978, pp. 13-21.

Glukhov, Y. "Solid Foundations for Soviet-Arab Friendship." *International Affairs,* No. 1, 1980, Moscow, pp. 95-101.
Golan, Galia. "The Soviet Union and the PLO." *Adelphia Paper,* No. 131. London: International Institute for Strategic Studies, 1976.
Goldman, Nahum. "Zionist Ideology and The Reality of Israel." *Foreign Affairs,* Vol. 57, No. 1, Fall 1978, pp. 70-82.
Gottlieb, Gidon. "Palestine: An Algerian Solution." *Foreign Policy,* No. 21, Winter 1975/76, pp. 198-211.
Griffith, William E. "The Fourth Middle East War, The Energy Crisis, and U.S. Policy." *Orbis,* Vol. XVII, No. 4, Winter 1974, pp. 1161-1188.
Handel, Michael I. *Israel's Political-Military Doctrine.* Occasional Paper, No. 30. Cambridge, Massachusetts: Harvard University, Center for International Affairs, July 1973.
Hareven, Alouph, ed. *Arab Positions Concerning the Frontiers of Israel.* Occasional Papers Series. Tel Aviv: The Shiloah Center for Middle Eastern and African Studies of Tel Aviv University, 1977.
Harkavy, Robert E. "Preemption and Two-Front Conventional Warfare: A Comparison of 1967 Israeli Strategy with the Pre-World War I German Schlieffen Plan." Unpublished paper delivered, Biennial Meeting of the Military Studies Section, International Studies Association at Carlisle, Pennsylvania, 1974.
Hoffman, Stanley. "A New Policy for Israel." *Foreign Affairs,* Vol. 53, April 1975, pp. 405-431.
Horowitz, Dan. "Israel's Concept of Defensible Borders." Jerusalem: *Jerusalem Papers on Peace Problems,* No. 16, 1975.
Hudson, Michael C. "The Palestinian Factor in the Lebanese Civil War." *MIddle East Journal,* Vol. 32, No. 3, Summer 1978, pp. 261-278.
International Labour Office, Geneva. *Action taken by the International Labour Office at its 59th to 64th Sessions.* Geneva, 1979.
Jervis, Robert. "Hypotheses on Misperception." *World Politics,* Vol. XX, April 1968, pp. 454-474.
Jonah, James O.C. "Peacekeeping in the Middle East." *International Journal,* Canadian Institute of International Affairs, Vol. XXXI, No. 1, Winter 1975/76, pp. 100-121.
Kelman, Herbert C. "Israelis and Palestinians: Psychological Prerequisites for Mutual Acceptance." *International Security,* Vol. 3, No. 1, Summer 1978, pp. 162-186.
Khalidi, Walid. "A Sovereign Palestinian State." *Foreign Affairs,* Vol. 56, No. 4, July 1978, pp. 695-713.
Klieman, Dr. Aharon, *International Guarantees and Secure Borders.* Research Project Paper. Tel Aviv: Tel Aviv University, no date given.
Klug, Tony. *Middle East Impasse: The Only Way Out.* Fabian research series, No. 330. London. January 1977.
Kollek, Teddy. "Jerusalem." *Foreign Affairs,* Vol. 55, No. 4, July 1977. pp. 701-716.
Leslie, Brigadier E.M.D. "Some Thoughts on International Peacekeeping." *Canadian Defence Quarterly*, Vol. 7, No. 3, Winter 1978, HIUER, pp. 18-22.
Mansour, Atallah and Stock, Ernest. "Arab Jerusalem after the Annexation." *New Outlook.* Vol. 14, No. 1, Jan/Feb. 1971, pp. 22-36.
McPeak, Col. M.A. "Israel: Borders and Security." *Foreign Affairs,* Vol. 54, No. 3, April 1976, pp. 426-443.
Organski, A.F.K. and Kugler, Jacek. "Davids and Goliaths: Predicting the Outcomes of International Wars." *Comparative Political Studies,* Vol. 11, No. 2, July 1978, pp. 141-180.
Pally, Sidney. "Cognitive Rigidity as a Function of Threat." *Journal of Personality,* Vol. XXIII, 1955, pp. 346-355.
Pelcovits, Nathan A. *Security Guarantees in a Middle East Settlement.* Beverly Hills: Sage Publications, 1976.

_____. "UN Peacekeeping and the 1973 Arab-Israeli Conflict." *Orbis,* Vol. XIX, No. 1, Spring 1975, pp. 146-165.
Pepitone, Albert and Kleiner, Robert. "The Effects of Threat and Frustration on Group Cohesiveness." *Journal of Abnormal and Social Psychology.* Vol. LIV, 1957, pp. 192-199.
Peres, Shimon. "Strategy for a Transition Period." *International Security*, Vol. 2, No. 3, Winter 1978, pp. 4-12.
Peresada, V. "Syria: A Land Renewed." *International Affairs* (Moscow), No. 4, 1976, pp. 108-115.
Perlmutter, Amos. "Begin's Strategy and Dayan's Tactics: The Conduct of Israeli Foreign Policy." *Foreign Affairs*, Vol. 56, No. 2, January 1978, pp. 357-372.
_____. "Crisis Management: Kissinger's Middle East Negotiations (October 1973, June 1974)." *International Studies Quarterly,* Vol. 19, No. 3, September 1975, pp. 316-343.
Pierre, Andrew J. "Beyond the 'Plane Package': Arms and Politics in the Middle East." *International Security*, Vol. 3, No. 1, Summer 1978, pp. 148-161.
Pomerance, Michla. "American Guarantees to Israel and the Law of American Foreign Relations." *Jerusalem Papers on Peace Problems,* No. 9, Jerusalem, 1974.
Postman, Leo and Bruner, Jerome. "Perception Under Stress." *Psychological Review*, Vol. LV, November 1948, pp. 314-323.
Potomov, V. "The Middle East: An Important Initiative." *International Affairs*, No. 2, 1976, pp. 120-123.
Quandt, William B. "The Middle East Crisis." *Foreign Affairs,* Vol. 58, No. 3, *America and the World Issues*, pp. 540-562.
_____. *Palestinian Nationalism: Its Political and Military Dimensions.* Santa Monica: Rand Corporation, 1971.
Ro'i, Yaacov. "US Role in the Middle East — A Soviet Perspective." Paper presented Shiloah Colloquium on Middle East and United States. Tel Aviv. March 1978.
Rosen, Steven and Indyk, Martin. "The Temptation to Pre-empt in a Fifth Arab-Israeli War" in *Orbis*, Vol. 20, No. 2, Summer 1976, pp. 265-285.
_____. "What the Next Arab-Israeli War Might Look Like." *International Security*, Vol. 2, No. 4, Spring 1978, pp. 149-173.
Safran, Nadav. "The War and the Future of the Arab-Israeli Conflict." *Foreign Affairs,* Vol. 52, January 1974, pp. 215-36.
Scherer, John L. "Soviet & American Behavior During the Yom Kippur War." *World Affairs,* Vol. 141, No. 1, Summer 1978, pp. 3-23.
Shahar, Haim Ben, Berglas, E., Mundlak, Y., and Sadan, E. *Economic Structue and Development Prospects of the West Bank and the Gaza Strip.* Santa Monica: Rand Corporation, 1971.
Shulman, Marshall D. "The Super-powers." *Survival,* Vol. XVI., No. 1, Jan/Feb. 1974, pp. 2-4.
Singer, David J. "Threat Perception and National Decision Makers." *Theory and Research on the Causes of War,* edited by Dan G. Pruitt and Richard C. Snyder. Englewood Cliffs, New Jersey: Prentice-Hall, Inc., 1969, pp. 39-42.
Smart, Ian M. "Military Insecurity and the Arab-Israeli Conflict: There is an Effective Alternative to the United Nations." *New Middle East,* No. 26, November 1970, pp. 28-32.
Smolansky, O.M. "Soviet Policy in the Middle East." *Current History*, January 1978, pp. 5-9; 38-39.
Soder, Karen. *Sweden's Neutrality Policy.* Ministry for Foreign Affairs, the Press and Information Department, Stockholm, 1977.
Sullivan, John D. "International Alliances." *International Systems: A Behavioural Approach,* ed. Michael Haas. New York: Chandler Publishing Co., 1974, pp. 99-122.

Tabory, Ephraim. "The Attribution of Peaceful Intentions to the Visit by Sadat to Jerusalem and Subsequent Implications for Peace." *Journal of Peace Research*, Vol. XV, No. 2, 1978, pp. 193-195.
Ullman, Richard H. "Alliance With Israel?" *Foreign Policy*, No. 19, Summer 1975, pp. 18-33.
Valdes, Toribio de. "The Authoritativeness of the English and French Texts of Security Council Resolution 242 (1967) on the Situation in the Middle East." *American Journal of International Law*, Vol. 71, No. 2, April 1977, pp. 311-315.
Watt, D.C. "Towards a Middle Eastern Settlement? The Policy of Ambiguity." *Political Quarterly*, Vol. 49, No. 1, Jan/March 1978, pp. 13-24.
Watt, David. "The European Initiative." *Foreign Affairs,* Vol. 57, No. 3, April 1979, *America and the World Issue,* pp. 572-588.
Wheelock, Thomas R. "Arms for Israel: The Limits of Leverage." *International Security*, Vol. 3, No. 2, Fall 1978, pp. 123-137.
Whetten, Lawrence L. "Changing Perceptions About the Arab-Israeli Conflict & Settlement." *The World Today*, Vol. 34, No. 7, July 1978, pp. 252-259.
Williams, Colin. *Jerusalem: A Universal Cultural and Historical Resource.* New York: Aspen Institute for Humanistic Studies, 1975.
Wiseman, Henry. "Lebanon, the Latest Example of UN Peacekeeping." *International Perspectives* (Canada), Jan/February 1979, pp. 3-7.
_____. "United Nations and UNEF II: A Basis for a New Approach To Future Operations." *International Journal*, Vol. XXX, No. 1, Winter 1975, pp. 123-45.
Yakubov, N. "The Soviet Union and the Arab East." *International Affairs* (Moscow), No. 9, 1974, pp. 26-36.
Yorke, Valerie. "Retaliation and International Peacekeeping in Lebanon" *Survival*, Vol. XX, No. 5, September/October 1978, pp. 194-202.
Zurayk, Constantine K. "Arab-American Relations: Dangers and Opportunities." *Arab Studies Quarterly*, Vol. 2, No. 2, Spring 1980, pp. 113-126.

Glossary

Alawite

A minority Shiite sect established in the ninth century whose doctrine and practices include some elements of Christian and pagan beliefs. Alawites are located primarily in northwest Syria as well as in pockets in Jordan and Lebanon. The Alawites believe Mohammed was a mere forerunner of Ali and the latter was an incarnation of Allah. It is usually considered an extremist sect.

Arab Defence Pact

The pact consists of two documents: "Treaty of Joint Defence and Economic Co-operation Among the States of the Arab League" of April 13, 1950; and the "Supplementary Protocol to the Treaty of Joint Defence and Economic Co-operation (and to the Military Annex) among the Arab States" of February 2, 1951. Its primary effect was to establish an economic and military alliance between the contracting states of Syria, Egypt, Jordan, Iraq, Saudi Arabia, Lebanon, and Yemen. Although it was agreed that an armed act of aggression against one is an act of aggression against all the signatory states, the Pact did not bind members to use force in defence of another signateur state but rather to "undertake to hasten to the aid of the State or States against whom an aggression is committed, and to take immediately, individually and collectively, all measures and to utilize all means available, including the use of armed force, to repulse the aggression and to restore security and peace." The government of Yemen added a reservation to Article 2 which stated: "As regards the provisions of Article 2, Yemen does not consider aggression to be aggression against any Arab State, unless it is an aggression against that State itself and not because it is bound by a treaty or agreements with any other state or because foreign troops exist in its territories for any other reason."

Arab League

The Arab League was created in 1945 by Syria, Jordan, Iraq, Saudi Arabia, Lebanon, Egypt, and Yemen. Its avowed purpose was to strengthen relations amongst the Arab states, in particular in the fields of economics, communications, cultural affairs, nationality/passport coordination, social programs and health, to mediate disputes between members and third parties, and to coordinate their respective national policies. Article 5 stated that any resort to force in order to resolve disputes arising between two or more member states of the League is prohibited. If a difference takes place between two states over independence, sovereignty, or territorial integrity, and if the parties in dispute have recourse to the Council (of the League) for settlement, the decision of the Council shall be obligatory.

Baath Party

This most important Arab socialist party was founded in 1943 by Michel Alfaq and Salah al-Din al-Bitar. The Baath Party became powerful in both Iraq and Syria under a common leadership. The Party later broke into two separate Baathist Parties, one Iraqi and one Syrian. The rift which separated the Parties had strong elements of ideological, political and nationalist-sentiment overtones. Several attempts at reconciliation have been attempted over the years of which none have been successful. A central tenet of Baathist ideology is the primacy of the "Arab nation."

Baghdad Summit

The most frequently described Baghdad Summit meeting was held from November 2-5, 1978, as a gathering of the members of the League of Arab States. Its purpose was to denounce "U.S. inspired Camp David Agreements for a separate Egyptian-Israeli peace." The participants established a $3.5 billion annual "war chest" to strengthen the front-line Arabs (those immediately in confrontation with Israel physically); and announced measures to be taken against Egypt (to commence when Egypt signed a peace treaty with Israel).

The major suppliers of the financial "war chest" were Saudi Arabia, Iraq and Kuwait ($2 billion of the $3.5 billion). Major beneficiaries included Syria ($1.85 billion); Jordan ($1.2 billion) and the PLO ($400 million). One-fourth of the PLO's funds were delegated to be spent in the West Bank and Gaza Strip areas.

This Summit meeting also decided to suspend Egypt from the Arab League, transfer the Arab League out of Cairo and boycott Egyptian products, all after Egypt would sign a peace agreement with Israel.

Disengagement Agreement (Israel-Syria, 1974)

This carefully negotiated agreement between Syria and Israel was signed on May 31, 1974. [Text may be found in U.N. Document S/11302/Add.1/Annex 1 (1974).] This largely American-initiated agreement provided for the separation of Israeli and Syrian armies while establishing demilitarized zones; enforced the cease-fire called for in U.N. Security Council Resolution 338; provided for repatriation of prisoners of war and bodies of the dead; and created UNDOF (United Nations Disengagement Observer Force) on the Golan Heights to monitor the separation agreement. It is not a peace treaty.

Druze

A small sect of Islam which has been called mystical and heretical. Druid people live mainly in the mountain areas of southern Lebanon, in Syria, as well as in Israel. The Druids are known for their independent character and are regarded as stout fighters and reportedly have served in various fighting capacities for both the Arab and Israeli military efforts since 1948. The name Druze derives from Al-Davazi, a missionary of Persian origin who brought about the conversion of the Syrian mountaineers to a belief in the divine origin of Fatimid Caliph al-Hakim.

Eretz Israel

The Hebrew term for the "Land of Israel." The translation, however, does not properly convey the strong emotional connotation which is associated with this word by the Jewish people. It is sometimes translated as "My Israel" or "My Home of Israel" and includes all areas currently known in international parlance as the West Bank and Gaza. The term is religious rather than political or legal. The Eretz Israel concept denies the possibility of a Palestinian homeland.

Green Line

The term used to describe the 1949 Armistice Line. This represents the old borders of Israel. The name was based upon an historical reality that a green writing implement was used to draw the 1949 line.

Gush Emunim

A small, extremist right-wing political party in Israel that calls for the establishment of Israeli sovereignty over all of the lands of Eretz Israel. The name Gush Emunim means "block of the faithful." Its controversial policies are based on religious ideology. This party is primarily responsible for controversial Israeli settlements in populated Arab areas of the West Bank.

IDF

The Israeli Defence Forces were established by the Government of Israel on May 26, 1948, through a government ordinance. The IDF replaced the underground armies of the Irgun and Haganah which had fought in the 1948 war against the Arabs and had previously conducted terrorist attacks against British and Arab targets. The IDF is simply the name given to the Israeli military establishment.

Jordan Rift

A valley (also called the Great Rift or the Rift Valley) surrounding the Jordan River and running north/south through the center of Jordan. The Rift itself extends from Lebanon to Mozambique with its lowest point at the Dead Sea (1300 feet below sea level).

Rabat Arab Summit

This name is used to describe the Seventh Arab Summit Conference, held in Rabat during October of 1974. The Resolution adopted at this summit is considered a watershed in the development of Palestinian demands for self-determination. Its five major operative paragraphs included the following: the Palestinians have a legitimate right to self-determination and a homeland; the PLO was the sole representative of the Palestinian people (previously the Jordanian government had been internationally recognized as such a spokesman) together with an affirmation of the right of Palestinians to an independent national authority under the command of the PLO; a pledge of support by the Arab states to the PLO; a call upon Jordan, Syria, the PLO, and Egypt "to devise a formula for the regulation of relations between them in the light of these decisions so as to insure their implementation;" and a pledge by Arab states to stay out of the "internal" affairs of the PLO.

This resolution was adopted unanimously and represented the first acceptance of the PLO by the Arab world as the sole Palestinian spokesman.

Red Line

This line refers to the Litani River in Lebanon. The name first appeared publicly in the Lebanese press and diplomatic circles in 1976. It represented the southernmost line for deployment in Lebanon of Syrian (Arab League) peacekeeping troops. It was feared that deployment south of this line would provoke a major Israeli reaction and a new Arab-Israeli war.

Rhodes Armistice Agreements

The 1949 Rhodes Agreements consist of four parts. Each is an armistice agreement but *not* a peace treaty resolving the underlying issues of the Arab-Israeli conflict. The first was signed between Israel and Egypt (February 24, 1949); followed by Israel and Lebanon (March 23, 1949); Israel and Jordan (April 3, 1949); and Israel and Syria (July 20, 1949). Each treaty established that disputes are to be brought before the United Nations Security Council and be resolved peacefully; armed forces are not to move against, plan to move against, or threaten to move against the forces of the other; and the right to security for each state was established. The agreements represented the termination of the Israeli War of Independence but not of the Arab-Israeli conflict.

Shiia

The Shiia Moslem sect is the largest minority group within Islam, having broken with the majority Sunni sect in a disagreement over the choice of Mohammed's heir.

The Shiias represent an overwhelming majority of the population in Iran and form sizeable percentages of population in Bahrain, Iraq, Pakistan,

Yemen, and India. There are strong pockets of Shiias in Lebanon (the south) and Jordan. It should be noted that the Shiia religious leadership has always exercised an enormous political influence over their people, unlike the Sunni religious leadership which has not been prone to such open political influence. Shiia Islam does not in the main differ on fundamental issues from the Sunni orthodox since they draw from the same ultimate sources. Shiia religious leaders have freedom to alter the application of law since they are regarded as spokesmen of the Hidden Imam.

Sunni
The overwhelming majority of Moslem believers are of the Sunni sect, followers of the Sunnah or orthodox manner of conduct of the Prophet Mohammed. Sunnis represent some 90 percent of Egyptians, 80 percent of Jordanians, 70 percent of Syrians, and even some 10 percent of Israelis (excluding the West Bank and Gaza). The Sunni doctrine is traditionalist and monotheistic.

U.S.-U.S.S.R. Joint Statement
On October 1, 1977, the United States and the Soviet Union issued a joint statement on the Middle East. It called for a reconvening of a Geneva peace conference before the end of 1977. Its importance includes the fact that it reopened the door for Soviet direct participation in the peacemaking process. It also presented the United States acceptance of the need to insure the legitimate rights of the Palestinian people. The Joint Statement was shortly thereafter disavowed by the United States, following which President Sadat made his initiative (November 1977) to Israel starting the events that were soon to lead to the Camp David process.

War of Attrition
This term refers to the undeclared, limited war waged between Egypt and Israel at the Suez Canal from 1967-70. The Egyptian strategy was to inflict substantial casualties upon Israel, thus pressuring Israel to withdraw from the occupied territories. The situation escalated with aerial dogfights between Israeli and Russian piloted planes. The United States called for a cease-fire in the Security Council of 90 days while continuous U.N. negotiations were conducted. Although the U.N. mediator Gunnar Jarring was unsuccessful in facilitating a formal agreement, the cease-fire continued past the 90 days and represented the termination of the War of Attrition (August 1970).

Index

Afghanistan, 18, 23, 25, 57, 72, 95, 100
Alawite, 70, 72, 196
Ali, Hassan, 126
Alliances and defense pacts, 24, 37, 51, 79, 114, 144, 150, 152, 177, 196
Arab Defence Pact, 50, 118, 196
Arab-Israeli wars (prospects and problems for the future), 25, 26, 47, 63, 75, 91, 99, 104, 126
Arab League, 153, 158, 196-197
Arab League Peacekeeping Force (Lebanon), 59, 70, 80, 85-87, 118, 182, 198
Arabs, 13, 15, 16, 17, 18, 21, 22, 31, 32, 34, 39, 40, 47, 51, 65, 84, 90, 92, 110, 114, 126, 130, 152, 186
Arab unity, 86, 87, 88, 158
Arafat, Yasir, 36, 59, 80, 157, 164
Arens, Moshe, 99, 143
Armistice Agreements (Rhodes, 1949), 61, 130, 198, 199
Arms sales, 14, 23, 24, 49
Assad, Hafez, 36, 38, 72, 74, 79, 86, 88, 134, 174
Austria, 15, 40, 91, 112, 130-163
Austrian State Treaty (1955), 140, 147, 149, 156
Autonomy talks, 91, 95, 143, 144, 155

Baath Socialist Party, 72, 88, 130, 197
Baghdad Meeting, 40, 61, 197
Bashan Plateau, 175
Begin, Menachem, 31, 36, 38, 39, 40, 50, 69, 74, 75, 96, 113, 125, 126, 132, 134, 170, 174, 184
Ben Gurion, David, 114
Benvenisti, Meron, 68
Bir Zeit University, 90, 131
Blum, Yehuda, 64
Brown, Harold, 56

Camp David process, 18, 23, 26, 39, 41, 68, 99, 181, 185, 197, 200
Carter, Jimmy, 16, 59, 69

China, 109, 161, 162
Christians, 80, 84, 87, 133, 182
Comprehensive settlement (full peace) 13, 14, 15, 21, 24, 25, 54, 88, 99, 102, 103, 110, 130, 153, 179, 187
Confederation, 40, 43, 163-173
Confidence-building, 21, 43, 99, 103, 104, 113, 130, 133, 134, 135, 152, 155, 173, 177, 180, 187
Congress of Vienna, 141
Council of Europe, 158
Cuba, 100, 132
Cyprus, 60, 162

Dayan, Moshe, 56, 57, 129, 134
Dead Sea, 61, 127, 185-186
Demilitarization, 115, 119, 138, 154, 155, 168, 173, 175, 177, 179, 187
Demographic variables, 51-56, 64, 93, 95, 96, 115, 129
Disengagement Agreements (1974), 75, 175, 197
Drobless, Matitiyahu, 93
Druze, 88, 182, 198
Dulles, John Foster, 150

Eastern Front, 32, 37, 47-50, 103, 117, 118, 177, 185
Economic issues and problems, 21, 23, 25, 26, 29, 38, 45, 56, 59-60, 63, 70, 76, 78, 79, 86, 93, 94, 102, 108, 130, 131, 132, 133, 137, 138, 144, 145, 148, 149, 151, 152, 153, 168
European Economic Community (EEC), 158
Egypt, 5, 8, 18, 32, 35, 37, 39, 40, 41, 45, 50, 51, 56, 65, 78, 79, 84, 91, 97-101, 108, 118, 130, 144, 153, 162, 172, 185, 200
Egyptian-Israeli Peace Treaty (process), 13, 23, 31, 32, 37, 41, 42, 45, 47, 50, 51, 56, 69, 70, 78, 97, 99, 118, 133, 185

211

Eretz Israel, 28, 36, 94, 129, 188, 198
Europe, 66, 95, 96, 112, 161, 186

France, 24, 56, 87, 144, 147, 162, 178

Gaza, 13, 14, 18, 40, 45, 51, 56, 64, 78, 85, 91, 92-95, 102, 103, 127, 138-173
German Assets (1949), 145
Germany, Federal Republic of, 56, 144
Germany, Democratic Republic of, 100
Golan Heights, 17, 18, 26, 50, 60, 61, 72, 75-76, 85, 86, 117, 172, 173-179, 197
Great Powers, 14, 22, 25, 29, 100, 112, 132, 133, 138, 149, 162, 178, 187
Greece, 162
Green Line, 115, 198
Guarantees (security), 74, 111, 113-114, 115, 119, 131, 147, 151, 154, 155, 156, 160-163, 177
Gulf States, 66, 97, 118, 131, 144
Gush Emunim, 93, 129, 157, 198

Haddad, Saad, 83, 84
Hague Peace Conference (1907), 141
Harkabi, Yehoshafat, 55, 119, 124
Hart, Liddell, 117
Hormuz, Strait of, 57, 66
Horn of Africa, 18, 100
Hula Valley, 47, 174
Hussein, King, 31, 36, 61, 63, 91, 134, 163, 167, 171

International Labor Organization (ILO), 93, 94
International Peace Academy (IPA), 5, 6, 7, 9, 16-19
IPA Middle East Task Force, 5, 6, 9, 13, 17, 18, 22, 23, 42, 43, 44, 130, 133, 134, 137, 144, 163, 164, 165, 179, 184
Iran, 18, 23, 25, 29, 31, 49, 57, 95, 118, 198
Iraq, 23, 29, 32, 37, 47, 49, 56, 59, 61, 70, 72, 74, 79, 87, 88, 90, 91, 100, 101, 117, 118, 130, 177, 197, 198
Israel, 5, 8, 13, 15, 16, 18, 21, 22, 23, 24, 31, 32, 34, 35, 37, 39, 40, 41, 45-60, 61, 63, 70, 74-79, 80, 83, 84, 86, 88, 90, 91, 92, 93, 97, 101, 105, 106, 110, 111, 112, 114-124, 127-129, 131-132, 137, 138, 144, 153, 156, 157, 162, 168, 169, 172, 174, 175, 177, 178, 179, 183, 184, 185, 186, 187, 188
Israeli Arabs, 54-56
Israeli Communist Party, 157

Japan, 66, 144, 161
Jarring, Gunnar, 200
Jerusalem, 45, 47, 51, 64, 65, 66-68, 76, 90, 93, 94, 103, 115, 119, 179-181, 186
Jewish lobby, 57
Jordan, 5, 8, 15, 32, 37, 45, 47, 49, 51, 60-70, 84, 93, 100, 112, 126, 148, 149, 153, 154, 155, 156, 157, 163-173, 181, 183, 186, 197, 198
Jordan River, 47, 60, 119, 166, 169, 198
Jordan Valley, 115, 127, 155, 198

Khalil, Mustapha, 50
Kissinger, Henry, 16, 17, 61
Kollek, Teddy, 179, 180
Korea, 161
Kreisky, Bruno, 59
Kuwait, 5, 65, 148

Lake Tiberias, 60, 61
Lebanon, 5, 17, 18, 26, 35, 45, 59, 63, 65, 70, 74, 80-88, 97, 114, 118, 125, 127, 148, 153, 172, 181-183, 198
Levy, David, 93
Libya, 23, 25, 59, 87, 100, 101
Limited Armament Zones, 40, 102, 111, 119, 154, 172-173, 175, 177, 178, 187
Litani River, 60, 74, 80, 83, 84-87

Meir, Golda, 69
Middle East sample, 5, 24, 25, 26, 42, 108, 127, 133, 137, 155, 164, 168, 173, 178, 179, 180
Minority groups, 79, 86, 117
Mobilization, 34, 45, 47, 115, 155, 178
Molotov, Vyacheslav, 145
Moscow Memorandum (1955), 146, 147
Moslem Brotherhood, 72
Moynihan, Daniel P., 56
Mugabe, Robert, 170

North Atlantic Treaty Organization (NATO), 161
Negotiation process, 38-43, 65, 143, 170
Neutrality, 15, 40, 43, 88, 137, 138-163
Nixon, Richard, 56, 109
Nuclear weapons and facilities, 23, 56, 59, 70, 74, 79, 101, 113

Oil, 18, 25, 26, 29, 31, 56, 65, 69, 92, 99, 100, 131
Organization of Petroleum Exporting Countries (OPEC), 23, 56, 57

Palestine Liberation Organization (PLO), 5, 8, 18, 21, 22, 23, 28, 31, 32, 36, 51, 55, 57, 61, 66, 70, 80, 83, 84, 86, 87, 88-97, 106, 107, 124, 131, 144, 152, 157, 159, 164, 167, 169, 170, 171, 181, 182, 185, 187, 197, 198
Palestine National Council, 97, 157, 169
Palestinian entity or state, 13, 15, 22, 31, 40, 42, 50-51, 54, 83, 84, 85, 90, 91, 102, 113, 119, 124, 125, 127, 132, 137, 138-163, 163-173, 180, 186
Palestinian self-determination, 13, 23, 26, 40, 42, 50, 72, 76, 79, 84, 90, 91-92, 95, 97, 99, 102, 106, 108, 125, 126, 127, 137, 144, 152, 159, 163, 178, 188, 198
Palestinians, 8, 13, 15, 21, 22, 23, 31, 32, 36, 41, 43, 51, 57, 64, 66, 80, 84, 85, 87, 88-97, 100, 106, 119, 125, 130, 131, 137, 138-173, 181, 183, 184, 185
Peace Now Movement, 42, 51
Peacekeeping, 16, 18 (*See* United Nations)
Perceptions, 14, 21, 22, 27-38, 42, 101
Peres, Shimon, 32, 69, 134, 146
Preemprive attacks, 63, 69, 74, 84, 102, 114, 117, 155, 157, 178

Rabat Summit, 61, 199
Rabin, Yitzhak, 68, 134, 174
Real Union, 165-166
Red Sea, 186
Rejectionist states, 66, 79, 144
Rhodesia, 135, 159
Right of return, 55, 124, 153, 156

Sadat, Anwar, 16, 23, 32, 36, 40, 108, 130, 134, 200
Saudi Arabia, 32, 40, 49, 51, 56, 57, 59, 65, 86, 117, 131, 144, 148
Security, 17, 26, 41, 47, 85, 96, 105-109, 136, 188-189
Security Council, 16, 18, 147, 149, 154, 159, 162
Settlements (Israelis), 63, 68, 76, 93, 103, 115, 118, 126, 127, 129, 145, 156, 174, 185
Shamir, Yitzhak, 96

Sharon, Ariel, 66, 75, 93, 126, 127
Shiia Moslems, 80, 85, 87, 88, 182, 199
Sinai, 61, 97, 99, 114
Smith, Ian, 135
Soviet Union, 16, 18, 23, 25, 31, 32, 37, 49, 50, 66, 72, 87, 91, 97, 99, 100, 101, 105, 112, 130, 131, 132, 142, 144, 145, 146, 147, 150, 156, 161, 162, 177, 178, 185, 200
Stalin, Joseph, 146
Sudan, 5, 101
Sunni Moslems, 70, 72, 80, 88, 182, 200
Sweden, 139-140
Switzerland, 15, 40, 140-163
Syria, 5, 8, 32, 35, 37, 38, 45, 47, 49, 50, 51, 59, 60, 61, 63, 70-79, 84-87, 100, 112, 118, 130, 153, 154, 155, 156, 172, 173-179, 183, 186, 197

Terrorism, 14, 51, 59, 60, 63, 88, 95, 104, 107, 124, 125, 127, 152, 157, 183
Thailand, 161
Third parties, 14, 17, 18, 24, 25, 35, 37, 60, 93, 107, 111, 133, 134, 144, 154-156, 171-179, 181, 189
Threats, 14, 32-38, 44-104, 105, 107
 capabilities, 27, 34-36
 intentions, 14, 15, 27, 36-43, 44, 45, 130, 133, 134, 136, 184
 primary military, 14, 109-124
 secondary military, 14, 124-129
 non-military, 14, 129-132
Time, the element of, 21, 23, 38, 39, 47, 87, 92, 126
Transitional stages, 24, 150, 152, 154-156, 157, 171, 172, 180, 189
Treaty of Guarantee (1959), 162
Treaty of Versailles, 141
Turkey, 29, 162, 182, 186

United Kingdom, 24, 126, 144, 147, 148, 162, 178
United Nations (UN), 8, 18, 94, 111, 151, 154, 156, 157, 158, 159, 172, 173, 175, 178, 180, 197, 200
UNDOF, 72, 172, 175, 177, 178, 197
UNEF I., 16, 172
UNEF II., 172
UNIFIL, 80, 83, 84, 86, 172
UNTSO, 18, 172
United Arab Kingdom Plan, 163, 167
United Arab Republic, 166

United Jewish Appeal, 93
United States, 16, 18, 23, 25, 29, 32, 37,
38, 41, 45, 47, 49, 50, 56-57, 59, 61,
68-70, 72, 74, 79, 83, 84, 85, 87, 90,
91, 92, 94, 95, 97, 100, 102, 112, 113,
117, 126, 130, 131, 132, 145, 147,
148, 150, 161, 162, 171, 177, 178,
179, 185, 197, 200

Vietnam, 132, 161

War of Attrition, 35,
Warsaw Pact, 146
Weapons, deployment of, 37, 115
  limitation of, 111, 138, 151, 154, 156, 178
  quality of, 34, 50, 100-101, 107, 112, 117, 119, 127
  quantity of, 35, 49, 119, 132
Weizman, Ezer, 56, 99
West Bank, 5, 13, 14, 18, 24, 31, 35, 38,
40, 45, 50, 51, 56, 60, 61, 63-65, 66,
68, 78, 85, 91, 92-95, 102, 103, 113,
114, 115, 117, 125, 126, 127, 137,
138-173, 180, 185, 197, 198

Yadin, Yigael, 41, 51
Yemen, 18
Yemen, Peoples Democratic Republic of, 23, 99, 100
Yom Kippur War, 16, 29, 45, 69

Zimbabwe, 170
Zionism, 74, 76, 78, 79, 85, 113

About the Author

John Edwin Mroz serves as Executive Vice President of the International Peace Academy, a professional educational institute that provides training for military officers and diplomats from 114 nations in the skills of peacekeeping, mediation, and negotiation. Mroz holds graduate degrees from the Fletcher School of Law and Diplomacy and has held a National Science Foundation teaching fellowship. He is a specialist in Soviet-American relations and Middle East military-political affairs and has lectured widely on these subjects.